Advance Praise for
A Godless Crusade

"Dr. Kradin's work is not for intellectual sissies. His conclusions are unambiguous and suggest thatAmerica is on life support—both body and soul."

—**John Budris**, radio host, WRKO 680 AM Boston;
editor, *Vineyard Style* magazine

"As with all of his work, Dr. Richard Kradin challenges us to examine the functioning of our society. *A Godless Crusade* is a thorough and compelling analysis from an extraordinarily honest American psychiatrist and academic."

—**Lucas Klein**, PhD, host, *Real Clear* podcast

"Dr. Kradin compellingly presents how neuroscience, philosophy, and religion contributed to woke progressivism and its disconcerting impact on our current sociocultural and political state of affairs. It's an important and relevant account to understanding the realities of our modern era."

—**Nina Salander**, PhD, clinical psychologist, author in *Cynical Therapies: Perspectives on the Antitherapeutic Nature of Critical Social Justice*

A GODLESS CRUSADE

THE PROGRESSIVE CAMPAIGN TO RID THE WORLD OF RELIGION

RICHARD KRADIN, M.D., M.L.A.

R

A REPUBLIC BOOK

A Godless Crusade:
The Progressive Campaign to Rid the World of Religion
© 2025 by Richard Kradin, M.D., M.L.A.
All Rights Reserved

ISBN: 978-1-64572-102-4
ISBN (eBook): 978-1-64572-103-1

Cover design by Jim Villaflores

R

Republic Book Publishers
New York, NY
www.republicbookpublishers.com

Published in the United States of America
1 2 3 4 5 6 7 8 9 10

Contents

Contents

Preface

THE CULTURAL ATTITUDES OF AMERICANS are arguably more polarized than at any time in recent history. Whereas most secular critics are inclined to avoid explanations for this phenomenon that are focused on religion, as philosopher Terry Eagleton has suggested, a society is truly secular only when its members are no longer agitated by religion.

Anthropologist Mircea Eliade referred to man as *homo religious*, indicating that expressions of what may be termed "religion" are observed in all cultures. Psychologist Carl Jung suggested that a *sui generis* religious impulse exists in the "collective unconscious" and cannot be eradicated. But with the advent of science and left-brained cognitive dominance, traditional expressions of religion have declined in American society, accompanied by a rise in neopaganism and immorality as defined by the Judeo-Christian ethic. As Napoleon recognized, the absence of religion tends to destabilize society.

Despite the widespread decline in religious observance in America, Eagleton's criterion for a secular society has not been achieved. Instead, what may be termed atheistic "functional religion" has been on the rise, primarily in the form of neo-Marxism/progressivism and its recent postmodern avatar "wokeism." Rooted in materialism, these movements lack an intrinsic spiritual component and compensate by selectively adopting utopian notions from the Judeo-Christian tradition. Indeed, philosopher Bertrand Russell designated Marxism as a restatement of Christianity. But absent a spiritual aspect, functional religion will invariably seek expression in political goals. Unwilling to share power, it is intolerant of competition in the public square and focuses on undermining alternative expressions of theistic religion, and in so doing attacks the traditional moral underpinnings of society. The goals of progressivism include consolidating power for the state, deconstructing biblical values of family and sex, criticizing Judeo-Christian religionists for being insufficiently devoted to social justice, and attacking the rule of law.

Christopher Lasch noted in the 1970s that a culture of narcissism has emerged in America, with an attendant increased emphasis on individual freedom. The American social movements of the 1960s focused on expanding the civil rights and freedoms of women and blacks, a trend that has increased over the last half century, together with political efforts at undermining the fabric of society. In contrast, the orthodoxies of the Judeo-Christian religions include polemics against self-centeredness and their definitions of both freedom and progress are based on the individual's identification with a transcendent power.

In *A Godless Crusade*, I will examine how reform movements in monotheistic religion, beginning with ancient Christianity, have inadvertently fostered the secularizing trends seen in today's society. The suspension of the particularisms of Judaism by early Christianity and the emphasis on personal religion in Protestantism resulted in an insidious infiltration of secular ideas within society that have contributed to today's culture wars. In truth, these are secularized restatements of past religious wars. As men are unable to agree on what is "moral," only a "revealed" set of values, which the Judeo-Christian ethic has traditionally provided, can be expected to preserve the moral fabric of society.

Introduction

What's past is prologue.

—WILLIAM SHAKESPEARE, *THE TEMPEST*

WHAT DOES IT MEAN TO BE FREE? It is impossible to define freedom without evoking the notion of slavery, as they are opposing archetypes within the human psyche. Despite this, in antiquity the prevalent social imaginary allowed free men to live in societies of slaves without experiencing ethical conflict. But post-Enlightenment Americans have been preoccupied with freedom since the founding of the nation, and its creation was marred by slavery in the agrarian South.

Currently, America is in the midst of a cultural revolution aimed at achieving unrestrained individual freedom. As philosopher R. R. Reno (2019) has argued, since the end of the Second World War secular humanists have viewed freedom in opposition to "strong ideas"—including nation, God, religion, and a defined moral code, which has resulted in a weakening of authoritative cultural institutions. But as Americans are discovering, when "strong gods" are abandoned, the unrestrained quest for individual freedom can result in societal chaos.

The idea of an "open society" began as a response by liberals to the twentieth-century totalitarianism that resulted in the enslavement

1

and death of millions, and in recent years, the notion of a border-less society has made strange bedfellows of Marxists and corporate globalists, who, while differing in their attitudes towards capitalism, agree that a new world order is necessary in order to counter ultra-nationalism.

As will be discussed, the freedom that characterizes monotheistic religion differs from both individual and political freedom, although at any given time all three notions can coexist in society, albeit with different emphases. Understanding how freedom and slavery are currently viewed in America's polarized culture is critical to understanding the nature of the conflict between progressives and conservatives. In the 1960s, America was enmeshed in an unpopular war in Vietnam and focused on defending individual freedoms. While political freedom was widely held to be a societal "good," the freedom that had traditionally been associated with identifying with an all-powerful "sovereign" was viewed as authoritarian and antiquated. Indeed, since the Enlightenment, sovereignal freedom was declared to be an impingement on individual freedom and identified with slavery. Nevertheless, this mode of freedom in its earliest manifestation can be seen in the book of Exodus, where Moses demands that Pharaoh free the Hebrews from slavery so they can worship God as their rightful "king" in the wilderness. Sovereignal freedom remains a behavioral goal for conservative religionists who profess belief in an almighty God.[1]

Marxism was conceived as a substitute for religion, and as a system of belief that opposes all impediments to freedom. Neo-Marxists view America as an imperialist "oppressor," i.e., as a nation that condoned slavery for the first century of its existence and that continues to subjugate marginal groups in society. They promote diversity, inclusion, and the redistribution of wealth as strategies that

---

[1] Here allow me to acknowledge my debt to Orlando Patterson, who laid out the tripartite division of freedom into personal, civic, and sovereign in his *Freedom in Western Culture* (Basic Books, 1991).

will transform America into a "utopia" in which all men are free to pursue their own pleasures. But in order to accomplish this, it is first necessary to convince Americans that the freedom of blacks, women, nonnormative genders, and the disabled is actively being undermined by reactionary conservatives.

The 1960s and '70s were characterized by protests for social justice inspired by Marxist ideas. When comprehensive civil rights legislation was passed by Congress, and the Vietnam War came to an end, most Americans naively imagined that the protests were at an end. But instead, the radicals of the '60s simply abandoned their revolutionary goals, and instead opted to continue the "revolution," not by violent means, but via the systematic infiltration of Marxist ideas into the culture. By the twenty-first century, they had succeeded in injecting neo-Marxist progressive ideas into the workings of the Democratic Party, government bureaucracies, the educational system, the news media, and large corporations. The culture had been "captured."

The goal of an "open society," however, was not limited to Marxists; others were also clamoring for increased freedoms. Western scholars adopted a postmodern philosophy that opposed "strong truths" that might impinge on the freedom of the individual, and in its place they promoted moral relativism and nonjudgmentalism as bulwarks against externally imposed limits. As a result, many Americans today labor under the illusion that freedom can only be achieved by opposing all limitations. They have naively embraced this idea without realizing that it will not guarantee their freedoms. Today, repackaged as "woke" progressivism, the revolutionary Marxism of the 1960s is well on its way toward dismantling America's institutions, and is waging ideological and political war on all authority, including God and morality. This "Godless Crusade" to rid the world of religion in pursuit of untrammeled freedom has already borne bitter fruit.

While bicoastal secular elites in America have materially benefited from the victories of progressive ideology, much of America has suffered. As sociologist Charles Murray argued in *Coming Apart*, the differences in elite "Belmont" and working-class "Fishtown" neighborhoods are not only material. Rather, the imposition of postmodern ideas by elites has wreaked havoc on the social fabric of America's working class, while elites quietly continue to adhere to "strong" values in rearing their own families, remaining largely immune to the consequences of the dystopia they have forcefully imposed on others (Murray 2012).

CHAPTER 1

The Truth

God is dead. God remains dead. And we have killed him.
How shall we comfort ourselves, the murderers of all murderers?
What was holiest and mightiest of all that the world has yet owned
has bled to death under our knives: who will wipe this blood off
us? What water is there for us to clean ourselves? What festivals of
atonement, what sacred games shall we have to invent? Is not the
greatness of this deed too great for us? Must we ourselves
not become gods simply to appear worthy of it?

—FRIEDRICH NIETZSCHE, *THE GAY SCIENCE*

Beauty is truth, truth beauty—that is all
Ye know on earth, and all ye need to know.

—JOHN KEATS, "ODE ON A GRECIAN URN"

"THE WORLD TODAY SPEAKS FOR ITSELF: by the evidence of its decay, it announces its dissolution. The farmers are vanishing from the countryside, commerce from the sea, soldiers from the camps; all honesty in business, all justice in the courts, all solidarity in friendship, all skill in the arts, all standards in morals all are disappearing" (Dodds 1963, 12).

These are the words of Cyprian, a third-century bishop of Carthage, but they describe what is transpiring in America today. The American economy is currently plagued by debt and inflation; commerce is beleaguered by opposing goals of globalism and protectionism; the military is stretched to its limits, its mission undermined by irrelevant social issues, and the justice system is tainted by partisan politics. America is in the midst of a "mostly peaceful" civil war that reflects its deep philosophical conflicts. Battle is being waged on authority, God, transmitted morality, and law and order, by "woke" secular humanists intent on transforming America into Godless society, one devoid of physical borders and cultural boundaries.

The West has been on a course toward denying God and metaphysical claims for centuries. In the eighteenth century, Enlightenment philosophers declared victory over the peripatetic scholastics of the medieval universities, whose *raison d'etre* was to reconcile reasoned metaphysical arguments for God's existence with Christianity. Today, we consider those scholastics to be benighted deniers of rational science. But some modern scholars continue to argue that the Enlightenment's claims against God and metaphysics were framed incorrectly (Burtt 2016). In the seventeenth century, the world was in the midst of a cognitive revolution, in which the metaphysical explanations for man's relationship to God were being challenged by a materialistic philosophy, one aimed at reframing man's role in the world. The prescientific Ptolemaic worldview was anthropocentric; it positioned man at the center of the cosmos, with the sun, moon, and planets all revolving around him (Hecht 2003). This cosmology situated man between God and nature, with the purpose of interrogating the mind of God in order to discern His reason for creation.

The emerging scientific worldview espoused by Galileo and Newton in the seventeenth century shifted this frame of reference. Man's role was now to investigate nature directly. As a consequence, Aristotle's

Figure 1: Evolving Perspectives on God, Man, and Nature

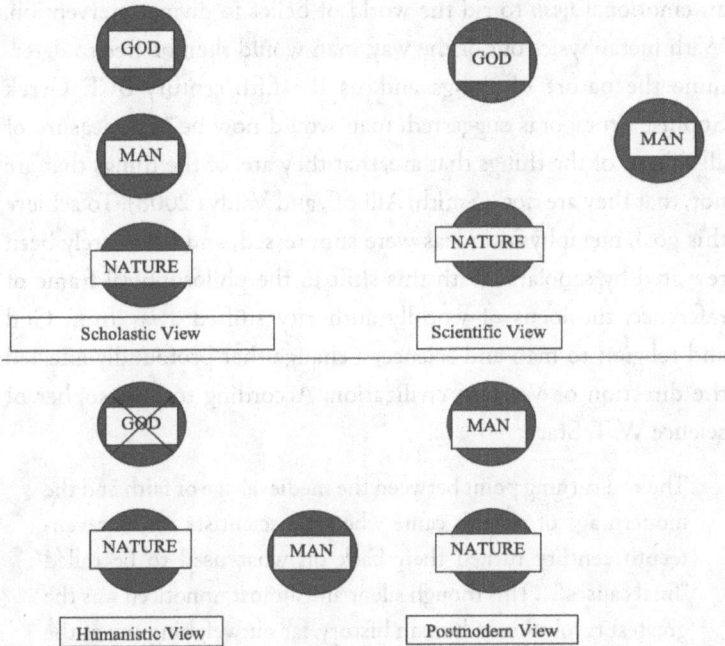

| Scholastic View | Scientific View |

| Humanistic View | Postmodern View |

metaphysical notions of purpose (*telos*)[2] and causality were replaced by mathematical descriptions of matter in motion (Burtt 2016). See Figure 1.

Although the functional explanations of nature by the scholastics were unquestionably incorrect, their metaphysical arguments for God and teleology could not be discredited by rational proofs, despite what later generations of students were led to believe. Instead, when the Enlightenment philosophers dismissed the search

---

[2] "Final cause," or *telos*, is one of the four types of causes described by Aristotle in the *Metaphysics*. This includes 1) material cause, 2) formal cause, 3) efficient cause, and 4) final cause. Final cause implies purpose, and this was used by Aristotle and medieval theologians to formulate rational arguments for God, monotheism, the soul, and morality. Those opposed to the notion of God argued against "final cause" but have never provided a convincing argument in this regard.

for God, meaning, and purpose as unscientific, they were expressing an emotional *wish* to rid the world of belief in divine intervention. With metaphysics out of the way, man would then be free to determine the nature of things and, as the fifth-century-BCE Greek Sophist Protagoras suggested, man would now be "the measure of all things: of the things that are, that they are, of the things that are not, that they are not" (Smith, Allhoff, and Vaidya 2008). To achieve this goal, metaphysical ideas were suppressed, and have rarely been revisited by scholars. With this shift in the philosophical frame of reference, the locus of worldly authority shifted away from God and religion to man and science, a change that profoundly affected the direction of Western civilization. According to philosopher of science W. T. Stace:

> The real turning point between the medieval age of faith and the modern age of unfaith came when the scientists of the seventeenth century turned their back on what used to be called "final causes."…This though silent and almost unnoticed was the greatest revolution in human history, far outweighing any of the political revolutions whose thunder reverberated through the world.… The conception of purpose in the world was ignored and frowned upon. The world according to this new picture is purposeless, senseless, meaningless. It came to be believed that moral rules must be merely an expression of our own likes and dislikes.… Therefore, morals are totally relative (Feser 2008, 225–26).

Unfortunately, this has misled generations to believe that no meaning can be found in life.

Secular humanists in the nineteenth century championed naturalist Charles Darwin's ideas concerning evolution, believing they provided proof that metaphysics can rationally be ignored, as Darwin's theory opposes not only creationism but teleology as well. But as philosopher Edward Feser (2019) argues in *Aristotle's Revenge*, all science relies on metaphysical assumptions. As man is apparently hardwired to think in terms of causality and purpose, metaphysical ideas cannot be expunged.

As the secular humanist project of discrediting God was slow to unfold, science and religion managed to coexist uncomfortably for centuries. But in its most recent iteration as progressive "woke" neo-Marxism,[3] secular humanism has adopted a militant stand, one that actively crusades against God and morality as symbols of "strong" authority that oppose freedom. In the late nineteenth century, German philosopher Friedrich Nietzsche (2012) proclaimed that "God is dead," and warned that being freed from authority would leave man with no moral compass with which to navigate the world. Nietzsche's warning has now been fulfilled, as Americans find themselves facing moral challenges with few available tools to address them.

The "Judeo-Christian ethic" has been the basis of American morality since the nation's founding, and together with the capitalist free-market economy, it has contributed to America's "exception-alism." Yet few are aware that the Judeo-Christian ethic is a recent concept. The term "Judeo-Christian" was coined in 1939 by English writer George Orwell (1968) to describe the moral vision shared by the two great Western monotheistic religious traditions. But the moniker ignores their critical differences. Judaism is based on a divinely revealed command morality. It is authoritarian by design, a clear example of philosopher Rusty Reno's "strong gods" (2019). Christianity, on the other hand, is a syncretism of Jewish revelation, Greek philosophy, and Roman law, and its increased emphasis on rationality and individual salvation inadvertently opened the door for "weak gods" to enter, during the Protestant Reformation (Wallis 1972).

---

[3] The terms "Progressivism," "woke," and "Marxism" are used interchangeably in this text because today they essentially overlap.

Since the Enlightenment, secular humanists have claimed that morality is the product of human reason, not divine revelation. By the twentieth century, "postmodern" philosophers were insisting, in line with Enlightenment philosopher David Hume, that morality is both subjective, and relative—that it is impossible to define objectively and cannot credibly be imposed by consensus—a distinctly "antiauthoritarian" stance favoring the uninhibited freedom of the individual. Consequently, the Judeo-Christian ethic is viewed as biased and aimed at preserving the status quo of conservative elites. In a pluralistic society, shared moralities are now judged as unwelcome impositions on the freedom of the individual, whereas moral stances that are nonjudgmental and favor diversity and inclusiveness are seen as fostering freedom. From this perspective, immorality cannot be defined except as a social construct that opposes the freedom of the individual. But such reasoning runs counter to the very purpose of morality, which is to provide a guide for how men are to behave with one another in a society. As philosopher Harry Frankfurt (2006b, 47) opines: "It is sensible to insist that moral truths are and must be stringently objective. After all, it would hardly do to suppose that the requirements of morality depend upon what we happen to want them to be, or upon what we happen to think they are."

No society can function effectively based on the idiosyncratic values of individuals, and the absence of a shared morality undermines political freedom. When morality is determined solely by self-interest, it can only function effectively if there is uniform conformity without opposition, or when imposed by the power of a state apparatus. When postmodern morality is imposed by the state, tolerance is extended only to like-minded individuals, while those who take issue with the elite/state consensus will be judged as "evil." Those who decry the current unequal administration of justice that appears to favor progressives while targeting conservatives must recognize that postmodern progressive ideology cannot be expected to extend tolerance to those who do not conform to its ideas and that it views punishment of dissenting conservatives as justified.

The present cultural revolution can be framed as pitting those whose values are rooted in postmodern moral relativism against those who adhere to the Judeo-Christian ethic.[4] But more accurately it is a conflict between those who imbue man and the state with the highest powers and those who remain loyal to a transcendent notion of sovereignal freedom. Sovereignal freedom is achieved by identifying with a power greater than oneself, be it the God of monotheism or a monarch imbued with divine powers, as ancient kings often were. The conservative adheres to a combination of sovereignal, political, and individual freedoms, whereas the progressive materialist splits the metaphysical category of sovereignal freedom and unconsciously confers its transcendental qualities onto the individual and the state (Patterson 1991). See Figure 2 on page 11.

Freedom never exists as a concept on its own; instead, the notion of freedom always evokes slavery, and *vice versa*. The championing of absolute personal freedom endows progressivism with the feeling-tone of a religion. However, the notion of unlimited personal freedom is an illusion that necessarily leads to unexpected modes of enslavement. The "free" individual who during the Covid epidemic insisted on the need for the universal wearing of face masks or vaccine mandates was enslaved to rules that encroached on individual freedom.

Since the French Revolution, the conflict between those who demand unlimited personal freedom and those who recognize its limits has been the core ideological difference between liberals and conservatives (Kirk 1953). For the last hundred years, liberalism in its various avatars—all motivated by a Dionysian impulse in

---

[4] There may be secularists who claim a belief in God, but that is doubtful. The God of both Judaism and Christianity requires a parallel belief in reward and punishment and the tenets of the Judeo-Christian ethic as determined by religious tradition. Present-day deists and agnostics do not fall into this category.

Figure 2: The Chord of Freedom

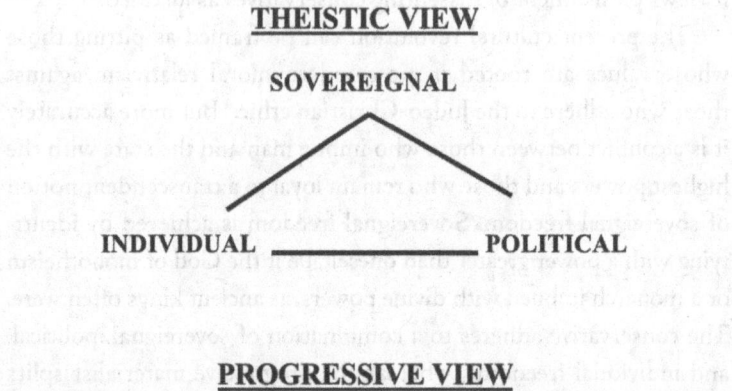

THEISTIC VIEW

SOVEREIGNAL

INDIVIDUAL _____ **POLITICAL**

PROGRESSIVE VIEW

INDIVIDUAL (sovereignal) _____ **POLITICAL (sovereignal)**

(Adapted from the work of Orlando Patterson, 1991)

the collective psyche toward unrestricted individual freedom—has dominated America's culture, including its art, laws, and habits. That domination was reflected in the post–World War II consensus that "openness" is the antidote to authority and totalitarianism, by favoring diversity over homogeneity, inclusiveness over exclusion, and open borders over closed ones.

This mindset was an emotional overreaction to the horrors of the last European world war. Yet it is questionable whether such thinking is the antidote to "fascism." Evidence against the open-versus-closed dichotomy is found in nature. All living forms must be permeable to the environment in order to obtain the elements required to sustain life and to excrete metabolites, but they must also establish effective barriers against potentially hostile environments. Finding the optimal balance between an open and closed system is the challenge, as the polar extremes of openness and closedness are incompatible with life. In this regard, a living society is no different from a living organism. An "open" society is no better equipped for success than one that is rigidly "closed."

While American society has prided itself on its relative openness, in recent years progressives have increasingly rejected the notion of any boundaries. As philosopher Terry Eagleton (2014) opined, the goal has increasingly been to replace "hard" religious values with "soft" secular ones. Neo-Marxists and globalists have recognized that changing a nation's political system is most effectively achieved by first capturing its culture (Corsi 2023). So the opening battles in the "Godless Crusade" have been fought under the banner of a "Culture War."

In his evaluation of the new American nation, nineteenth-century French observer Alexis de Tocqueville (2000) concluded, "Liberty cannot be established without morality, nor morality without faith," and he was referring to an authoritative morality, not the postmodern subjective one. But "strong" beliefs are waning in twenty-first-century America, as a 2022 Gallup poll reports:

> Belief in God has fallen the most in recent years among young adults and people on the left of the political spectrum (liberals and Democrats). These groups show drops of 10 or more percentage points comparing the 2022 figures to an average of the 2013–2017 polls. Most other key subgroups have experienced at least a modest decline, although conservatives and married adults have had essentially no change.
>
> The groups with the largest declines are also the groups that are currently least likely to believe in God, including liberals (62%), young adults (68%) and Democrats (72%). Belief in God is highest among political conservatives (94%) and Republicans (92%), reflecting that religiosity is a major determinant of political divisions in the U.S. (Gallup 2022).

While interest in religion has diminished, the desire to be viewed as "virtuous" by others has apparently increased. However, culturally determined virtue is rarely motivated by deeply held beliefs. Instead, it is often the result of peer and political pressures. This fosters conformity and leads to shared perceptual distortions, as Hans Christian Andersen suggested in the tale of "The Emperor's New Clothes."

Formulating accurate assessments of reality depends on access to facts. Unfortunately, few people have contact with facts that occur at a distance, and consequently most of us depend on others entrusted to provide us with them. In the past, this was the role of the "free" press. A good journalist was expected to dispassionately report facts and then leave it to the public to interpret them. While this ideal was rarely achieved, it was in theory the goal. But during the recent Covid-19 pandemic, not only the public but medical professionals as well found it impossible to discern what was true about the disease because the "facts" being provided were more often propaganda than truth.

Today, rather than attempting to provide facts, many journalists work to conceal facts that do not support the progressive ideological narrative, justifying their ill-conceived effort as virtuous opposition to "reactionary authoritarian forces" in society. As a result, Americans today are ill-informed and inundated with more false "facts" about what is transpiring than at any time in recent history. The little-discussed truth is that journalism has long been the propaganda arm of the state. An insight into how it is manipulated by political forces was recently offered by Ben Rhodes, a Deputy National Security Advisor during the Obama administration, in a statement to the *New York Times*: "'All these newspapers used to have foreign bureaus,' Rhodes told the *Times* in May. 'Now they don't. They call us to explain to them what's happening in Moscow and Cairo. Most of the outlets are reporting on world events from Washington. The average reporter we talk to is 27 years old, and their only reporting experience consists of being around political campaigns. That's a sea change.... They literally know nothing'" (Samuels 2016).

What Is Truth?

What is truth? This age-old question cynically posed by Pilate during the trial of Jesus has in recent years been revived by post-modern philosophers and those who purposefully choose to distort truth for political advantage. In the fifth century BCE, Plato (2001) argued that Truth was a supernal Form, an eternal and unchanging archetype. In the *Republic* he described man's grasp of the truth as a shadowy approximation of Truth and argued that it was the philosopher's task to seek beyond the obvious to encounter Truth itself. Plato insisted that only the immutable Truth is "real," whereas all that is subject to change is "false"—a perspective that modern philosophers term *realism*. Like the monotheistic religionists, Plato equated Truth with a supreme Being. But this notion of Truth has been rejected by postmodernists as excessively "strong," as it lacks the relativistic ambiguity required to appease their desire for unlimited personal freedom.

The Enlightenment philosophers believed that truth exists, but unlike the scholastic philosophy and the traditional Christianity that they were rebelling against (and also unlike Plato and Aristotle), they also believed that truth was limited to the material world and could only be discerned through empiric observation. This denial of metaphysical truths, known as "nominalism," is the basis of Western materialistic science. But as Feser argues, the nominalist worldview is fraught with rational inconsistencies, and abandoning Platonic "realism" may have been the "single greatest mistake ever made in the history of Western civilization" (Feser 2008, 51).

Beginning in the early twentieth century, scientific rationality was challenged by the probabilistic uncertainties of the quantum world. Schrodinger's wave equation indicated that particles were located probabilistically in space rather than in discrete locations, and Heisenberg's uncertainty principle demonstrated that participation in the act of observation ultimately affects what is being observed and that we live in a universe in which outer reality cannot be clearly separated from subjectivity. But at the scale of everyday reality, quantum rules needlessly complicate the assessment of the physical world. One does not require quantum mechanics or relativity theory to describe the behavior of objects in motion in the everyday world. Instead, these activities are well described by Newtonian mechanics, which assumes that objects are discrete and unaffected by observation (Feynman 2011). The postmodern inclination to challenge the obvious harkens back to the ancient Sophists who challenged the institutions of ancient Athenian society rhetoric, for which Plato denounced them as more concerned with words than truth (Rommen 1998). In response to postmodern nihilism, Frankfurt (2006b) insists, "Truth-seeking and truth-telling must be rewarded, and their inverse must be punished. Truth is truth whether or not anyone believes it or even knows it." Cultural critic John Gray (2003, 55) concurs and has opined that "the postmodern denial of truth is the worst kind of arrogance. In denying that the natural world exists independently of our beliefs about it, postmodernists are implicitly rejecting any limit on human ambitions. By making human beliefs the final arbiter of reality, they are effectively claiming that nothing exists unless it appears in human consciousness.

The current cultural revolution pits the postmodern philosophy of progressives against conservatives who continue to believe that truth exists and is worthy of pursuit. Nietzsche recognized that this controversy posed a choice between living with a sense of meaning and nihilistic chaos. Postmodernism discounts man's innate inclination to seek meaning, ignoring the fact that this impulse cannot be suppressed. It is an *opus contra naturam* and as such is ultimately doomed to fail, because nature imposes real limitations. Nor can man's thirst for meaning be expunged. But the archetypal reaction against authority and the irrepressible impulse toward unachievable freedom in the human psyche is also real and cannot be eradicated.

As such they are fated periodically to reemerge. The demise of post-modernism may not occur in the immediate future, but ultimately Dionysian impulses must give way to Apollonian ones that strive for truth and order.

Identifying truth requires both the will to pursue it and hard work. Today many view truth-seeking as excessively arduous, as the collective will of the present culture has been eroded and now values convenience over truth. As the conservative educator James Wilson (2017, 321) has opined, "The relentless hum of goodwill serves to distract us from the fact that we no longer believe the truth could be anything greater than the crude intractable matter we seek to control in the name of bodily comfort; we begin to suspect, as it were, that if silence should fall upon our mind and our hearts for a moment, we might awaken to discover the world and ourselves are alike devoid of meaning."

Lies

Lies oppose truth, and virtually all religious traditions view lying as immoral. But as journalist Ralph Keyes (2004) suggests in *The Post-Truth Era*, truth today is increasingly viewed as flexible, and lying as acceptable. According to a 2023 *New York Post* article, lying is commonplace among America's youth: "A new survey found that of all generations, those born between 1981 and 1996 are the biggest culprits of lying in the workplace and on social media.... The findings showed that millennials were the worst offenders, with 13% copping to being dishonest at least once a day. By contrast, only 2% of baby boomers, those born between 1946 and 1964, fibbed once per day" (Lefroy 2023).

This is what can be expected from a culture that embraces moral "relativism," in which lying is tacitly sanctioned, and few are held accountable. While the Judeo-Christian ethic views truth-telling as critical for personal integrity and lying as a serious character flaw, neither character nor integrity have meaning for those who reject truth as excessively "rigid." But as Nietzsche (2003) recognized, lying erodes one's ability to trust others. As he stated in *Beyond Good and Evil*, it is "not that you lied to me but that I no longer believe you [that] has shaken me."

When truth is relative and relationships are conducted at a distance on social media, the need to trust others is diminished. Nevertheless, the quest for truth has sustained Western civilization, and in its absence it must be expected to decline.

The Neurobiology of Truth

The mind has a propensity to distort reality to accord with preconceptions and emotional biases, a phenomenon that has been termed "truthiness." This tendency allows a person to ignore facts that "feel" wrong. It is a widespread phenomenon, and it is common today to hear people claim that something is true simply because it "feels right." But when *truthiness* replaces *truthfulness*, constructive dialogue is impossible.

Psychologists attribute this to "confirmation bias," the tendency to interpret reality in a way that is consistent with one's preexisting beliefs, and to seek only information that confirms them. But this begs the question as to why this should be the case. In *The Master and His Emissary*, neuropsychiatrist Iain McGilchrist (2018) details how information is normally processed differently by the right and left cerebral hemispheres of the brain. The right hemisphere grounds sensory experiences in the body, orients the person in space, and generates mental images rooted in sensations. It also mediates intuition and contributes to the construction of metaphor and to mythopoesis. Much of what is termed the "unconscious" can be attributed to activities mediated by the right brain (Joseph 1992). The primary role of the left hemisphere, on the other hand, is to re-present images generated initially by the right brain and then "translate" them into conscious language-dependent cognitions that are the bases of speech and the written word.

While the left hemisphere can re-present information from the right hemisphere accurately, at times the functional cooperation between the two hemispheres is skewed. Bi-hemispheric cooperation can be biased by excessive intellectualization or conversely by imaginings, or by drugs and disease. In the laboratory, when the activity of the right hemisphere is experimentally silenced by inhibiting neural transmission across nerve bundles that connect the hemispheres, the left hemisphere continues to autonomously create narratives divorced from physical reality. When confronted with facts that do not align with this fabricated narrative, the unopposed left brain will resist this information and instead continue to insist on its version of reality (McGilchrist 2018).

This propensity to create narratives divorced from reality is termed "confabulation," a phenomenon classically observed in Wernicke's syndrome, a form of brain damage due to nutritional deficiency often seen in chronic alcoholism, and with other forms of brain injury. Damage to the right frontal lobe is a constant feature in these cases. Confabulation is distinguished from lying, as it is not purposeful deception. But confabulating individuals will present blatantly false information, although their narratives may appear coherent, internally consistent, and plausible to an unbiased observer (Damasio 2000). And they themselves believe them.

The conclusion to be drawn from this is that left-hemispheric dominance favors the construction of false narratives that are rigidly adhered to. Might this account for "truthiness" and abstract narratives that do not jibe with reality? The answer is uncertain, but the question merits consideration.

Truthiness and Immaturity

As noted, "truthiness" reflects a dissociation between rationality and feeling-toned imaginings. While observed in all age groups, it is most often seen in childhood, where it reflects the immaturity of the developing brain. In contrast to the development of other mammals, human brain maturation occurs predominantly *ex utero* and continues for the first three decades of life (Sapolsky 2017). As a 2017 bulletin of the American Academy of Child and Adolescent Psychiatry states, "Pictures of the brain in action show that adolescents' brains work differently than adults when they make decisions or solve problems. Their actions are guided more by the emotional and reactive amygdala and less by the thoughtful, logical frontal cortex. Research has also shown that exposure to drugs and alcohol during the teen years can change or delay these developments." While this does not mean that teenagers should be excused for their actions, it does suggest that they are not well positioned to make important decisions.

The capacity of the left brain to represent reality depends on "instruction" of the nervous system via a strategy that Nobel laureate Gerald Edelman (1987) termed "neural Darwinism." According to this theory, the brain includes a "primary" neural repertoire at birth that subsequently undergoes experiential postnatal "pruning" in which selected neural pathways are strengthened via repeated use while others drop out through disuse. The end result is a mature adult brain with a "secondary" neural repertoire that exhibits limited plasticity throughout life.

The nervous system's ability to assess reality depends on experience-based neural instruction by parents, teachers, and caretakers. But when children are encouraged to accept fantasy over reality, or when their experience is constrained by overly protective caretakers, normal mental maturation may be impeded. Sheryl Wilson and Theodore Barber (1983) examined the childhood antecedents responsible for fantasy-proneness in later life and found them to include "a parent, grandparent, teacher, or friend who...reinforced the child's fantasies."

Progressive pedagogues promote mental immaturity by indoctrinating impressionable youth with false notions of unrealistic potential and by censoring uncomfortable truths that conflict with these narratives. Neurotically fearful parents limit their child's exposure based on what they misperceive as the "harmful" effects of reality. Unfortunately, as developmental milestones are time-dependent, once critical maturational time points have passed, it may be impossible to reverse deficits fully. In this regard, adults subjected to "brainwashing" as children in Communist China and who subsequently emigrated to free societies have reported substantial difficulties accepting truths that conflicted with their early indoctrination (Lifton 2014).

The response of college students to the recent terrorist attacks on civilian Jews in Israel provides a cogent example of how difficult it may be to assess reality properly in the face of ideological indoctrination. Israel was founded as a Jewish state in response to the destruction of six million European Jews in the last century, an event that culminated two millennia of European anti-Semitism. Israel's statehood was approved by a majority vote of the United Nations at a time when the world recognized that it was impossible for Jews to live safely as a minority either in Christian Europe or in Islamic countries.[5]

Nevertheless, progressive ideologues insist on labeling Israel a "colonial power" that "oppresses" Palestinians, while ignoring the reason for its founding. Its critics also discount the facts that Israel has not occupied Gaza or the West Bank since the early 2000s and that Palestinians have consistently refused to accept Israel or the presence of Jews in what they insist is the Islamic world.[6] Progressives ignore

---

[5] The Islamic countries that bemoan Israel as a colonizing power might well be asked what has become of the Jews that inhabited their lands for centuries. The answer is that they were expelled from these countries once Israel was declared a state and that there are virtually no Jews left in what had been their ancestral homes.

[6] Any honest observer of this conflict knows that the Palestinians have no interest in making peace with Israel. Organizations such as Hamas and Hezbollah are Islamist, and like the former Islamic State, they seek the recreation of an Islamic caliphate, a theocracy free of Jews and Christians and subject to *sharia* law. Narratives that deny this fact are either ignorant or disingenuous.

the multiple attempts by Palestinians and surrounding Arab states to destroy Israel through unprovoked wars and terrorism, as well.

In the October 2023 terrorist attack on Israelis, Hamas Islamists barbarically raped and massacred over one thousand Israeli men, women, and children, including babies, with no other goal than to rid the land of Jews, and they did so with the approval and assistance of noncombatant Palestinians, including employees of the United Nations working in Gaza. Indeed, the notion that Hamas and the Palestinian people are distinct is a fantasy, one apparently shared by the progressive Biden administration, which continued to insist on an unrealistic "two-state solution."[7]

Despite these documented facts, many college students on progressive university campuses have been indoctrinated to believe that Israel is a "colonizing oppressor" state composed of "privileged whites" who are persecuting people of color—despite the fact that dark-skinned Sephardic Jews of Middle Eastern and African descent make up 55 percent of the Israeli Jewish population, and are physically indistinguishable from Palestinians. Sheltered from reality and indoctrinated into a culture of moral relativism, these elite students are unable to recognize the lack of moral equivalency between barbaric acts of terrorism directed at innocent citizens and the response of a beleaguered nation-state charged with defending its citizens. This is sobering evidence of how distorted the conceptions of reality have become for many of America's youth.

When, following the October 7 massacre, the presidents of Harvard, M.I.T., and the University of Pennsylvania were questioned before Congress and asked to explain the anti-Israeli and anti-Semitic activities on their campuses and why they were unwilling to condemn terrorism, murder, rape, and infanticide or to acknowledge the scapegoating of Jewish students on their campuses, they refused

---

[7] A similar fantasy was created for the German people, who progressives in the West insisted were distinct from the Nazi regime, despite substantial evidence that most Germans enthusiastically supported Hitler's policies.

to provide an acceptable answer. The subsequent outrage in response to their perceived moral bankruptcy on the part of the public and many large donors rapidly forced the white female president of the University of Pennsylvania to resign. But the Harvard president, a progressive black woman, continued to receive the support of the Harvard faculty for over a month, until she too was forced to resign, not on account of her responses to Congress but because she was found to have committed serial instances of plagiarism in her publications. When she did finally step down, she attributed her resignation to "racism," and the board of the Harvard Corporation offered no apologies for its delayed and weak response to public accusations of institutional anti-Semitism.

Mob Mentality

In recent years, America has witnessed numerous political protests by progressives in which people have been killed and private property damaged. While Americans have a constitutional right to assemble, they do not have the right to kill or destroy property in doing so. Nevertheless, these protests were perceived as morally justified by local progressive lawmakers and those in Washington, DC, ostensibly on account of their support of "social justice," and there were few legal repercussions for protesters who committed criminal acts. On the other hand, many conservatives who participated peacefully in the January 6, 2021, election protests at the Capitol routinely received lengthy jail sentences for simply being on the wrong side of the cultural divide, raising serious concerns about a two-tiered criminal justice system.

Regardless of whether protests occur on the left or right of the political spectrum, what is unquestionably true is that people in groups show a diminished capacity to assess situations rationally and to curb violent behavior (Le Bon 1899). This phenomenon was described in the nineteenth century by the French philosopher Lucien Lévy-Bruhl, who termed it "participation mystique" and attributed it to a collective lowering of rational consciousness.[8] According to Swiss psychoanalyst Carl Jung (1976), "A group experience takes place on a lower level of consciousness than the experience of an individual. This is due to the fact that, when many people gather together to share one common emotion, the total psyche emerging from the group is below the level of the individual psyche. If it is a very large group, the collective psyche will be more like the psyche of an animal, which is the reason why the ethical attitude of large organizations is always doubtful. The psychology of a large crowd inevitably sinks to the level of mob psychology."

Mistrust of mobs runs through the history of political philosophy. Plato criticized Athenian democracy[9] because of the propensity of a numerical majority to ignore the rights of others and to embrace policies that are not necessarily in the best interests of society.[10] This mistrust of direct democracy was shared by America's Founding Fathers, who opted to create a democratic republic rather than leave the fate of the new nation to the whims of the majority. As Polybius suggested in the second century BCE, oligarchy inevitably tends to change to democracy, democracy to mob rule, and mob rule to tyranny (Fox 2006). In the nineteenth century, Tocqueville (2000) remarked that "I know no country, in which, generally speaking, there is less independence of mind and true freedom of discussion than in America." Indeed, the group experience of democracy can lead to the suppression of free discourse and the negation of personal liberties, as it did during the French Jacobin revolution, which began as a democracy but quickly devolved into a Reign of Terror and finally into Napoleon's tyranny.

[8] It has been suggested that participation in groups may activate primitive precognitive modes of communication.

[9] See The Statesman, 302b, 302e-303a (Plato 1925).

[10] Plato's animus toward democracy was in part personal. His uncle had been executed by a democratic government, and his mentor Socrates was also executed by a democratic regime that accused him of corrupting the morals of Athens's youth. See The Apology (Plato 2001).

Censorship

In the fifth century BCE, Socrates introduced dialogue as a path toward seeking truth (Waterfield 2023). Freedom of speech was guaranteed by America's Founding Fathers and it has undoubtedly contributed to American "exceptionalism." But the recent demands for increased "democracy" by progressives have been accompanied by concomitant calls for censoring dissenting speech. Convinced of the superiority of their ideas, progressives do not believe that those who disagree with their agenda should be allowed to voice their opinions publicly. This has been most evident in America's higher educational facilities, which in the past were the guardians of free speech: "A new nation-wide survey found that 80% of students self-censor on their university campuses, with a significant portion feeling intimidated to speak on controversial topics in class or to a professor. A large percentage of students believe that it is acceptable to 'shout down' and silence speakers on campus that hold opposing views" (Camp 2022). This rise in censorship reflects an emerging totalitarian impulse in American society that has resulted from progressive ideas of "freedom."

Government Lies

Lying to the public has always been part of how leaders govern. In Renaissance Italy, the courtier Niccolò Machiavelli (1847) advised rulers to mask their true intentions and to "act against mercy, against faith, against humanity, against frankness, against religion, in order to preserve the state." While it is a long-standing strategy, deception reached new heights in the twentieth century, when totalitarian governments implemented propaganda to manipulate citizens.

In *1984*, George Orwell presciently described the unscrupulous manipulation of truth. Orwell was a left-wing journalist who grew disenchanted with communism when he recognized that Stalin had betrayed the socialist cause in the Spanish Civil War. In *1984*, the state interrogator O'Brien informs Winston, the ill-fated protagonist, "We are not interested in the good of others, we are interested solely in power." He goes on to explain how truth and reality can be bent in any direction that the state decides: "You believe that reality is something objective, external, existing in its own right.... When you delude yourself into thinking that you see the same, you assume that everyone sees the same thing you do. But I tell you, Winston, that reality is not external. Reality exists in the human mind, and nowhere else. Not in the individual mind, which can make mistakes, and in any case soon perishes: only in the mind of the party, which is collective and immortal. Whatever the party holds to be truth, *is* truth" (Orwell 1983, 118). O'Brien's argument illustrates how postmodern philosophy has provided the intellectual justification for totalitarianism.

In *Live Not by Lies*, Christian journalist Rod Dreher argues that totalitarian governments prefer to achieve their goals by manipulating minds, tending to use force only as a last resort. To control their citizenry, totalitarian governments depend on the assistance of the news media to censor truth and to disseminate pro-government propaganda. In progressive culture, truth is viewed as fluid and relative, meeting the "weakness" criterion that Reno has laid out (Reno 2019). When citizens cannot reconcile their experience with what their governments are telling them is true, they may become demoralized and placid, which is precisely what is currently occurring in America, where an increasingly totalitarian progressive Democratic Party has co-opted the major media and information technology platforms to tailor the information that the public is allowed to consume. They have been successful because the public has been lulled by distractions and conveniences. As Dreher notes:

> Soft totalitarianism...makes use of advanced surveillance technology not (yet) imposed by the state, but rather welcomed by consumers as aids to lifestyle convenience—and in the

post-pandemic environment likely needed for public health. It is hard to get worked up over Big Brother when you have already grown accustomed to Big Data closely monitoring your private life via apps, credit cards, and smart devices, which make life so much easier and more pleasurable. In Orwell's fictional dystopia, the state installed "telescreens" in private homes to keep track of individual lives. Today we install smart speakers into our homes to increase our sense of well-being (Dreher 2020, 11).

If Americans are to regain a proper relationship to truth, they must be willing to examine ideas and attitudes that have become deeply entrenched within the culture because of progressive propaganda and question whether they benefit society. This includes deeply embedded positions on race, sex, abortion, crime, diversity, inclusion, equity, and freedom. Only the return of strong moral principles is likely to reverse the trend toward civilizational decline and dissolution.

CHAPTER 2

Religion and Science

Science can purify religion from error and superstition.
Religion can purify science from idolatry and false absolutes.

—POPE JOHN PAUL II (1988)

THE TERM "RELIGION" IS DERIVED from the Latin *re ligare*, which means to reestablish a connection—that is, to renew the bond between man and God (Griffiths 2000).

Prior to the Reformation, it was virtually impossible to imagine a public profession of atheism in Western society, and a formal concept of "religion" did not exist. But as Christianity began to fragment, scholars saw a need to define what religion is, and it soon became clear that no single definition addressed all of its possible manifestations.

In the sixteenth century, historian Edward Herbert suggested that a *monotheistic* religion should satisfy five conditions:

1. Belief in the existence of a supreme deity
2. Worship of that deity

3. The cultivation of virtue
4. Repentance for wrongdoing
5. Belief in reward or punishment in this life or the next

There were Enlightenment thinkers who embraced the notion of a creator God but did not believe in divine intervention, or in reward and punishment in the next life. For the most part, these "Deists" continued to adopt the Judeo-Christian ethic as their guide for how to behave in society. Thomas Jefferson (2004) was a Deist who created his own Bible by cutting Jesus's sayings from the New Testament and pasting them into a book, expurgating all references to miracles and whatever else he judged to be "irrational." Jefferson viewed Jesus not as a divine being but as a teacher of morality and a role model for how to conduct one's life.

Inventing "Religion"

In the early twentieth century, the pioneering sociologist Emile Durkheim defined "functional religion" as "those practices that tend to unite a people into a moral community" (Griffiths 2000). This definition potentially included systems of belief organized around a strong unifying atheistic ideology—Marxism, for example. Eagleton has suggested that a cardinal feature of functional religion is reliance on political action to realize its goals, and this explains why progressivism, which qualifies as a functional religion, is seemingly preoccupied with political activism. In the absence of God, "woke" religion has no other way to achieve its goals than in the political arena. But a godless progressive religion cannot abide competition from traditional religion and therefore progressives see it as their duty to oust Christianity and Judaism from the public square and replace them with the new atheistic—in fact, misotheistic, i.e., God-hating—religion. Thus, the need for a "Godless Crusade."

Despite obvious differences from traditional religions, a misotheistic functional religion intent on denying God must remain tethered to theistic values, although it will be predisposed to manipulate these for its own ends. All misotheistic functional religions are skewed restatements of theistic values. It is noteworthy that there are atheists who hold no animus toward theistic religion. While they do not believe in God, they remain tolerant of those who do. However, because of its political aims, a misotheistic functional religion like progressivism cannot abide expressions of theistic religion in the public square, and it will take every opportunity to attack religious values by deriding the observance of religious holidays[1] or, as has occurred recently, by labeling traditional religionists as potential domestic terrorists (Gray 2018). Much of the progress in this regard has been achieved by distorting First Amendment guarantees of religious freedom and applying "separation of church and state" in ways the nation's Founders never intended.

Some conservatives do not recognize the functional religious basis of progressive culture and cannot comprehend why it is focused on politicizing society, or why its rise has been accompanied by an attendant rise in anti-religious sentiment directed against Christians and Jews. They remain puzzled about why the progressive justice system targets churches for lawsuits, labels Catholics "domestic terrorists," exhibits blatant anti-Semitism, and attacks pro-lifers. They fail to appreciate the anti-religious animus of progressivism because it is rarely openly admitted. Instead, progressives often wrap themselves in a cloak of Christian compassion in an effort to co-opt the Judeo-Christian ethic, while concomitantly undermining the religious freedoms of observant Christians and Jews.

"Woke" Religion

"Woke" is the most recent iteration of postmodern neoliberalism, with roots in three areas of overlapping thought: 1) Marxism,

---

[1] The holiday of Christmas has been a prime target, while the concocted holiday of Kwanza is encouraged.

2) the post–World War II neoliberal tradition, and 3) the post-'60s emphasis on "identity." It is a functional religion that, like Marxism itself, aims at deconstructing the foundations of American society by insisting that America's institutions are "oppressive" and should be uprooted. It views race as the most obvious example of this, but also supports other "oppressed" groups, including women, LGBTQ+, and the disabled. It holds "white privilege" responsible for these injustices, but as investigative journalist James Simpson notes, "'White' does not mean white. 'White' in radical deconstruction means anyone of any race, creed, nationality, color, sex, or sexual preference who embraces capitalism, free markets, limited government, and American traditional culture and values. By definition, these beliefs are irredeemably evil and anyone who aligns with them is 'white' in spirit and thus equally guilty of white crimes'" (Simpson 2021, 61).

"Woke" notions of social justice are to be distinguished from those of biblical social justice (Neusner and Chilton 2009; Pluckrose and Lindsay 2020). Whereas biblical social justice seeks fair treatment for marginalized groups in society, "woke" social justice aims at deconstructing the *source* of these injustices, which it imagines to be *all* of America's institutions. According to Critical Race Theory (CRT), which applies Marxist critical theory to blacks and other identity groups, only the "oppressed" are in a position to define the socio-economic–political disparities in society, and their perspectives must be deferred to. There is no room for difference of opinion or compromise with anyone who challenges "woke" ideas. It is a puritanical, intolerant, and overtly racist religious movement.

"Woke" social justice adopts the ideas of Harvard philosopher John Rawls (1971), who argued that 1) each person has an equal right to the most extensive basic liberties, and 2) social and economic inequalities should be arranged so that they are to the greatest benefit of the least advantaged. The "woke" notion of "equity," which must be distinguished from equality, insists on equality of outcome, a notion that can be traced back to Rousseau and the radical Jacobin leaders of the French Revolution. It is distinct from the Enlightenment notions of social justice that characterized the Civil Rights Movement and the early feminism of the 1960s.

"Woke" relies on the four pillars of postmodernism: 1) the social construction of self, 2) moral relativism, 3) cultural deconstruction, and 4) globalization. As we have seen, it adopts Marxist critical theory, calling for the "ruthless criticism of everything existing" (Marx 1843). In this regard it shares what Paul Ricoeur termed a "hermeneutic of suspicion" (Felski 2012) with the ideas of Marx, Freud, and Nietzsche, who insisted that one must first deconstruct ideas to arrive at their "real" meaning. "Woke" views classical Marxism as having failed by having focused excessively on economic disparities rather than on the dichotomous division of society into "oppressed" and "oppressor."

"Woke" ideology seeks out power disparities and finds them everywhere. It manipulates language through "political correctness" to silence opposition and to shame opponents for lacking sufficient compassion for the downtrodden—something it borrows from the prophetic traditions of the Hebrew Bible and that was accentuated in the Christian Gospels. As a misotheistic secular ideology, "woke" exploits the Judeo-Christian ethic to support its claims, while concomitantly distorting that ethic to consolidate political power. It insists on deconstructing traditional society, but offers few ideas for how to rebuild it. Instead, it provides platitudes such as "Build Back Better," without defining what such terms mean. It is a nihilistic ideology, one fueled by envy, greed, and hatred, that aims to punish conservatives and those who continue to espouse the Judeo-Christian ethic.

"Woke" is antithetic to the values of theistic religion. While it can superficially claim to offer compassion toward those it judges as "oppressed," that "compassion" is accompanied by vicious attacks on anyone who does not agree with it. Its recent support for Islamic terrorism and anti-Semitism belies its feigned "compassion." Instead, "woke" is a perversion of the Judeo-Christian ethic, which is based on repentance and forgiveness. Though it is apparently an uncomfortable truth for many, "woke" ideology and the Judeo-Christian traditions are irreconcilable. As philosopher Henry Frankfurt opines, "When such a (irreconcilable) conflict arises...there may be no way to deal with it, in the end, other than to separate or to slug it out.... [This is] just a fact of life" (Frankfurt 2006b, 51).

It is not possible to understand the zeal of "woke" religionists without addressing their underlying psychology. As we have seen, it is impossible to discuss freedom without evoking the notions of slavery and oppression, which explains why "woke" ideology insists on the presence of persistent "systemic racism" and other forms of "slavery" in society. The monotheistic religions include the idea of "sovereignal freedom," i.e., freedom as relationship to an all-powerful metaphysical deity. But as the secular "woke" religionist consciously denies metaphysical ideas, all transcendent impulses within the psyche must be denied and repressed. But those impulses necessarily reemerge in disguised form and imbue the "woke" religionists' desire for freedom with a feeling-tone that is normally associated with the worship of a transcendent deity. This "return of the repressed" explains the strong feelings expressed by "woke" religionists and other secular functional religionists.

Culture and Religion

Although the origins of "woke" progressivism can be traced to ideologies of the nineteenth and twentieth centuries, precursors can be identified in antiquity. Anthropologist Mary Douglas, who examined the influence of culture on religion, described the ancient Israelite religion as the expression of an "enclave" culture aimed at distinguishing itself from its pagan neighbors. According to Douglas (2001), enclave cultures are ill disposed to imagery, and she attributed the Hebraic notion of an aniconic deity to that fact. Judaism shares with Islam the notion of an aniconic God. Christianity, although by its own claims also a monotheistic tradition, is viewed by the other Abrahamic faiths as tainted by polytheism as a result of the doctrines of the Trinity and the Incarnation.

Unlike Judaism, Christianity is a syncretistic religion; it combines elements of Judaism with Hellenistic philosophies. Greek philosophy emphasized the freedom of the individual, a notion largely foreign to the ancient Israelite religion, but one that exerted a profound influence on early Christianity. By imagining Jesus as a divine object of worship, Christianity reintroduced the pagan myth of an iconic God. Indeed, it is noteworthy that some early Christian theologians, including Origen and Clement, deeply influenced by the Neoplatonic notions of an aniconic God and aversion to the physical world, eschewed emphasis on the Incarnation and Resurrection in their theological musings.[2]

Like Aristotle's perspective on the *polis*, the enclave culture of Judaism viewed freedom of the individual primarily in relation to God and community and posited that it could only be achieved within the context of the demands of the Law. By contrast, by the fourth century Christianity defined individual freedom in relation to "Natural Law," as interpreted through the Greco-Roman traditions (Rommen 1998). Although Christianity interpreted the Natural Law through the divinely revealed Ten Commandments, the particularisms of Judaic Law were abandoned as overly restrictive impediments to freedom, and emphasis was redirected toward interpreting the Law through the rational perspectives of Greco-Roman philosophy. As a result, the details of daily activities of the Christian would not be defined by the Law as they were for the Jew, thereby limiting the authority the Law, and providing an increased degree of individual freedom.

Judaism calls for belief and obedience to the Law. The Jewish religionist is allotted free choice, but that freedom must be exercised with

---

[2] Origen was a major figure in the early Church. However, his theological ideas would eventually be condemned as heretical and his writings burned.

respect to the Law. While Pauline Christianity retained the Judaic emphases, the new religion was transformed by Greco-Roman influences that shifted the focus from belief, faith, and obedience toward what would become our modern secular notions of rationality and individual freedom (Rommen 1998). By assuming a diminished distance between the mind of man and the divine Mind, Christianity inadvertently opened the door to the possibility of a secular "religion of humanity."

Following Aristotle, Eagleton notes that ultimate freedom can only be attributed to an entity with no limits, which is how the God of monotheism is conceived (Eagleton 2014). The orthodoxies of monotheistic religion teach that the only genuine freedom available to man is achieved through acceptance of divine authority and contemplative effort, that is, as sovereignal freedom. When man imagines himself to be the "measure of all things," he in fact embraces a grandiose fantasy. The flaw in this principle is portrayed in the biblical story of the Tower of Babel, in which man's plan to "build us a city and a tower, whose top may reach to heaven" and to "make a name" for himself is undone through divine intervention, or in Goethe's story of the "Sorcerer's Apprentice" who recognizes too late that his power to control nature is limited.

The difficulty in accepting authority greater than oneself is as old as mankind. In Ezekiel 29:3, Pharaoh informs Moses and Aaron that "The Nile belongs to me; I made it for myself." In Exodos 5:2, he asks contemptuously, "Who is the Lord, that I should obey him and let Israel go?" The story of the Exodus is the transition from one form of sovereignal freedom—that is, from the Hebrews' slavery under a divine Pharaoh—to their service to God. Indeed, when God discusses his plan for the exodus of the Israelites, it is framed as the defeat of the gods of Egypt. As God states in Exodus 12:12 (KJV), "Against all the gods of Egypt I will execute judgment." But in today's secular and increasingly self-absorbed culture, the notion of being in service to another is interpreted as an onerous form of bondage.

Reno has addressed how different perspectives on freedom determine how authority is experienced, either as a useful guideline or as an oppressive imposition: "Authority is not the same as power. Power compels by force, while authority directs our lives because we assent to its commands.... Political philosophy calls this fusion of the power of command with free assent [to] legitimate authority. In its most effective forms, legitimate authority issues commands, we accept and internalize, taking responsibility for pressing them forward, improvising, and even criticizing for the sake of achieving the commanded goal.... If we see authority as illegitimate, however, conformity to it grates. We feel commands as bondage...our obedience is not free" (Reno 2016, 32).

Indeed, the rejection of authority and constraints on individual freedom are seen in American trends toward decreased religious observance, decreased willingness to marry, and diminished desire to have and to raise children. This unwillingness to make commitments is antithetical to Judeo-Christian religious values—and perhaps to the very survival of our civilization. In the absence of stable relational bonds and a sustaining rate of procreation, an uncommitted atheistic secular society is unlikely to survive.

Psychoanalyzing Religion

In the early twentieth century, the new field of "scientific" psychology addressed the topic of religion and, in keeping with the secular bias of the times, viewed it unsympathetically. Most clinical psychologists today continue to find fault with religion, seeing it as an arcane source of psychological conflict and stigma.

Sigmund Freud is widely regarded as the father of modern psychotherapy. He was a *fin de siècle* neuropathologist who developed an interest in hysteria and other neuroses, conditions that today would be classified as somatoform, or psychosomatic, disorders. Freud was a secular humanist, an atheist who proudly referred to himself as a "Godless Jew" (Gay 1987). However, he maintained strong cultural ties to Judaism and credited the independence of his thought to having been an "outsider" in anti-Semitic Viennese society. Many of Freud's psychoanalytical ideas can be traced to Rabbinic Judaism, although he rarely credited them to it (Kradin 2016). Like other physicians of his time, Freud viewed himself as an adept of Darwin's thought; he called himself a "biologist of the mind" (Sulloway 1979).

Freud's writings exhibit his troubled relationship with religion in general and with Judaism in particular. Like other pioneers of the new social sciences, he displayed an interest in the origins of religion, and he attempted to discover its source through the method of psychoanalysis. Psychoanalysis was rooted in Freud's sexual theory of the neuroses and the "incest taboo." In *Totem and Taboo*, he proposed that religion had begun with a primordial act of parricide that triggered oedipal guilt and the need to seek forgiveness from the deceased and spiritualized "father" (Freud 1989). Freud provided no objective evidence to support this claim, and critics argued that the theory was baseless and failed to explain how a single event in the ancient past might be transmitted to future generations, considering what was then known about Mendelian genetics and Darwinian evolution.

However, Freud continued to insist that psychological experience could be intergenerationally transmitted via Lamarckian evolution, a theory that allowed for the transmission of acquired events, but one that had been rejected by most scientists of Freud's time. Interestingly, in the late twentieth century, scientists discovered that historical experiences could indeed be transmitted *epigenetically* and intergenerationally in laboratory animals and possibly in man as well (Dupont, Armant, and Brenner 2009). But this does not prove that Freud's theory concerning the origin of religion is correct.

In his final opus, *Moses and Monotheism*, Freud speculated on the origins of Judaism in particular. As in *Totem and Taboo*, he suggested that the ancient religion began with a murder, in the case of Judaism the murder of an Egyptian Moses by a band of pagan slaves that he had led out of Egypt (Freud 1989; Freud 2010). Like his previous explanations for religion, this account was dismissed by scholars and religious leaders, who viewed it as heretical. But it was yet another example of Freud's ability to devise a compelling mystery.[3]

The Future of an Illusion was Freud's major polemic against religion. In it he suggested that religion represented an aberrant assessment of reality, an "illusion" rooted in a childlike need to escape from existential anxieties about disease and death by imagining the protection of an omnipotent "father" deity. According to Freud, "The whole thing [religion] is so patently infantile, so foreign to reality, that to anyone with a friendly attitude to humanity it is painful to think that the great majority of mortals will never be able to rise above this view of life" (Freud 1975).

In the spirit of the Enlightenment *philosophes* and many of his fellow scientists, Freud insisted that mankind's progress required that religion yield to scientific materialism[4] and hinted that in the future psychoanalysis might serve as a suitable replacement: "Our knowledge of the historical worth of certain religious doctrines increases our respect for them but does not invalidate our proposal that they should cease to be put forward as the reasons for the precepts of civilization. On the contrary! Those historical residues have helped us to view religious teachings, as it were, as neurotic relics, and we may now argue that the time has probably come, as it does in an analytic treatment, for replacing the effects of repression by the results of the rational operation of the intellect."

---

[3] Freud was a gifted writer. In gymnasium he was awarded the Goethe Prize for his writing. It has been suggested that his clinical case histories have some of the suspense of the turn-of-the-century genre of detective stories, such as Conan Doyle's *Sherlock Holmes*.

[4] Freud rejected metaphysical concepts but was apparently blind to the fact that psychoanalysis is replete with them.

Freud's assessments of religion are considered simplistic by students of religion. He shows little awareness of the subtleties of the theological arguments offered for the existence of God by great thinkers such as Aristotle, Maimonides, and Aquinas. Instead, reading the Hebrew Bible's descriptions literally, Freud imagines God anthropocentrically, as "an old man sitting on a throne in the heavens," an image more suitable for children than for someone of mature intellect, and one rejected by theologians dating back to antiquity.

Freud was a misotheist, who exhibited a hostile bias against religion and those who believed in it (Baggini 2003).[5] In *Why Did Freud Reject God?*, psychoanalyst Ana-Maria Rizzuto concludes that Freud's feelings about religion were tainted by anger with his father for having failed to defend himself against anti-Semitic attacks, as he described in a confession to his colleague Wilhelm Fliess (Rizzuto 1998). Experience in psychoanalysis with those who find religion distasteful often shows that their hostility is rooted in anger at the patriarchal authority in general (Kradin 2016). Freud shares with today's progressives the desire to discredit God, religion, and authority, and as we shall see, the modern field of psychotherapy has supported this agenda.

In his early psychoanalytical writings, Freud (1953–1974b) mused that religious ideas and rituals shared features with the neuroticisms of obsessive-compulsiveness, including "magical thinking" meant to ward off danger. This idea may have gained prominence in Freud's mind because of his acquaintance with Judaism's preoccupation with ritual purity, which has been viewed with distaste by rationalists since antiquity. But as Douglas (2005) argues in *Purity and Danger*, in the ancient world impurity was considered an ontological source

---

[5] Freud's wife was descended from prominent Rabbinic families, and she was positively inclined toward observing Jewish rituals. Freud forbade her to do so in his house, evidence of his hostility toward religious practices even with his immediate family.

of danger and part of a complex symbolic system that equated life with God and impurity with divine absence and death.[6] Freud was a rationalist who attempted to demythologize religion and to rid mankind of the "irrational." But as a depth psychologist, he might have realized that is an impossible task; irrationality represents an innate aspect of man's psychological repertoire and as such cannot be eradicated.

Archetypes and the Collective Unconscious

C. G. Jung was a protégée of Freud's and a prominent figure in the early psychoanalytical movement. A Swiss psychiatrist and the son of a Protestant theologian, he maintained a lifelong interest in myth and the psychology of religion. Unlike Freud, he conceived of religion as a *sui generis* impulse within the human psyche, one arising from the "collective unconscious" that mediates transpersonal experience.[7] Jung rejected Freud's reductive explanation of God and religion as products of infantile experience, insisting instead that they were adaptive aspects of man's psychological repertoire. This difference of opinion was a critical factor in Jung's eventual break with Freud, and it inspired Jung to develop a distinct mode of psychological investigation that he termed "analytical psychology" (Jung 1989).

Adopting Plato's notion of the Forms, or archetypes, Jung postulated that religious sensibility was mediated by the archetype of Self, which he conceived as the central organizing element in the human psyche.[8] His clinical work with psychotic patients and his detailed

---

[6] In the ancient Israelite religion, death was considered the greatest source of impurity, and aspects of this belief have been carried over into modern Judaism.

[7] By 1923, Freud conceived of a tripartite mind with ego, superego, and id. Jung's conception was more complex, including not only Freud's personal unconscious, which was essentially isomorphic with the id, but also the "collective unconscious," an aspect of unconscious process shared by the entire species.

[8] Jung's archetypes are based on the Platonic notion of the Forms. His definitions of the term continued to evolve and evaded absolute clarity as they oscillated between metaphysics and psychologisms.

analysis of dreams suggested there was an irrepressible activity within the unconscious capable of generating images that were experienced as mediated by a transcendent "force."[9] This Self, according to Jung, was the source of "numinous" images in dreams and visions that recapitulated the symbols of different religious traditions. While these could accord with acquired religious beliefs—for example, an old man sitting on a throne for Jews or the Virgin Mary for Catholics—they could also take on untraditional forms, including images of theriomorphic beings— part man and part animal[10]—or geometric designs such as circles, both kinds of images experienced by the dreamer or visionary as numinous (Jung 1912).

Jung made no theological claims for his conception of the Self, although at times in his writings he came close to doing so. Like Freud, he insisted that he was neither a metaphysician nor a mystic. But he did suggest that when fleshed out by narratives, symbols, and rituals, the images generated by the Self were the psychological bases of religion. Jung also saw a role for the Self in the psychotherapeutic process. In his treatments of psychotic patients, he noted that the images generated by the Self, often circles or mandalas, appeared in a patient's dreams and drawings immediately prior to recovery. Like the nineteenth-century American psychologist and philosopher William James, he argued that religious experience had pragmatic therapeutic value, and he encouraged patients, whenever possible, to reconnect to their religions of origin in order to augment the healing process. His ideas were adopted by William Griffith Wilson, aka Bill W., as the basis of the twelve-step programs that call on addicted individuals to form a relationship with a "higher power" as a path to recovery (Wilson 1957).

---

[9] Modern research suggests this activity is likely mediated primarily by the right cerebral hemisphere.

[10] Ezekiel's vision of the celestial chariot (*merkavah*) with the images of a lion, ox, eagle, and man is an example of a theriomorphic image. "Numinous" is a term that Rudolf Otto coined to suggest a sense of awe.

Religion, Science, and Scientism

In *Two Cultures*, English author C. P. Snow (1959) noted that modern academia is divided between the arts and sciences, and that their respective scholars exhibit non-overlapping worldviews. The current educational emphasis on math and science has resulted in the dominance of a positivist materialistic philosophy that eschews all metaphysical references. This extremely positive valuation of science, termed "scientism," has led to the denigration of other areas of study. In 2011, President Obama promoted math and science as the roadmap to the future.

> Nations like China and India realized that with some changes of their own, they could compete in this new world. And so, they started educating their children earlier and longer, with greater emphasis on math and science. They're investing in research and new technologies. Just recently, China became the home to the world's largest private solar research facility, and the world's fastest computer.
>
> We know what it takes to compete for the jobs and industries of our time. We need to out-innovate, out-educate, and out-build the rest of the world. We have to make America the best place on Earth to do business (Obama 2011).

Note Obama's emphasis on science and math as the answer for "doing business," a topic that will be revisited later.

Despite this enthusiasm for science as the key to future world success, some of the world's greatest scientists have rejected scientism. Isaac Newton, who pioneered the current mechanistic approach to science in the seventeenth century, devoted much of his extensive writings to religion and was clearly a believer, as can be seen from the following quote: "We are therefore to acknowledge one God, infinite, eternal, omnipresent, omniscient, omnipotent, the creator of all things, most wise, most just, most good, most holy. We must love him, fear him, honor him, trust in him, pray to him, give him thanks, praise him, hallow his name, obey his commandments, and set time apart for his service, as we are directed in the third and fourth Commandments" (Burtt 2016, 282).

When confronted with the intrinsic uncertainties of quantum theory, Albert Einstein, the twentieth-century theoretical physicist who discovered the dualism of light, as well as both special and general relativity, quipped that "God does not play dice with the universe." For these men, science was the approach to unlocking the secrets of the universe, not an exercise aimed at denying God, a way to impose man's will on nature through technology, or the key to the future success of capitalism.

Interestingly, atheists are more likely to be found among humanities scholars (Gross 2008). This should be no surprise, as scholars in the humanities are primarily engaged in a world of constructed symbols and ideas, whereas physical scientists are focused on a world created by other forces.

By virtue of the science that has developed as an analytical process in the West, in contrast to the holistic "sciences" of the East, its explanatory powers are by definition limited to statements about the material world. Unfortunately, too many Western scientists view metaphysical statements as "unreal," in error. As the late Cornell philosophy professor E. A. Burtt noted, "Metaphysics they [Western scientists] tended more and more to avoid, so far as they could avoid it, so far as not, it became an instrument for their further mathematical conquest of the world" (Burtt, 2016, 303).

In the twentieth century, scientists investigating nature at the atomic level were discovering phenomena that defied rational explanations. They found that light behaves as both a wave and a particle and that there is "spooky action" at a distance, reminiscent of the paradoxes reported by religious mystics. Heisenberg demonstrated that it was impossible to define the position and momentum of a particle simultaneously, which led some to conclude that there was no definite "truth."

Some astrophysicists have suggested that the physical world is a unitary energy field in which matter coalesces at various points, an idea reminiscent of panentheism, a Kabbalistic theory in which God both transcends creation and is identified with it (Päs 2023). Theoretical physicist David Bohm (1984) proposed that matter continuously emerges from a nonobservable "implicate order," which accords with the Kabbalistic claim that the universe is constantly newly created. These are a few of the obvious nexuses between metaphysical speculation and the physical world, suggesting that they may share in an undefined meta-intelligence.

As Western science is limited to empirical observation of the physical world, it can neither confirm nor refute claims for metaphysical entities, including God (Davies 2021). Nevertheless, some modern philosophers have argued that in the absence of material evidence, God does not exist. But as the Nobel laureate physicist Richard Feynman (1998, 36) stated, "Science cannot disprove God, and a belief in science and religion is consistent.... There are very many scientists who believe in God, in a conventional way. Their belief in God and their action in science is thoroughly consistent." Feynman argued that whereas belief in metaphysics has been undermined by modern science, the moral claims of religion have largely been unaffected. However, when the moral claims of religion are largely left unscathed by science, its metaphysical claims may result in cognitive dissonance. But while empiricism is the basis of Western science, it does not exhaust man's ways of "knowing" the world. While cognition is a defining feature of human rationality, it does not hold an *a priori* privileged position over other ways of perceiving the world. Belief in the metaphysical is as much a part of man's mental repertoire as is rationality, and one need not give priority to one over the other, except to say that they are suited to different tasks. Neither rationality nor faith has a final claim on truth, and what is irrational is not "unreal."

The late Harvard anthropologist Stephen Jay Gould (1999) opined that science and religion are best viewed as "non-overlapping magisteria," each with its own truth claims. The point is that the commonly held idea that faith is irrational is false. Rather, faith is often the affirmation of belief arrived at through both rational and other modes of knowing. William James suggested that faith was a function of the "will to believe," and that as a long-standing part of man's mental repertoire, it likely serves an adaptive purpose (James 2017).

Indeed, the Judeo-Christian traditions contend that the optimal approach to God includes both reason and faith, and as noted, reason can lead to faith. Conservative educator James Wilson has suggested that religious contemplation ideally includes *logos* and *mythos*, arguing that man expresses the essence of his nature and describes his path toward Truth through stories (Wilson 2017). Indeed, the synthesis of reason and faith may equate with the "wholeness" that some view as the essence of mental health (Storm 2015).

Problems exist on both sides of the conflict between science and religion. Religionists are ill advised to deny truths that have been definitively established by science. The Bible is not a science text, and it can be accepted as divinely inspired without the need to embrace scientifically indefensible positions. Metaphysical arguments for *why* are different from scientific ones that address *how*. Virtually all religious traditions recognize that aspects of their canonical texts are allegorical, and that one must distinguish those that are literally factual from those that are not. For example, it is generally accepted that the world was not created in six twenty-four-hour days, despite the literal reading of Genesis, and that God did not plant dinosaur bones in the earth to fool modern paleontologists. The insistence, in some quarters, that literal interpretation of such passages is required to sustain religious belief makes it easy for secular scientists to dismiss fundamental religionists as benighted.

The monotheistic traditions hold that divine revelation is ongoing, and science does not contradict that belief. If God created man, he could have used evolution to do so and still infused him with an element of divinity that is absent in other animals. Many passages in the Bible are read allegorically by staunch believers, and the story of Adam and Eve should qualify as one. On the other hand, as British intellectual C. S. Lewis suggested, scientists should be the first to agree that much of what is taken to be scientifically conclusive today will require revision in the future (Feynman 2011). Like religion, science is witness to continuing revelation, and to conclude that it is inerrant is to fall into the error of scientism. Lewis condemned scientism and opined that when properly conceived science is a subtopic of religion. Oxford scholar Michael Ward summarizes Lewis's thoughts on the matter:

> He believes science to be a fundamentally imaginative enterprise. He argues that scientific statements, because they tend to be univocal and strive to be verifiable, are actually rather small statements, all things considered. He argues that there is always a mythology that follows in the wake of science and that both scientists and non-scientists should take care not to put excessive weight on particular scientific metaphors. We should hold our scientific paradigms with a due provisionality because new evidence may always turn up to overthrow those paradigms. Even the best and most long-lasting paradigm is merely a lens or linguistic stencil laid over reality, not reality itself. This humility in relation to the facts about the physical universe is a virtue similar to the one we should exercise before the mystery of God (Ward 2013, 7).

French philosopher Blaise Pascal argued that belief in God is reasonable and cannot be rationally criticized. He conjectured that the risks of being mistaken about the potential consequences of an eternity in heaven or hell favor wagering on God's existence and behaving accordingly. Atheists have criticized "Pascal's wager" by arguing that the potential outcomes he posits are imaginary, but they cannot know this for a fact; rather, it's their opinion. Ultimately, the question of God and belief is a matter of faith and one's philosophy (Baggini 2003).

William James (1963) argued that those who believe in God experience personal benefits that cannot be denied. Although it is not fashionable to discuss these benefits in medical scientific circles, numerous studies have demonstrated that people who practice religion report an improved quality of life, improved physical health, live longer, and experience less anxiety and depression (Koenig 2012).

Psychological Types

In *Psychological Types*, Jung (1972) developed a classification of personality types based on his reading of history and clinical experience. He divided people into those whose attitudes were primarily outer-directed (extroverts) versus inner-directed (introverts). He further divided these extroverts and introverts into those who experience their environment primarily via "thinking" versus "feeling," or "intuition" versus "sensation," referring to these as functions. According to Jung, everyone has a dominant attitude as well as primary and auxiliary functions, so that there are, for example, introverted feeling/intuition and extraverted thinking/sensation personality types. He posited that mental health was achieved by integrating as many functions into one's personality as possible—with rare exceptions, only three configurations were possible—which was his notion of psychological "wholeness." Jung further opined that neurosis could result from an excessively one-sided typology, for example, excessive thinking.[11]

Jung's system of typological classification has been popularized as the Myers-Briggs Type Indicator, which is widely used as an

---

[11] According to Jung, it is only possible to integrate three of the four, with the remaining function referred to as "inferior" and unavailable to consciousness but still capable of influencing unconscious activities.

assessment tool by institutions, and his concept of extroversion/ introversion has been adopted by modern personality theory (Hayes and Joseph 2003; Douglas 2005). A person's typology determines how he or she experiences the world, but it also creates barriers to understanding those whose typologies differ from one's own. Extroverts report different interests than introverts, thinking types find it difficult to understand feeling types, and so forth. Jung noted that when typologies differ greatly, there is an inclination to denigrate or deny the experience of the "other."

Jung posited that typology was key to religious experience and that those with certain typologies were incapable of valuing what is immaterial and transcendent, and therefore prone to denigrating religious experience. According to Jung, this group was most often composed of extroverted thinking/sensation types, as they are outwardly directed, inclined to filter their experience through rational thought, and lacking well-developed intuition (Jung 1972). Jung further suggested that Freud exhibited this typology and that explained why he was ill disposed toward religion.

Because of the increased focus and value placed on intellectualization in today's society, extroverted thinking/sensation types have increased and they are often in positions of power and authority.[12] Jung suggested that the current skewed reliance on left-brained rationality in managerial society is changing how we evaluate the world, and he warned that ignoring other modes of experience would prove detrimental: "Rational truths are not the last word, there are also irrational ones. In human affairs what seems impossible by way of the intellect has often become true by way of the irrational. Indeed, all of the greatest changes that have affected mankind have come not by way of intellectual calculation, but by ways which contemporary minds either ignored or rejected as absurd, and which were

---

[12] Jung believed that typology was both innate and acquired. For this reason, there are individuals whose innate typology may be distorted by early developmental influences and education.

recognized long afterward because of their intrinsic necessity. More often than not they are never recognized at all, for the all-important laws of mental development are still a book of seven seals" (Jung 1972, 69).

As increased attention to the activities of the left brain inhibits those of the right brain, the capacity to appreciate religious symbols, images, and metaphor can be expected to diminish (McGilchrist 2018). Whether in time this will lead to a reconfiguration of the human nervous system, one favoring rationality, agnosticism, and atheism, is uncertain, but the possibility cannot be discounted.

Paradoxically, excessive rationality can activate irrationality in unpredictable ways. As Jung wrote, "Old Heraclitus, who was indeed a very great sage, discovered the most marvelous of all psychological laws: the regulative function of opposites. He called it *enantiodromia*, a running contrariwise, by which he meant that sooner or later everything runs into its opposite" (Jung 1972, 72). This may explain the odd ideas that one often observes in hyperrational individuals. Irrational aspects are commonly seen in obsessional personalities who characteristically intellectualize and rationalize experience (Salzman 1977).

Jung also voiced serious concerns about the inability of the psyche to adapt to the rapid advances in technology that had been occurring over the last two hundred years. Despite the plasticity of the nervous system, biological adaptation is slow, and technologies can outpace the nervous system's capacity to process them, resulting in psychological disturbances, including feelings of being overwhelmed, anxious, and depressed. According to Jung, rapid changes in technologies are the leading cause of neurosis today. In a 1949 letter to a friend, he wrote that "at the bottom of all these problems [the great problems of our time] lies the development of science and technology, which has destroyed man's metaphysical foundation.... Technology and 'social welfare' provide nothing to overcome our spiritual stagnation, and they give us no answer to our spiritual dissatisfaction and restlessness, on account of which we are threatened from within as from without" (Jung 1973).

Why We Can't Keep Up

The recent increase in mental disturbances reported by young people tracks temporally with the introduction of the internet and social media (Twenge 2023). The speed with which digital images are presented over the internet has resulted in decreased attention spans and addictive behaviors. According to a recent study, "Social media has a reinforcing nature. Using it activates the brain's reward center by releasing dopamine, a 'feel-good chemical' linked to pleasurable activities such as sex, food, and social interaction. The platforms are designed to be addictive and are associated with anxiety and depression and even physical ailments" (McLean Hospital 2024).

America's teens currently spend up to nine hours a day on social media platforms, 60 percent of that time on mobile devices (Asano 2017, 1). Social media has become the primary mode of communicating with others, while in-person interactions have diminished. As man is a social animal, the reduction in time spent interacting with others in person is at odds with his nature.

The "Objective Psyche"

Jung based much of his theoretical musings on his work with psychotic patients, whose inability to distinguish hallucinations from waking reality intrigued him. He concluded that these imaginal experiences were manifestations of an "objective psyche," that aspect of unconscious experience that results in observable physiological changes. He noted that that the hallucinations of schizophrenics were invariably accompanied by physiological activities indistinguishable from those observed in response to objective "real" events. For example, the eye movements of schizophrenics while hallucinating are processed by the brain as though it is tracking real objects moving in the visual field. For the schizophrenic, what others judge to be imaginary is objectively real.

Non-schizophrenic individuals who report religious visions also insist that what they have experienced is real. Their visions are experienced as tangible and described as awe-inspiring, or as a merger with something greater than themselves, the *mysterium tremendum et fascinans*, the phrase that Rudolph Otto used to describe mystical experience (Otto 1936). In *The Varieties of Religious Experience*, William James (1963) noted that mystics who report such visions often spend the remainder of their lives attempting to understand what occurred to them.

Individuals under the influence of hallucinogenic drugs also report numinous ineffable experiences, and it has been suggested that visions triggered by the ingestion of psychedelic plants, including ergots and the ritual drink soma, may have been the impetus for the religious experiences that have evolved into the organized traditions that we recognize today (Hancock and Kreisberg 2010).

CHAPTER 3

The Evolution of Religion

The Christian ideal has not been tried and found wanting.
It has been found difficult; and left untried.

—G. K. CHESTERTON

The God of the Old Testament is arguably the most unpleasant
character in all fiction: jealous and proud of it; a petty, unjust,
unforgiving control-freak; a vindictive, bloodthirsty ethnic cleanser;
a misogynistic, homophobic, racist, infanticidal, genocidal, filicidal,
pestilential, megalomaniacal, sadomasochistic, capriciously
malevolent bully.

—RICHARD DAWKINS (2006)

THE TRANSITION FROM POLYTHEISTIC to monotheistic religion is
a factor that contributed to the modern notion of progress. Pagans
lived in a world rooted in the repetitiveness of nature. Whereas the
inevitability of change was recognized by Heraclitus in the fifth
century BCE, the notion of circular time (*kairos*) dominated the
pagan's calendar and his psychology. The statement in Ecclesiastes

1:9 that "there is nothing new under the sun" epitomizes how time was viewed in the ancient world.[1] In contrast to today, tradition was lauded, while novelty was viewed with suspicion. Indeed, as Hesiod suggested, it was widely believed that the world was regressing, rather than progressing, over time—from a primordial "Golden Age" to a degraded leaden present.

Paganism

Pagans imagined a world inhabited by gods that they identified with nature: the sky, the earth, rivers, seas, and so forth, were all imagined as mediated by innumerable gods and spirits.[2] Daimons, like the one that visited Socrates, served as intermediaries between the individual and the gods,[3] and the pagan world was brimming with spiritual life, in contrast to the inanimate material world that would increasingly dominate the minds of men after the Enlightenment. As nature is universal, pagans were inclined to embrace regional gods from other traditions as their own gods, just with different names. Zeus, the sky god of the Greek pantheon, was equated with the Roman god Jupiter; Hermes, the messenger of the gods, with Mercury; Poseidon, the god of the seas, with Neptune; and so on. Religious syncretism and tolerance were staples of pagan religion, and religious differences rarely resulted in conflict.

Unlike Christianity, pagan religion was not based on a system of beliefs. There was no pagan "credo." Instead, it was focused on *praxis*, that is, on public rituals and animal sacrifices. These were aimed at

[1] Although Ecclesiastes is part of the canon of the Hebrew Bible, it is generally classified as "wisdom literature," which tends to parallel the "wisdom" of pagan culture and does not include substantial references to religious ideas.

[2] Monotheism would replace these gods with angels who served as "messengers" (*angelos*) for the supreme God and who mediated his wishes for the behavior of nature.

[3] Socrates's daimon is described as a helpful spirit. Daimons, which could be either good or bad spirits, would be renamed "demons" by the early Christians and equated with evil because of their association with paganism.

appeasing the gods and ensuring the safety of the community (Fox 2006). Those who refused to participate in the sacrificial cult were condemned as "atheists." Indeed, this was the usual charge brought against Christians in the Roman Empire who refused to sacrifice to the gods or to the emperors, who after Julius Caesar were also often accepted as "divine."

Despite the public expressions of polytheism, some ancient Greek and Roman philosophers, including Plato and Aristotle, conceived of a supernal Being who transcended the pantheon of lesser gods. Based on rational argument, they imagined this Being as unitary and perfect, the combination of essence and existence, omnipresence and omniscience, as the source of truth, and therefore "the highest Good." This "God of the philosophers" shared features with the God of the monotheistic religions and would contribute to Christianity's idea of the natural law.

Monotheism

During the twelfth dynasty in Egypt, a form of proto-monotheism emerged in which Aten, the sun disc, was imagined as a supreme god. During the reign of Amenhotep III, Aten was worshipped among other gods, but he became the supreme god of Egypt during the reign of Amenhotep IV, who changed his name to Akhenaten to reflect the worship of this new supreme deity.

Aten was conceived as the creator of all peoples, whose concern for mankind was mediated by the pharaoh, early evidence of the inseparable relationship between religion and the "divine right of kings." However, scholars differ as to whether the worship of Aten was monotheistic or an example of monolatry, in which a supreme god is worshipped along with lesser gods.

Aten's reign as supreme god was short-lived. The Aten religion was poorly received by the polytheistic Egyptians, and it was abandoned following Akhenaten's death. Scholars have suggested that Moses, the biblical deliverer of the Israelites, who according to tradition was raised as a prince of Egypt, may have been influenced by the religion of Aten, but the question remains unresolved (Assmann 2005).

Judaism

According to biblical tradition, Abraham was the first monotheist, and the father of the Jews, Christians, and Muslims, alike.[4] The Hebrew Bible introduces Abraham as a Mesopotamian pagan who was commanded by God to leave his home and travel to the land of Canaan. A covenant is cut[5] between God and Abraham, in which Abraham is promised that his descendants will inherit the land and that all the nations of the world will be "blessed through him."[6]

Both the biblical narrative and archeological evidence suggest that Jewish monotheism evolved over centuries from paganism, through a series of transitions from henotheism, the worship of God as one god among others; through monolatry, i.e., the favored worship of one God above all others; and finally to monotheism, which denies the existence of all but a single supreme deity. But most scholars agree that monotheism was only firmly established in Judaism by the fifth century BCE, and following the Babylonian exile.

Monotheism posits a creator God who transcends space and time. According to strict monotheistic conceptions, as expostulated by the medieval Jewish philosopher Maimonides, despite the many anthropomorphic descriptions of God in the Hebrew Bible, He must be imagined as devoid of all conceivable forms. All biblical anthropomorphic references are explained as metaphors and attributed to the Bible's "speaking in the language of men." According to the apophatic

---

[4] The name Avraham is derived from the Hebrew phrase *av hamon*, which means "father of many."

[5] In the language of the Hebrew Bible, one "cuts" a covenant (*brith*). This may refer in part to the cutting in two rituals: the "covenant of the pieces" and circumcision.

[6] This promise, which is found in the Genesis, is the basis upon which Jews claim Israel as their rightful homeland.

tradition explicated by the Neoplatonist philosopher Pseudo-Dionysius the Areopagite in the fifth century, all "positive" statements about God must be rejected as limiting and false.

The aniconic God of the philosophers poses a psychological challenge for worshipers. Efforts at bridging the gap between man and God were addressed by medieval Kabbalists who reintroduced mythic elements into Judaism by imagining the Godhead (*Ein Sof*, i.e., "Without End") in Neoplatonic terms as an indescribable "Source" that emanates a chain of vessels (*sefirot*) with "attributes" that can be approached through intellect and imagination via contemplation, prayer, and imitation. But unlike the Neoplatonists, who conceived of the emanations from the Godhead as spontaneously "overflowing," the Kabbalistic Godhead was conceived as "willing" these emanations to occur, with the ultimate aim of creating man and the physical world. Man's soul was conceived as an extension of God, a microcosm of His divinity, and capable of imitating the intellectual and emotional attributes with God through an *imitatio Dei*.

The Kabbalistic worldview imagines a theurgic dynamic system in which man's actions evoke flows of divine energy from the Godhead. When a Jew fulfills the divine commandments, offers prayer, or repents his sins, these actions are thought to initiate an efflux of positive divine energy into the world, whereas disobedience impedes the "spiritual energy flow" and disrupts the imagined integrity of the Godhead.

As historian of Jewish religion Menachem Kellner notes, Maimonides's philosophical concept of God and the concept of the Kabbalist mystics are superficially incompatible (Kellner 2006). Maimonides had attempted to demythologize Judaism by denying the ontology of the Jewish soul, angels, or any other intermediary that could be imagined in corporeal terms. For Maimonides, Judaism was a religion of the intellect, and the Jewish practitioner was to obey the Law and rationally contemplate the mind of God, which, following Aristotle, was the path to accessing the "Active Intellect."

From a practical perspective, Maimonides's efforts were unsuccessful. Judaism as practiced today remains an amalgam of rational thought and the mystical contributions of the Kabbalists. Both are represented in the liturgy and practices of normative Judaism, reflecting the irreducible need to satisfy the insistent impulses of two distinct modes of mental experience.

The Law

According to the biblical creation myth, the first man was given the single commandment to refrain from eating from the Tree of the Knowledge of Good and Evil in the Garden of Eden and sinned by failing to obey God's command.[7] By tradition, God revealed 613 biblical commandments to Moses at Mount Sinai; 248 commandments for what must be done, and 365 commands for what must not be done.[8] These commandments delineated in the Law (*Torah*) guide the daily practices of normative Jewish life. Unlike Christianity, which is an orthodoxy, i.e., a system of *right* belief, Judaism is primarily an orthopraxis, one of correct action. The laws of Judaism govern all aspects of daily life, but in order to fulfill them, the practitioner must maintain a high degree of mindfulness and exert free will in making appropriate choices. The ability to curb one's instinctual desires is central to the morality of Judaism.

While the Jewish religionist is encouraged to make rational efforts at understanding the commandments, he is to accept that they cannot all be rationalized. Nevertheless, as they reflect divine revelation, they are to be accepted (*kabbalat ol*, "accepting the yoke") in

---

[7] Freud, undoubtedly influenced by Jewish tradition, viewed sublimation as the highest form of psychological defense against the bestial forces of the unconscious id and the ideal endpoint of a successful analysis.

[8] Many of these commandments are limited to actions related to the Temple ritual and currently cannot be practiced.

the service of fostering self-control and moral behavior.[9] Rather than a random set of statutes, the Law constitutes a complex interconnected system that creates a "path" (*halacha*) for ethical behavior (Kradin 2021).

Christianity accused Judaism of inhibiting spirituality and limiting personal freedom by emphasizing adherence to the Law (Nirenberg 2013). However, Judaism is not just a set of legalisms; rather, it includes a substantial spiritual focus and a notion that freedom is only achieved through service. Normative Judaism is a "strong" authoritative system, according to Reno's classification (Reno 2019). For this reason, it is antithetical to the "weak" and fluid tenets of progressive ideology. Until recently, Judaism escaped the hostile attacks of progressives because of its minority status, while Christianity, as the dominant religion, has drawn their ire. However, as radical Islamists have increasingly allied themselves with the politics of the Left, there has been a revival of anti-Semitic vitriol directed against Jews and the state of Israel.

Freedom

Americans have always been obsessed with freedom, though the term is rarely critically defined. But it is clear that the idea of freedom arose in reaction to the institution of slavery (Patterson 1991). According to the Hebrew Bible, the ancient Israelites were redeemed from slavery and the pagan practices of Egypt by divine intervention for the purpose of receiving the Law at Mount Sinai.[10] The Exodus is celebrated today as commemoration of the ancient Israelites' liberation from physical

---

[9] The tradition refers to this as *kabbalat ol*, which means "accepting the yoke," analogous to oxen responding to the direction of their driver. The idea is comparable to the term *Islam*, which means "to submit."

[10] Torah, often translated as Law, means "instruction." The Law in Judaism exists as both a written law and an oral law, the latter meant to expound the details of what is written. Normative Jews follow both sets of Law in practice. Throughout this text Law is used to refer to both generically.

bondage, but freedom in Jewish religious terms has a distinct meaning from freedom as understood in secular society.

Large numbers of people were routinely enslaved in antiquity. Many were women and children captured during war (whereas defeated men were regularly killed). It is estimated that as many as 30 percent of the population of the Roman Empire in the first century were slaves (Arnheim 2022). One could be enslaved to an individual for unpaid debts, or be in bondage to the state, as the ancient Israelites were to Pharaoh. Household slavery was accepted by both Judaism and Christianity in the early centuries, but unlike in the pagan world, slaves were expected to be treated with respect and compassion by both Christians and Jews. Indeed, the Law indicates that injuring a slave is cause for his immediate manumission, which contrasts with the harsh treatment of slaves described in the prebiblical Babylonian Hammurabi Code.

However, the Israelites were not freed from bondage in Egypt to do as they pleased; rather, as we have seen, they were liberated for the express purpose of serving God. As Exodus 9:13 (NKJV) states, "Thus says the Lord God of the Hebrews: 'Let My people go, that they may serve Me.'" Indeed, Hebrew makes no distinction between "slave" and "servant" (*eved*). Freedom in Judaism is sovereignal and conceived as a covenantal relationship between man and God. The notion of personal freedom to do as one wishes, as freedom is generally understood today, is foreign to Judaism. Instead, man's freedom equates with his ability to choose freely to adhere to the demands of the Law or not. The Hebrew Bible says that the Israelites were asked whether they wanted to receive the Law and responded, "We will do (the Law), and then we will understand [it]," a statement of their unconditional service to God.

Exclusivity

Like other religions in the ancient world, the ancient Israelite religion was a Temple-based sacrificial cult in which worshippers were required to maintain themselves in a state of purity in order to participate. Ritual impurity was common and unavoidable, and not in itself sinful, but it required a ritualized purification ceremony before a sacrificial offering sacrifices could be brought to the Jerusalem Temple. In Leviticus 20:26 (ESV), God commands, "You shall be holy to me, for I the Lord am holy and have separated you from the peoples." The Hebrew term for "holy" (*kodesh*) means "separate," and the Israelites were commanded to live as a community apart from their pagan neighbors as a "nation of priests" who were to serve as a moral example for the surrounding nations.

One of the differences between Maimonides and the mystical Kabbalists was how they interpreted what it means to be "holy." According to Maimonides, holiness is a legal construct determined by the specifics of the Law, whereas the Kabbalists imagined holiness as an ontological state of person, place, or thing. Indeed, this argument continues within the modern denominations of Judaism to this day (Kellner 2006).

According to the Hebrew Bible, God commanded the ancient Israelites to eliminate the indigenous Canaanites and destroy their places of worship in order to purge the land of their immorality. The land was regarded as ontologically holy, and it was understood that God would not tolerate immoral behavior from those living in it. The Israelites would also be "vomited" from the land if they were to lapse into the immoral practices of their pagan neighbors.

Modern readers, disturbed by this call to genocide, have used the conquest of Canaan to question the morality of Judaism and the God of the Hebrew Bible, labeling the Jewish God as one of "vengeance" rather than "love." Progressive ideologues are quick to label Israel's hostile actions against its enemies as "genocide" and to express their horror of the "oppressive" and "exclusive" behaviors described in the Hebrew Bible. But these same critics readily excuse the Communist Chinese oppression of Muslim Uyghurs and ignore the violence of fundamentalist Islamists against nonbelievers, betraying their Marxist leanings and anti-Semitic sentiments.

Jewish Law was not created for either Christian or secular society. It is specific to Judaism, and many of the moral positions prevalent today are foreign to it. The biblical commandment to remain separate from "other nations" was designed to ensure an ethical way of life for Jews. In contrast to Christianity, Jewish Law insists that it is inappropriate to be merciful to those who purposefully seek to kill you or who actively seek to undermine your moral standards.

Judaism recognizes that behaviors must be contextualized; as Ecclesiastes 3:1–8 says, there is a time to make love, a time to hate; a time to make peace, a time for war; and so forth. As Rabbi Joseph Soloveitchik argued:

> The Torah has always taught that man is permitted, indeed has a sacred obligation to defend himself. With the verse, "If a thief is caught in the act of breaking in" (Exodus 22:2), the Torah establishes the halakha that one may defend not only one's life but his property as well. If the thief who comes to take the property is capable of killing the householder (should the householder not comply with his demands) the householder may rise up against the criminal and kill him. For good reason the Torah relates that two of its great heroes, Abraham and Moses, took sword in hand to defend their brethren…. This behavior does not contradict the principle of loving kindness and compassion. On the contrary. Passive position without self-defense may sometimes lead to the most awesome brutality (Soloveitchik 2006, 39).

This differs radically from the progressive approach to crime, which allows thieves to steal without penalty, while punishing those who defend their lives and property from criminal violence. The current rise in crime in America is stark evidence of how progressive "morality" that often claims to borrow from Judeo-Christian morality has failed. Those who insist that Israel should not be allowed to defend itself against enemies that wish to destroy it refuse to recognize that Jewish Law differs from progressive notions of how war is to be waged. Indeed, inclusivity is opposed to normative Jewish values, as are the aims of "equity" and "diversity," as we shall see. Although Judaism is the source of biblical social justice, progressive social justice is antithetical to it.

In the fourth century BCE, Alexander the Great conquered the Persian empire, and Judea was incorporated into the Hellenistic world. Alexander was arguably the first "globalist," whose goal was to impose Hellenism on his diverse empire. In 167 CE, the Seleucid king, Antiochus Epiphanes, attempted to suppress the practices of Judaism by imposing Hellenistic rationality on the population of Judea by force. Antiochus objected to those "particularisms" of the Law that had no rational basis, for example, circumcision and the dietary laws, which separated Jews from their Hellenized neighbors. The effort to abolish the particularisms of Judaism was supported by Hellenized Jews who wished to assimilate into the ambient culture—much as one finds "Hellenists" today, as Jews who support progressive ideals and anti-Israel stances. The revolt against the Seleucids was in part a civil war that pitted conservative Jewish religionists against reforming Hellenists, and—in an early example of asymmetric warfare—the conservative Judeans succeeded in throwing off their Seleucid yoke, a victory that is celebrated today as the festival of Chanukah.

In 62 BCE, Judea again lost its independence, this time to Rome. Tensions between Rome and the Jews grew, leading to war in 66 CE. Despite stiff resistance, Judea was defeated, and the Jerusalem Temple—the center of the sacrificial cult of Judaism—was destroyed (Rogers 2021). Hundreds of thousands of Jews were reportedly killed in the revolt that ended in 73 CE, and many were transported to Rome as slaves for imperial building projects.[11]

---

[11] Of these building projects, the most widely recognized today is the Flavian Amphitheater, better known as the Coliseum.

The vacuum created by the loss of the Jerusalem Temple and the exile of Jews from their homeland following a second unsuccessful rebellion against Rome in 132–135 CE allowed a little-known apocalyptic Jewish messianic sect, the Christians, to flourish and eventually to gain hold of the Roman Empire.

Apocalypse

"Apocalypse" is Greek for "revelation." Beginning in the second century BCE, a genre of literature emerged within Judaism that focused on eschatology, i.e., the end-time. These writings were based loosely on the writings of the Hebrew prophets and addressed what would occur to the Jews at the end of the world. The apocalyptic literature adopted a pessimistic perspective on man's fate by insisting that man was beyond redemption and that God's final judgement was imminent. The end-time was viewed as the culmination of a heavenly conflict between the spiritual forces of good and evil (Collins 1984). Except for the book of Daniel,[12] apocalypses were excluded from the Hebrew biblical canon, but they were widely read during the intertestamental period and exerted a profound influence on early Christianity.[13] In 1947, the chance discovery of the two-thousand-year-old Dead Sea Scrolls in a cave at Qumran allowed scholars to examine the texts of a historical apocalyptic sect directly rather than from excerpts alluded to in other texts. The sect responsible for the Dead Sea Scrolls, usually identified as the Essenes, apparently

---

[12] Scholars believe that Daniel was likely written during the time of the Judean revolt against the Syrians in the second century BCE. Certain tropes in the Gospels are likely based on Daniel, including the idea of the "Son of Man" (*bar enosh*) arriving on the clouds to judge man. The canon of the Hebrew Bible was likely established sometime in the second century CE.

[13] The appellation "Son of Man" appears repeatedly in the book of Ezekiel where it simply means "a man." But in Daniel and the Enochian apocalyptic literature, it implies a quasi-divine being. The Gospel reference to the "Son of Man arriving on the clouds" (Matthew 24:30) is a direct reference to Daniel 7:13: "In my vision I saw one who looked like a *son of man*. He was coming with the *clouds* of heaven."

lived as monastics in the Judean desert and believed that they were engaged in a spiritual battle between the forces of "light and darkness." Although distinct from the early Christians, their ideas show substantial areas of overlap.

Christianity

Modern-day scholars maintain that a normative Judaism did not exist before the emergence of Rabbinic Judaism following the destruction of the Jerusalem Temple in 70 CE. Instead, different views and practices coexisted, albeit with tensions, in the time of the Second Temple. By the first century, there was widespread antagonism toward Roman rule in Judea and the Galilee. Brigands (*lestei*) roamed the countryside and dagger-wielding zealots (*sicarii*) engaged in political assassinations of the collaborating ruling class.[14] The Jews anxiously hoped for a messiah who would deliver them from Roman oppression and restore political freedom to their beleaguered nation.

The term "messiah" (*moshiach* in Hebrew; *christos* in Greek) means "anointed with oil." The Hebrew Bible describes the oil-anointing of kings, the high priest, and even Temple vessels, but since the second century BCE the term has been used to refer to a future redeemer. In the first century, who or what the Messiah would be was uncertain. While most expected a hero who would restore the political autonomy of Judea, some speculated that the Messiah would be a divine being who would usher in the eschatological Kingdom of God, and with it the final judgment of man and the resurrection of the dead. Historian of Jewish mysticism Gershom Scholem referred to the former as the "restorative" Messiah, the latter as the "utopian" Messiah.

According to first-century historian Josephus, Judea saw several unsuccessful "messiahs" during the years prior to the Jewish War of

---

[14] Some scholars have suggested that Judas Iscariot may have been a member of the *sicarii* based on the similarity between the terms.

66–73 CE, all summarily executed by Rome.[15] One failed messianic claim centered on the Jewish general Simon bar Kokhba during the Second Jewish War of 132–136 CE After that war was lost, Bar Kokhba was executed, and Judea was renamed Palestine by the Roman emperor Hadrian, who rededicated Jerusalem as the pagan city Aelia Capitolina.

The emerging Rabbinic movement adopted a reserved attitude toward messianism.[16] Although the arrival of a Messiah continues to be a cardinal tenet of normative Judaism, the Babylonian Talmud, a compendium of Jewish Law that was finally redacted in the sixth century, offers vague and disparate descriptions of what the messianic age will look like. According to Maimonides in the twelfth century, the Messiah will be a man who restores Jewish sovereignty and rebuilds the Jerusalem Temple. In the Mishneh Torah, an early code of the Law, he writes that "the great advantage [of the messianic age] is that we will be relieved of the oppression of wicked regimes." He never entertains the idea that the Messiah might be a divine figure, but it is likely that Jews in first-century Palestine held a variety of opinions on that topic—as evidenced by the apocalyptic literature.

The ministry of Jesus of Nazareth occurred sometime between 30 CE and 36 CE, the *terminus ad quem* being the documented removal of Pontius Pilate from his role as prefect of Judea, more than thirty years prior to the destruction of the Jerusalem Temple. Controversy persists as to whether Jesus claimed to be the Jewish Messiah or viewed

---

[15] Josephus was a Jew, belonged to a priestly family, and had commanded the Jewish rebellion in the Galilee. However, he deserted and threw in his lot with Vespasian and Titus, the Roman generals who were executing the war on the Jews. He became the court historian for the Flavian emperors, and virtually all that we know about the conduct of the Second Jewish War and the politics of the time are from his writings. His account has been questioned for its veracity, but the broad outline, at least, appears to be accurate.

[16] It is generally assumed that the rabbis were the continuation of the pre-70-CE Pharisaic movement, although this remains controversial. What is often overlooked is that the Rabbinic movement developed after the emergence of early Christianity in the late thirties CE.

himself as divine. There is certainly no documentary evidence that he intended to create a new religion. Arguments for his role as a divine Messiah were based on typological readings of the Greek translation of the Hebrew Bible, the Septuagint (Levine and Brettler 2020).[17]

Scholars agree that Jesus was a Jewish teacher from the Galilee who preached repentance, practiced water baptism, and proclaimed the imminent coming of the Kingdom of God. And it is evident from the Gospel sayings that he held a more liberal notion of individual freedom than his Jewish peers. Jesus left no writings; the earliest extant "Christian" writings are letters of Paul that date to the forties and fifties CE. While Paul never knew Jesus in the flesh, he preached the message that belief in Jesus's death and resurrection was the path to salvation and freedom. Some scholars question whether Paul's letters hold Jesus to be divine. In any case, unlike the dominant Jewish conception of the Messiah as a political redeemer, the Pauline Messiah was imagined as the source of spiritual rather than civic freedom. Whereas the prophesied role of the Messiah as political liberator was not discounted, the early Christians imagined that political liberation would occur with Christ's return (*parousia*).

Christianity spread in urban centers of the Roman Empire, primarily through the conversion of freed slaves and "God-fearers," pagans attracted to the morality of Judaism but unwilling to embrace its dietary restrictions and circumcision requirement. Sociologist Orlando Patterson (1991) argues that the notion of interior freedom through salvation described by Paul played a major role in accelerating the growth of the new religious cult in a slave society. But despite rapid growth, Christianity would remain a minority religion

---

[17] As Levine and Brettler point out, the translation of certain terms from Hebrew into Greek led to controversy as to their meaning. One famous example is from Isaiah 7:14, where the Hebrew word *almah* was translated into Greek as *parthenos*, with the former generally translated as "young woman" and the latter as "virgin." This led to interfaith arguments concerning whether Isaiah had prophesied that Jesus would be miraculously conceived by a virgin, as Matthew 1:23 (ESV) indicates: "Behold, the virgin shall conceive and bear a son, and shall call his name Immanuel."

within the Empire until the fourth century, when Constantine established it as a "favored religion" through the Edict of Milan in 313 CE (Stark 1996).

The links between early Christianity and the politics of the Roman Empire have not been fully explored. Independent scholar Joseph Atwill (2011) suggests in *Caesar's Messiah: The Roman Conspiracy to Invent Jesus* that Christianity may have been "invented" by the Flavian emperors to discourage future militaristic messianic uprisings against Rome. He presents evidence that the Gospel texts describe events that reference the Jewish War in 66–73 CE, forty years after Jesus's death. Atwill hypothesizes that Josephus, with the assistance of other Flavian court Jews, may have penned the Gospels in an effort to create a religious movement with a peaceful Messiah favorably disposed to Rome. He supports this conclusion with physical evidence, showing that some of the prominent figures in the early Church were members of the imperial family and that Christian symbols were used on Flavian coinage. Admittedly, this is an outlying "conspiracy theory" but it raises interesting questions concerning how early Christianity may have been linked to Roman state politics.

But whatever its origins, Christianity offered a new mode of "freedom" that targeted the individual. Christianity adopted secular ideas about freedom from Stoicism and Cynicism, philosophies that originated in Greek paganism. In Christianity, salvation was not primarily a promise offered to an *ethnos*, as it was in Judaism, but instead targeted the individual who professed faith. Like Jews, Christians continued to link their freedom to the notion of God as sovereign, in much the same way that Romans worshipped their emperors, beginning with Augustus.

As Patterson (1991) repeatedly points out, the notion of freedom—be it individual, sovereignal, or civic—is inextricably linked to both the idea and reality of slavery. Thus, it is not coincidental that "woke" ideology emphasizes not only individual freedom but also "systemic racism." Freedom requires the abolition of slavery;

it is impossible to achieve one without the other. To insist that blacks, women, LGBTQ+, disabled groups are "oppressed" is equivalent to saying that they remain enslaved, and as a result freedom cannot be achieved while slavery persists. The fact that there is little legitimate evidence for this supposed "oppression" is ignored, as it is a necessary fantasy. To the extent that religion continues to insist on sovereignal freedom, it must be replaced by loyalty to the state.

In the fourth century CE, secular and religious sovereignal freedom merged under Constantine. The emperor actively engaged with the early Church and assumed a decisive role in resolving the theological Arian controversy, by approving the final form of the Nicene Creed (325 CE), which claimed that Christ was divine and co-substantial as "Son" with the "Father." Whether Constantine ever abandoned his pagan beliefs is uncertain, but he undoubtedly recognized the political advantages of unifying the empire under a single new religion. He was supported in that goal by Eusebius, the bishop of Caesarea, who wrote in his hagiographical *Oration in Praise of Constantine*: "There is one God, and not two or three, or more: for to assert a plurality of gods is plainly to deny the being of God at all. There is one sovereign; and his word and royal law is one." Cooperation between state and church would characterize the Roman Empire and its successor, the Holy Roman Empire, for the next thousand years, and the spiritual Kingdom of God would be tainted by the political aims of empire (Bardill 2012).

The Reformation

In 1517, corruption in the Roman Church[18] led the German Augustinian monk Martin Luther to criticize the Papacy in 95 theses that he nailed to the door of the Wittenberg Castle Church (Eire 2016).

---

[18] The most irksome form of corruption was the sale of "indulgences," which promised to shorten the time of a soul in purgatory for a price. The monies were used to finance the construction and furbishing of St. Peter's Cathedral in Rome. Luther viewed the promise as false, mercenary, and contemptible.

The purpose of the posting was to announce a disputation in which Luther would argue his opinions against the selling of indulgences that promised individuals salvation in return for a financial donation to the papacy. The debate never took place; instead, the theses were judged heretical, and Luther was denounced by Rome. Shielded from punishment by his political patron, Frederick III of Saxony, Luther inadvertently founded a new Christian denomination, known today as Protestantism. It claimed freedom from papal influence; saw scripture, interpreted by the individual, as the only authority (*sola scriptura*); and preached salvation through faith alone (*sola fide*), as opposed to the traditional role for good "works."[19]

Luther's reformation also signaled the end of the influence of Aristotelian philosophy on Christian theology. Luther did not refute the arguments of scholastic luminaries such as Thomas Aquinas, who had offered detailed proofs for the existence of God, the soul, and morality; he simply dismissed them as unnecessary, by emphasizing the exclusive role of faith for salvation.

By dismissing the role of philosophy on theology, Protestantism also discounted Aristotle's concept of causality and paved the way for Enlightenment philosopher David Hume to deny the reality of cause and effect in defiance of everyday experience, and to argue that morality has no *a priori* rational basis but is merely the rationalized expression of individual "passions."

Like Paul, Luther was plagued by concerns about his own salvation. As psychoanalyst Erik Erikson (1995) described in *Young Man Luther*, Luther was by his own confession scrupulous in his performance of "works," but suffered from crippling doubts as to whether his actions would save him. Like Paul, he cured himself by shedding his concern with "works" and placing his trust in salvation on faith alone.

---

[19] "Works" roughly correlate with obeying the non-particular commandments of the Law and good deeds.

The Reformation conflict with the Roman Church fostered the emergence of the European nation-state and diminished the role of both the pope and the Holy Roman Emperor in the politics of Western Europe. Protestantism would be an impetus for modern secularism. Its emphases on individuals reading the Bible directly, on salvation only through faith, and on predestination favored an ethic of individualism and hard work that would become the incentive for mercantilism and capitalism (Weber 2002). The freedom of the individual would become paramount, although loyalty to God was expected to persist. But Christianity had inadvertently opened a Pandora's box; the Reformation would pave the way for the Enlightenment, the various "religions of humanity," and—ultimately—godless wokeism.

Since the fourth century CE, Christianity in its various forms has been the world's dominant religion, with Judaism, numerically speaking, a minor faith. While the Judeo-Christian ethic emphasizes their commonalities, their differences have contributed to today's cultural revolution—as we shall see in the following two chapters.

CHAPTER 4

The Judeo-Christian Ethic:
A Study in Contrasts

God is good all the time. Every time.

—RUSSELL WILSON (2024)

I form the light, and create darkness: I make peace, and create evil:
I the Lord do all these things.

—ISAIAH 45:7, KING JAMES VERSION

When his life was ruined, his family killed, his farm destroyed,
Job knelt down on the ground and yelled up to the heavens, "Why
God? Why me?" and the thundering voice of God answered,
"There's just something about you that pisses me off."

—STEPHEN KING (1999)

THE TERM "JUDEO-CHRISTIAN ETHIC" emphasizes the shared moral values of the two major monotheistic religions of the West. But the two religions are not in complete agreement. And in fact, neither religious tradition is homogeneous in its own beliefs and practices. For that reason, in what follows I refer to "normative" Judaism and Christianity, by which I mean these religions as they were conceived of and practiced prior to the Reformation in the case of Christianity, and in the case of Judaism prior to the eighteenth-century Jewish Enlightenment, i.e., the *Haskalah* movement. These reform movements introduced new liberal and secular ideas at odds with the normative, or orthodox, versions of the two religions.

Christianity began as an apocalyptic sect of Judaism, and the teachings of Jesus were consonant with those of first-century Pharisaic Judaism. Although the Gospels are critical of the Pharisees, scholars have recognized that Jesus's ideas about the Law and the resurrection of the dead concord with those of the Pharisees, and the minor differences between them likely represented unresolved internecine arguments in first-century Judaism rather than a major rift (Sanders 1985). The primary commandments of Christianity, to "love God" and to "love your neighbor as yourself" are both found in the Hebrew Bible, and the latter is related to "the Golden Rule," to "do unto others as you would have them do unto you" (Neusner and Chilton 2009). However, Jesus did call for a greater degree of stringency than was practiced by most Jews in the first century in his teachings on divorce, anger, and wealth, apparently in preparation for what he preached as the imminent arrival of God's Kingdom (Sanders 1985).[1] But despite what some Christian theologians have suggested, there is little indication that Jesus intended to abrogate the Law. In Matthew 5:17–18 (ESV), Jesus said, "Do not think that I have come to abolish the Law or the Prophets; I have not come to abolish them but to fulfill them. For truly, I say to you, until heaven

---

[1] Despite the many negative references to Pharisees in the New Testament, most scholars today believe that Jesus was either himself a Pharisee or closely related to them in his message—sharing their belief in the resurrection of the dead, and in punctilious observance of the Law. It should be remembered that some of the most antagonistic relationships occur within families.

and earth pass away, not an iota, not a dot, will pass from the Law until all is accomplished."

But like other messianic movements, Christianity did offer a liberal perspective on the Law. In the seventeenth and eighteenth centuries, the messianic movements of Sabbatai Zevi and Jacob Frank, respectively, included efforts to reform the Law and devalue its authority. Scholem suggested that Sabbatian "messianic anomia" was the inspiration for the emergence of Reform Judaism in the nineteenth century (Scholem 1995).[2]

The beliefs and practices of the earliest post-Easter Jewish Christians are not entirely known. But according to the book of Acts, Jewish Christians in Jerusalem apparently continued to participate in the Temple's sacrificial cult. The Jewish Christians of the early Jerusalem Church, the Ebionites, likely lived communally in poverty[3]—according to the Gospels, Jesus, advising a wealthy young man, warned, "It is easier for a camel to go through the eye of a needle than for a rich man to enter the kingdom of God" (Luke 18:25 NKJV). Acts 5:1–11 describes the punitive deaths of Ananias and Sapphira for deceptively holding back money from the Christian community. In Romans, Paul describes taking up donations from newly converted Gentile communities for the "poor saints" in the Jerusalem Church. Unlike Christianity, Judaism frowned on asceticism and celibacy and discouraged donating more than a fifth of one's earnings to charity to avoid lapsing into poverty and becoming a burden on the community.

Socialism was part of early Christian communal life, but following the adoption of Christianity as a favored religion by the Roman emperors, it did not persist as the norm. Nor was the Marxist goal of ridding the world of poverty a goal of either Judaism or Christianity.

---

[2] The Reform movement that began in the early nineteenth century no longer holds the Oral Law as normative, and the conservative movement has emphasized egalitarianism.

[3] The term *evyonim* means "the poor."

Rather, as Deuteronomy 15:11 (NKJV) states, "For the poor will never cease from the land; therefore I command you, saying, 'You shall open your hand wide to your brother, to your poor and your needy, in your land.'"

Christian Ambivalence on the Law

The first indication of a change in Christianity's perspective on the Law is found in Paul's letters. A Roman citizen born in Tarsus, a pagan city within the Roman Empire (and present-day Turkey), Paul claimed that he had been a scrupulous observer of the Law, a Pharisee who had persecuted Christians for their beliefs prior to experiencing a vision of the risen Christ while traveling on the road to Damascus. Transformed by this vision, Paul was baptized and subsequently preached the salvific role of Jesus's death and resurrection to the Gentiles.

Despite the passage of two thousand years, controversy persists concerning Paul's attitude toward the Law. His opinions appear to vary in his letters to different congregations. While having been scrupulous in keeping the Law, he was evidently disturbed by what he experienced as its stifling effects. As he writes in 2 Corinthians 3:6: "He [Christ Jesus] has made us competent as ministers of a new covenant—not of the letter but of the Spirit; for the letter kills, but the Spirit gives life." In Galatians 2:19–21 he writes: "For through the law I died to the law so that I might live for God. I have been crucified with Christ and I no longer live, but Christ lives in me. The life I now live in the body, I live by faith in the Son of God, who loved me and gave himself for me. I do not set aside the grace of God, for if righteousness could be gained through the law, Christ died for nothing."

Christian theologians have referred to these statements to support the position that Paul renounced the Law. However, some scholars disagree. As historian of religion Paula Fredriksen (2017) opines, Paul interpreted the resurrection of Jesus as proof that the prophesied resurrection of the dead had begun and that the Kingdom of

God was in the process of appearing—in what scholars have termed a "partially realized eschatology." For Paul, the coming Kingdom would not be limited to Jews but would also include Gentiles who professed a belief in the God of the Jews—comparable to what the Hebrew prophets had forecast.

As Paul intimates in his letter to the Romans, the Jews who had been chosen by God according to Scripture would continue to live under the Law, but strict observance would not be required of Gentiles. According to Paul, all that was expected of Gentiles was that they accept the God of Jewish history, reject idolatrous worship, and follow the tenets of what the rabbis termed the Noahide Laws, the basic commandments that essentially represent Judaism stripped of its particularisms—circumcision, dietary laws, laws of impurity, and so forth.[4]

As Christianity spread through the pagan world, its ties to Judaism and the Law grew weaker, and when Jesus failed to appear for the Second Coming during the lifetime of the early Christians, increased emphasis was placed on the "world to come," with the Law and "this world" relegated to positions of secondary importance. However, Christianity never abandoned the notion of a divinely revealed Law. Instead, it melded the revealed Ten Commandments, which were the essence of Jewish Law, with the ambient Greco-Roman law, creating a synthesis that would become known as "the natural law." Unlike Jewish Law, which was to be obeyed as divine commandments, regardless of whether man judged it rational or irrational, Christian natural law would be dependent on reason (Rommen 1998).

---

[4] The Seven Noahide Laws were meant to apply to God-fearing Gentiles. They represent the basis of a universal morality that does not include the particularisms that only Jews are expected to observe. Although this sounds like a limited obligation, each of the seven laws has multiple ramifications, so that the morality of Jews and Christians is meant ultimately to be essentially identical. It is noteworthy that one of these laws is to create a legal system so that lawbreakers can be punished and societal stability achieved.

Early Christianity viewed the Law as excessively authoritarian and inadequately spiritual. A new notion of personal "freedom" increasingly demanded a dominant role for rationality as opposed to faith. As Christian theologian Matthew Rose (2024, 47) observes: "Under Paul's influence, Christian belief turned increasingly inward untethered from concrete commandments, suspicious of ritual observance, enamored of theological speculation, and vulnerable to hypocrisy and laxity.... The ambition of modern theologians to free Christianity of 'Jewish legalism' was a formula for moral anarchy... and it contributed to the dulling of Christian consciences, which often slumbered in the presence of grotesque injustice."

By parting with the Law, Christian morality opened itself to changing ideas as to what might be judged "rational" in the future. From adherence to an objective divinely revealed morality, Christianity shifted to a morality that was increasingly subjective, especially after the Enlightenment. This allowed new ideas to infiltrate churches, leaving them susceptible to emerging secular influences in the ambient culture that opposed the Judeo-Christian ethic.

Beyond Good and Evil

Judaism—like Islam, the other major religion that is strictly and indubitably monotheistic[5]—insists that there is one God, and that what man interprets as "good" and "evil" is authored by Him. Isaiah 45:7 (KJV) states, "I form the light, and create darkness: I make peace, and create evil: I the Lord do all these things."[6] Berachot 9:5 insists that "man is obligated to give thanks for evil as he does for goodness" (Talmud Bavli 2012). This idea is problematic for Christians and others who have been taught to believe that "God is Good"

---

[5] As we have seen, the other Abrahamic faiths view Christianity as tainted by polytheism through the doctrines of the Trinity and the Incarnation.

[6] This verse from Isaiah occurs in the Christian liturgy in modified form as "I make peace and create everything" in order not to emphasize the ability of God to "create evil."

or that "God is Love," fostering a strict compartmentalization of good versus evil.[7] As 1 John 4:8–10 states: "Whoever does not love does not know God, because God is love. This is how God showed his love among us: He sent his one and only Son into the world that we might live through him. This is love: not that we loved God, but that he loved us and sent his Son as an atoning sacrifice for our sins." The Gospel of Mark quotes Jesus as saying, "No one is good—except God alone" (Mark 10:18).

The Christian emphasis on God's goodness has been traced to the influences of Platonic and Aristotelian thought, which conceive of a "Prime Mover" whose existence and form are perfectly united. But the philosopher's notion of "good" is not an emotional attribute; rather, it refers to the imagined perfection of God (Waterfield 2023).

Jews and Christians living in the Hellenized world were versed in Platonic ideas and made efforts to reconcile them with their beliefs. In first-century Alexandria, Philo, a Hellenized Jew, attempted to interpret the Mosaic Law through Plato's philosophy. He introduced the idea of the *logos*, that is, the "rational word," which was subsequently adopted by the author of the fourth Gospel in its famous prologue. Philo read the Law as allegory, an approach that would become standard within the Church. An example of Philo's allegorical reading of the Hebrew Bible was his interpretation of the law that prohibited eating pork to mean that man should avoid acting "piggishly," but he continued to insist that the Law must be practiced literally, according to Jewish tradition.[8] While Philo's writings were adopted by the Church Fathers, they were ignored by the rabbis.

---

[7] This is not to suggest that God is evil; rather, the implication is that essentially God transcends all dualities as experienced by men.

[8] The rabbis addressed this mode of interpretation by insisting that while the Hebrew Bible could be interpreted allegorically, the literal meaning (*p'shat*) must always be considered a valid interpretation—which may be why Philo adhered to the strict interpretation with respect to ritual behavior.

As an apocalyptic sect, Christianity had a radically dualistic perspective on good and evil. In Judaism, *ha-satan* (Satan) is a prosecuting angel with no independent power apart from that granted to him by God. He makes his only appearance in the book of Job, where he makes a case against the steadfastness of Job's faith. But in the synoptic Gospels, Satan has morphed into the ontological source of evil (Pagels 1981). A comparable radical dualism is seen in "woke" progressivism, which divides the world into "oppressed" and "oppressors," equating them with good and evil, respectively.

Although Jews believe that God created the world with love, they do not *equate* God with love. Instead, He is transcendent of all dualities. While in Judaism, God's "emanated" characteristics include love and strictness, he is primarily represented as a God who reconciles these opposites, as a God of justice who also shows compassion and mercy.[9]

The book of Job is what theologians refer to as a theodicy; it addresses why bad things happen to good people. Job challenges God to explain why, although free of sin, he has been afflicted with a series of sufferings. He demands, as it were, his "day in court" to refute the charges against him. Job's "comforters" encourage him to inspect his actions and identify the sin that has caused his suffering, but Job insists that he is blameless.[10] Finally, God appears as a voice out of a whirlwind to answer Job:

---

[9] These statements highlight the conflict between the Maimonidean and Kabbalistic concepts of God. According to Maimonides, to speak of God's emotions—which would include love—is to attribute anthropomorphic characteristics to an ineffable formless One. The Kabbalists do speak of God's love, strictness, anger, and so forth, and these concepts persist in normative Judaism. (Christian theologians such as Thomas Aquinas would define the love they ascribed to God as an act of the will rather than an emotion.)

[10] Much has been written about whether Job deserved his suffering or not. The rabbis were critical of Job's questioning God concerning his fate. While there are other instances of man questioning God in the Hebrew Bible, including Abraham's questioning God concerning the elimination of Sodom and Gomorrah and Moses's wondering why God allowed the Israelites to suffer, their concerns were for others and not for themselves.

Brace yourself like a man; I will question you, and you shall answer me.

Where were you when I laid the earth's foundation? Tell me, if you understand.

Who marked off its dimensions? Surely you know! Who stretched a measuring line across it?

On what were its footings set, or who laid its cornerstone—while the morning stars sang together and all the angels shouted for joy?

Who shut up the sea behind doors when it burst forth from the womb, when I made the clouds its garment and wrapped it in thick darkness, when I fixed limits for it and set its doors and bars in place... (Job 38:3–10).

God's answer continues at length, but never addresses Job's question directly. Instead, he reframes it. His answer is reminiscent of Isaiah 55:8: "My thoughts are not your thoughts, neither are your ways My ways." God makes no effort to justify his actions to Job; instead, he reminds him of his omnipotence, and that his concerns extend to all of creation, not just to man. The difficulty that men have in reconciling themselves to the existence of evil is ultimately man's limitation. The question of evil is often used by atheists to justify their lack of belief. But humility is required in order to accept a greater authority than oneself—something the atheist is unable to accept.

Judaism offers a defined path toward ethical perfectibility, based on obedience to the Law; man must struggle to attain it, but it is recognized that he will rarely succeed. As Rabbi Joseph Soloveitchik argued in *The Lonely Man of Faith*, it is man's fate to struggle with his desire to control and dominate nature and others, while also accepting his concomitant need to participate in relationships with God, man, and nature. The *imitatio Dei* in Judaism requires recognizing the reality of evil in an imperfect world and responding to it accordingly. As Soloveitchik explained: "Judaism with its realistic approach to man and his status within existence, understood that evil does not lend itself to being obscured or glossed over, and that every attempt to diminish the import of the contrast and cleavage in existence will not bring man to inner peace or to comprehension of the existential secret. Evil is a fact that cannot be denied" (Soloveitchik 2006, 4).

On the other hand, the Christian *imitatio Dei*, which since Augustine in the fifth century has viewed God as the *summum bonum* (highest good) and evil as a *privatio boni*, (privation of good) compels man to embrace loving-kindness irrespective of the situation, leaving him ill-prepared to confront harsh realities.

World opinion on the current war between the Islamic terrorist organization Hamas and the Jewish state highlights the difference between these traditions. The Law prescribes the right of self-defense, including killing those who are attempting to kill you. Judaism does not insist on "turning the other cheek" or seeking what is good in the face of evil. Currently, the Israeli military response to terrorism is being hampered by the dominant bias—Christian in origin but adopted by progressives for their purposes—toward promoting peace, whereas Judaism recognizes that peace is rarely possible until an enemy has been soundly defeated. One of the tenets of Judaism is the command in Deuteronomy 25:19 to "erase Amalek"—the archetype of the anti-Semitic enemy. (Interestingly, unapologetic willingness to defend themselves was the attitude of most Christian nations prior to World War II. Judaism rejects the currently prevailing Christian pacifism as both naïve and dangerous.)

Progressives, like Amalek, are set on attacking God and religion. To further their Godless Crusade, "woke" progressives apply emotional blackmail, playing on the consciences of Christians who are theologically sensitive to accusations of lacking compassion for the "oppressed." When it suits their purposes, progressives espouse "loving-kindness" as the only acceptable response to behaviors that are undermining the morality of society. But their "love" extends only to those who agree with them. Those who resist are seen as legitimate targets for hatred and hostility, an attitude that mimics that of first-century apocalyptic sects who viewed the world as a battle between forces of "light and darkness." They do their best to enlist Christians as allies in their fight—but only temporary allies. Ultimately, their goal is to rid the world of religion.

Progressives reject setting limits and enforcing laws as "authoritarian." They use claims of the "oppression" of the disadvantaged to justify anti-social behaviors, and they have succeeded in convincing many of America's idealistic youth that it is "kind" to tolerate behaviors that disrupt society. On the other hand, Judaism teaches that compassion is never the proper response to immorality. Rather, those guilty of behaving badly are to be held accountable as the Law prescribes; only then can they potentially be offered the opportunity to repent their deeds and receive forgiveness.

A Bridge Too Far?

For the true Christian to be less than perfectly "good" is to miss the mark, which is the definition of sin. But when perfection is the goal, the ego is prone to repress flaws and create what Jung referred to as "the shadow"[11] (Jung 1976). The shadow is a normal and unavoidable aspect of the psyche, but it may become problematic as it carries with it a predisposition to "projection," that is, the misattribution of repressed flaws to another. The goal of the religious "cure of the soul," as well as of psychotherapy, is to recognize one's projections and to reintegrate them into consciousness, so that choices can be made consciously. But when the *imitatio Dei* requires one to become perfectly "good," it is an *opus contra naturam*—and one that few can bear without excessive shadow formation and projection. Such efforts are all too likely to result in what psychoanalysts refer to as a

---

[11] For those better acquainted with Freudian nomenclature, the Jungian "shadow" roughly corresponds to the unconscious or id.

"false self," in which one is dissociated from his or her own true feelings, rather than a transformative ethical achievement.

The current cultural revolution is laden with hostile projections coming from "woke" progressives who embrace a rigid perfectionistic vision of how they are to behave. The ideals suggested by "woke" progressivism are impossible to achieve. After all, how is a "woke" white male who has been indoctrinated to hate "white privilege" and "toxic masculinity" supposed to reconcile the cognitive dissonance? The only possible path available is to dissociate from one's true identity and project one's self-loathing onto others. This is a recipe for dangerous paranoid behavior, as we shall see.

The projections of "woke" progressives can appear hypocritical, and in some cases they most assuredly are. Yet it is likely that many adherents to "woke" ideology are genuinely unaware of their projections, as the latter can only serve as effective ego defenses when maintained only dimly consciously. And when projections cannot be identified and withdrawn, the only available paths toward resolving hostilities are divorce or war.

Two Kinds of Social Justice

Diversity, equity, and inclusion (about which see in detail in chapter 7) are not aspects of normative Judaism. In fact, they are opposed to its core principles.

Judaism is a religion rooted in Law, and it recognizes that a society cannot function cooperatively when laws are not enforced. As Deuteronomy 16:18 (ESV) says, "You shall appoint judges and officers in all your towns...." Those who criticize Judaism for its focus on "the letter of the Law" tend to ignore the compassionate stances that it adopts in its interpretation. Biblical talion law dictums such as an "eye for an eye," which were literally enforced in pre-monotheistic societies (and in current Islamic *sharia* law), were interpreted in Rabbinic tradition as monetary compensation for damages, not as calls for physical mutilation. Indeed, the criteria required to impose capital punishment by a Jewish court were so strict as to make it almost impossible to execute a perpetrator. According to the Talmud, a court that sentenced "[more than] one person in 70 years was considered murderous." But as the Law was divinely ordained, it could not be abrogated.

Judaism is the historical source of social justice, which, as previously noted, must be distinguished from the current social justice of "woke" ideology. The tenets of biblical social justice, as traditional liberals recognize it, can be found in the "Holiness Code" of Leviticus chapters 17–26, which includes a series of instructions concerning how to treat the poor, the widow, the orphan, and aliens: "When a stranger sojourns with you in your land, you shall not do him wrong. You shall treat the stranger who sojourns with you as the native among you, and you shall love him as yourself, for you were strangers in the land of Egypt: I am the Lord your God." (Leviticus 19:33–34 ESV)

This idea has cynically been adopted by progressives to justify their open borders policy and illegal immigration. But they ignore the fact that the biblical immigrants were not breaking the law, unlike most of those coming to America today, who are claiming legal asylum under false pretenses. When biblical commandments do not support their agenda, progressives either ignore or denigrate them. Consider Leviticus 19:11–16 (ESV), which states: "You shall not steal; you shall not deal falsely; you shall not lie to one another. You shall not swear by my name falsely, and so profane the name of your God: I am the Lord.... You shall do no injustice in court.... I am the Lord."

Laws passed in progressive states allow individuals to steal substantial amounts with impunity. But stealing is not limited to taking the material possessions of others. Illegal immigrants also steal opportunities from those who wish to come to America legally and from the citizens that already live here. Illegal aliens lie when they falsely claim asylum, and the Judeo-Christian ethic demands truth. But progressives view truth as subjective and malleable and laws as too strict and unforgiving.

Judaism demands that the Law be applied equally to all individuals without exception. While the disenfranchised are meant to be treated compassionately, they are nevertheless to be judged by the same criteria as others when they commit a crime. Leviticus 19:15 commands, "Show neither partiality to the weak nor deference to the mighty, but judge your neighbor justly." This opposes the progressive insistence that exceptions be made for "oppressed" classes when they break the law. Progressive social justice is not biblical social justice; it is its opposite, and those who support lawlessness out of a sense of "compassion" are misguided—and contributing to the immoral breakdown of society.

The same thing can be said about progressive "sanctuary cities," which afford illegal aliens refuge from the law. The Hebrew Bible calls for establishing cities of refuge for those who commit involuntary manslaughter, so that they can escape the revenge of the victim's family members. But those who willfully commit homicide are afforded no refuge. The First Book of Kings describes how Joab, a general in King David's army who had murdered several men, was taken from the "horns of the altar," where he had sought sanctuary, and killed there: "When the news reached Joab, who had conspired with Adonijah though not with Absalom, he fled to the tent of the Lord and took hold of the horns of the altar. King Solomon was told that Joab had fled to the tent of the Lord and was beside the altar. Then Solomon ordered Benaiah son of Jehoiada, 'Go, strike him down!'" (1 Kings 2:28–29)

Judaism does not condone shielding criminals from punishment, and it differs from historical Christian practice in this regard. From the fourth until the seventeenth century, a person could hide in an English church for up to forty days, and in some instances indefinitely, regardless of his crime (Shoemaker 2011). Sanctuary in the Christian world was unconditional and synonymous with "refuge."

Progressives base the legitimacy of modern sanctuary cities on this Christian practice.

The Triumph of the Victim

Critical Theory divides society into "oppressors" and "oppressed." The notion that one is "oppressed" implies a power differential that cannot be changed. Once one accepts the label of "oppressed," it is easy to identify as a "victim." The psychology of victimhood is timeless. In ancient Greek myth, the Titan Prometheus offended the gods by bringing fire to man without the gods' permission and was punished by Zeus. But rather than apologize in order to end his suffering, Prometheus insisted that he had been treated unfairly and chose to continue to suffer punishment, as it allowed him a perceived moral victory over Zeus. For those who consider themselves to be powerless, moral masochism can be the only available path to overcoming helplessness.

Writing in 1924, Freud attributed moral masochism to a desexualized form of masochism arising from an unconscious sense of guilt that can only be assuaged by suffering. He also recognized that the masochistic victim role can be a powerful strategy for manipulating and defeating others (Freud 1924). The nexus between religion and masochism was explored by nineteenth-century anthropologist James Frazer in his magisterial *Golden Bough*, in which he recognized the archetypal motif of the suffering and dying god in the myths of agrarian societies and attributed the defining myth of Christianity to it (Frazer 2019).

By all accounts, Rome was a brutal occupying force of first-century Judea, and Josephus described how the Jews were oppressed by heavy taxation and physical intimidation (Josephus 1981). In the Gospels, Jesus names a powerful demon "Legion," in what may be a thinly veiled reference to the armed Roman occupiers. But successful rebellion was not deemed possible. The only path to victory was a moral one—which Jesus's followers believed had been accomplished by his death and resurrection.

The messianic idea that the early Christians preached was a moral triumph of the weak over the powerful rather than a physical victory over Rome. As Paul wrote to the Corinthians, "God hath chosen the foolish things of the world to confound the wise; and God hath chosen the weak things of the world to confound the things which are mighty." (1 Corinthians 1:27 KJV) The early Christians searched the Hebrew Bible for prophecies of a crucified Messiah and believed they had found them in the "Suffering Servant" passages of Isaiah 53.

> He was despised and rejected by mankind, a man of suffering, and familiar with pain.
> Like one from whom people hide their faces he was despised, and we held him in low esteem.
> Surely he took up our pain and bore our suffering, yet we considered him punished by God, stricken by him, and afflicted.
> But he was pierced for our transgressions, he was crushed for our iniquities; the punishment that brought us peace was on him, and by his wounds we are healed.

Although modern biblical scholars argue that these verses more likely referred to the oppressed Israelite nation than to a suffering Messiah, they were embraced by early Christians as a typological proof text for Jesus's role as the suffering Messiah (Levine and Brettler 2020).

"Woke" Sado-Masochism

The current politics of grievance and victimhood derive their religious authority from Christianity. But "woke" progressivism offers no hope for redemption; instead, victim status is deemed immutable and cannot be redeemed. It is a form of moral masochism.

Masochism is never an isolated behavior; it is always one half of a sadomasochistic dynamic. The "oppressed" victim is not redeemed as he is in Christianity; his persistent covert hostility precludes redemption. Instead, he is transformed into the sadistic "oppressor" of others, while his apologetic "guilty" victim now assumes the "oppressed" masochistic role. It is a porous, ever-shifting dynamic.

In the aftermath of the George Floyd riots, whites could be seen groveling before once "victimized" blacks, seeking forgiveness for racist crimes they never committed. By allowing themselves to willingly bow and scrape before the aggrieved "victims," they assumed the moral masochist's superiority, signaling their "virtue." The entire dynamic is a neurotic nonproductive attempt to create a religious redemptive experience.

God and Man

One stark difference between Judaism and Christianity is the latter's claim that God was incarnated as the man Jesus. Whereas Judaism argues for a relationship between man and God, the physical and psychological distance between them is viewed as insurmountable. The aniconic God of Judaism insists on this separation, whereas the Christian incarnated God provides man with an imagistic bridge to divinity. But in doing so, Christianity opened the door to the possibility of a "religion of humanity." Indeed, progressive religion is a distorted restatement of Christianity, but one that imagines man rather than God as omnipotent (Hayek 1988). But worshipping man is a solipsistic exercise that ultimately leads to sociopathy. Wherever one looks in progressive society today, one detects this phenomenon. After all, if what is transpiring is genuinely virtuous, why is there so much societal turmoil and corruption?

Progressive "Morality"

Morality is meant to be a guide to what is "good." But when the Aristotelian ideas of "formal" and "final" causes were rejected by the Enlightenment philosophers and the command morality of Judaism and the natural law of Christianity were dismissed as irrational and antiquated, the ability to distinguish good from bad was undermined (Feser 2008). Progressives deny the possibility of defining shared moral values, claiming that morality is relative and whatever the individual chooses to adopt. But moral values must be shared if they are to serve as a stabilizing force in society. A self-serving "morality" of convenience only promotes decadence, not decency.

If there is any doubt about that, consider the progressives' positions on terrorism, abortion, aberrant sexuality, and so forth. In *Performance*, a 1970 movie starring Mick Jagger in his premiere as an actor, he delivers a line that characterizes what is transpiring today: "Nothing is true, everything is permitted." Those are said to have been the last words of Hassan-i Sabbah, the leader of an eleventh-century group of assassins. In the absence of God and a moral code, everything goes.

CHAPTER 5

Universalism Versus Particularism

Nationality is a good thing to a certain extent, but universality is better. All that is best in the great poets of all countries is not what is national in them, but what is universal.

—HENRY WADSWORTH LONGFELLOW

The universality of moral concern is not something we learn by being universal but by being particular.... There is no road to human solidarity that does not begin with moral particularity—by coming to know what it means to be a child, a parent, a neighbor, a friend. We learn to love humanity by loving specific human beings. There is no short-cut.

—RABBI JONATHAN SACKS (2020)

A COMPETITIVE PSYCHOLOGICAL IMPULSE drives man to set himself above his fellow man, while an opposing drive strives to level difference and seek equality. This conflict between hierarchical and leveling impulses can be noted in virtually every society and even in nonhuman primates (McMahon 2023). It is noteworthy that the ancient Greeks, who by most contemporaneous accounts were fiercely competitive, also created the first political democracies.

Darwinian evolution, which informs much of modern scientific thought, demonstrates that when left to its own devices, nature invariably yields unequal outcomes. Indeed, natural selection is based on inequalities; it requires unequal initial conditions and yields unequal outcomes. According to Darwin's theory, those differences that prove adaptive are more likely to be propagated. But modern man is disinclined to accept the laws of nature. When in his dotage Darwin was asked about the future of mankind, he professed pessimism, observing that the natural law of "survival of the fittest" was being undermined by those who refused to accept inequities. The desire for equal outcomes—equity—is the professed goal of progressives, but as Darwin recognized, it is an unnatural fantasy.

All-Inclusive?

The Judaic and Christian traditions diverge on the idea of inclusion. As an enclave culture, Jews chose to remain separate from their neighbors. Nevertheless, Judaism does include a universal message that is presented in the prophetic literature. Jews were commanded to set a moral example for the world, while remaining physically separate from their neighbors. Isaiah 49:6 (KJV) refers to Israel as a "light" to the nations: "He said: 'It is a light thing that thou shouldest be my servant to raise up the tribes of Jacob, and to restore the preserved of Israel: I will also give thee for a light to the Gentiles, that thou mayest be my salvation unto the end of the earth.'"

Inclusiveness, as Christianity—and progressivism—conceive of it, is foreign to normative Judaism, which emphasizes the importance of differentiating between "kinds" (*minim*) and insists on maintaining differences. As Genesis 1:24 says: "And God said, 'Let the land produce living creatures according to their kinds: the livestock, the creatures that move along the ground, and the wild animals, each according to its kind.' And it was so."

90

This idea of maintaining "separateness" in Judaism extends to not planting different species together in one's fields, not mixing linen and wool in a garment, and not intermarrying with Gentiles. There are classes of Jews that are forbidden to intermarry—for example, a priest and a widow. This conscious strategy of exclusivity is aimed at maintaining holiness—as we have seen, the Hebrew word for "holy" (*kodesh*) means separate. From that perspective, inclusiveness is neither natural nor beneficial.

Since antiquity, Judaism has been criticized for its exclusivity. As first-century Roman historian Tacitus wrote of the Jews:

> Moses, wishing to secure for the future his authority over the nation, gave them a novel form of worship, opposed to all that is practiced by other men. Things sacred with us, with them have no sanctity, while they allow what with us is forbidden. In their holy place they have consecrated an image of the animal by whose guidance they found deliverance from their long and thirsty wanderings. They slay the ram, seemingly in derision of Hammon, and they sacrifice the ox, because the Egyptians worship it as Apis. They abstain from swine's flesh, in consideration of what they suffered when they were infected by the leprosy to which this animal is liable.... We are told that the rest of the seventh day was adopted, because this day brought with it a termination of their toils; after a while the charm of indolence beguiled them into giving up the seventh year also to inaction.

This contempt for Judaism was widely shared in the pagan world. The notion of Israel as God's "chosen people" is central to the self-image of Judaism, but historically it has invited envy and ill will. The biblical narrative makes it clear that the Jews were not chosen for any inherent superiority. As Deuteronomy 7:7 (NKJV) says, "The Lord did not set His love on you nor choose you because you were more in number than any other people, for you were the least of all peoples." Instead, they were "chosen" to serve God for inexplicable reasons and to advertise God and morality to the pagan world. Nevertheless, there is an unquestionable sense of moral superiority that many observant Jews will admit to, because of their having remained faithful to the Law, because of living an ethical life, and—perhaps most critically—because of the survival of the Jewish people, persisting through the ages in the face of hardships in their faithfulness to God, their obedience to the Law, and their status as a people set apart. When Frederick the Great asked an advisor for proof of God's existence, he was told, "The Jews, Sire."

The above description applies to Orthodox Jews but differs substantially from what is currently believed and practiced by Reform Jews, who comprise 90 percent of Jews in America—although they remain a minority in Europe and Israel. Reform Judaism originated in nineteenth-century Germany in response to the emancipation of Europe's Jews. Unlike Law-observant Orthodox Jews, Reform Jews have embraced Christian universalism, expurgating Judaism of its particularisms in an effort at making Judaism more compatible with the dominant culture of Western Europe and America. Reform Judaism divested itself of the dietary laws, strict Sabbath observance, most of the Oral Law, and expurgated the synagogue liturgy of references to both a Messiah and the resurrection of the dead. Although Reform Jews do not accept Jesus as divine, the practical differences between Reform Judaism and Christianity, especially mainline Christianity, are relatively few. In recent years, American Reform Jews have embraced progressive ideas of an "open society" that are more aligned with the universalistic positions of Christianity than with traditional Judaism.

In recent years this has resulted in eroding support for the modern state of Israel. America's Reform Jews are increasingly willing to label Israel an "oppressor" state and to ignore the refusal of Palestinians to acknowledge Israel's right to exist. The infiltration of progressive ideas into Reform Judaism has been problematic, but the same thing is also happening to liberal Christian denominations (Miles 2021).

A 2021 Pew Research Center study highlighted the sociopolitical differences between Orthodox and Reform Jews in America today.

Religion is not central to the lives of most U.S. Jews. Even Jews by religion are much less likely than Christian adults to consider religion to be very important in their lives (28% vs. 57%). And among Jews as a whole, far more report that they find meaning in spending time with their families or friends, engaging with arts and literature, being outdoors, and pursuing their education or careers than find meaning in their religious faith. Twice as many Jewish Americans say they derive a great deal of meaning and fulfillment from spending time with pets as say the same about their religion....

Orthodox Jews are a striking exception to many of these overall findings. They are among the most highly religious groups in U.S. society—along with White evangelicals and Black Protestants—in terms of the share who say religion is very important in their lives. A plurality of Orthodox Jews say that being Jewish is mainly about religion alone (40%), and they are the only subgroup in the survey who overwhelmingly feel that observing halakha is essential to their Jewishness (83%). Fully three-quarters of the Orthodox say they find a great deal of meaning and fulfillment in their religion, exceeded only by the share who feel that way about spending time with their families (86%). And 93% of Orthodox Jews say they believe in God as described in the Bible.

Roughly one-third of US Jews say they believe God gave the land that is now Israel to the Jewish people, while 42% do not believe Israel was literally given by God to the Jews, and one-quarter of US Jews say they do not believe in God or a higher power.... Belief that God gave Israel to the Jewish people is much more common among Jews by religion than among Jews of no religion, but it is a minority opinion among both groups (Pew Research Center 2021).

The politics of Reform Jews have historically been and currently remain closely aligned with those of the progressive Democratic Party. A disproportionate number of American Jews vote the Democratic party line, whereas the Orthodox are more likely to support conservative Republican candidates. As the Pew study notes:

> Pew Research Center surveys, including the 2020 study, show that Jews are among the most consistently liberal and Democratic groups in the U.S. population. Seven-in-ten Jewish adults identify with or lean toward the Democratic Party, and half describe their political views as liberal.
>
> This general inclination toward the Democratic Party and liberal values goes hand-in-hand with disapproval of former Republican President Donald Trump. In this survey, conducted roughly five to 12 months before the 2020 presidential election, nearly three-quarters of Jewish adults disapproved of the job Trump was doing as president, while just 27% rated him positively—far below the 65% who approved of President Barack Obama's job performance in 2013.
>
> Orthodox Jews, however, stand out as a small subgroup (roughly one-in-ten Jewish adults) whose political profile is virtually the reverse of Jews as a whole: 60% of Orthodox Jews describe their political views as conservative, 75% identify as Republicans or lean toward the GOP, and 81% approved of Trump's job performance at the time of the survey.
>
> Jews by religion are considerably more likely than U.S. Christians to identify with or lean toward the Democratic Party; they look much more similar to religiously unaffiliated Americans in this regard, with Democrats making up about two-thirds of each group. Among Christian subgroups, only Black Protestants show higher levels of Democratic support (86%).

As can be seen from this exhaustive survey, the political attitudes of Jews track directly with their level of religious observance.

When recently, in response to the terrorist attacks in Israel and the anti-Semitic protests by "woke" progressives around the world,

Elon Musk suggested that American Jewry was in part responsible because of having supported the policies of "woke" progressives, he was accused of anti-Semitism. But Musk was correct. One cannot expect to promote groups that support anti-Jewish and anti-Israeli policies and then cry anti-Semitism when these groups turn on you, or accuse others of anti-Semitism when they happen to notice. (Reform Jews do not speak for Law-observant Jews, though most of whom reject the current "woke" progressive agenda.)

Marxism and the Jews

Karl Marx was born into a Jewish family that had converted to Christianity for economic reasons prior to his birth. The common claim that Marx was a Jew is incorrect; in fact it represents a subtle racial form of anti-Semitism, implying that despite being raised as a Christian, Marx remained a Jew. Marx was a rabid anti-Semite and a misotheist. The affinity that Jews have shown for Marxism may be attributed to their biblically informed concern for social justice and their long-standing mistreatment in Christian Europe (Podhoretz 2009). Poor Eastern European Jews, for example, saw Marx's wish to alleviate the burdens of the oppressed as the only path out of their economically deprived situation. But Jews' penchant for Marxist utopian ideas is misguided and has led many of them to support progressive causes that are antithetical to the core beliefs of normative Judaism.

Progressive Jews consistently overlook the fact that anti-Semitism has been a staple of Marxism from its inception. As we shall see, many of the leaders of the Frankfurt School, a group of Marxists who had played an important role in the American Left following World War II, were Jews who were either confessed atheists or misotheists. While progressive Jews are comfortable condemning right-wing anti-Semitism, which they associate with Nazism and white supremacy, they have been forgiving of left-wing anti-Semitism. Since the 1960s, Islamic and black nationalist causes have been aligned with Marxist ideology, and their agendas have been consistently both anti-Semitic and anti-Israel. Despite consistent support for Israel by Republican conservatives and their condemnation of anti-Semitism in recent years, liberal American Jews have found it difficult to vote for conservatives, even in the face of glaring progressive anti-Semitism.

This self-defeating stance likely stems from Jewish self-hatred and a wish to assimilate into the dominant secular culture. Reform Jews have expressed a continuing desire to support the causes of minority groups even in the face of blatant anti-Semitism (Kahane 1972). Following the terrorist attacks on Israel and anti-Semitic protests on university campuses and urban streets, many nontraditional Jews have continued to support progressive policies.[12] As a recent National Survey of Jewish Voters poll showed:

> Approximately 47% of younger Jewish voters, aged between 18–35, feel that Joe Biden is overly supportive of Israel, according to the latest November 2023 National Survey of Jewish Voters, conducted by the Jewish Electorate Institute with GBAO Strategies. This contrasts sharply with the generally favorable view of the older Jewish electorate towards the President's handling of the war between Israel and Hamas. According to the survey, only 18% of American Jews between the ages of 36 to 65 thought that Biden was "overly supportive." The religious stream with the highest support for Israel is the Conservative movement, with 89% approval for Biden's support for Israel, as opposed to 81% of the Orthodox and 79% of Reform Jews (Jerusalem Post Staff 2024).

Liberal Theology

Universalism and inclusivity were familiar ideas to the pagans who converted to Christianity in the first centuries. These values were

---

[12] This may be changing as a sizable minority of American Jews voted for Donald Trump in the 2024 presidential election.

part of the Hellenism that Alexander the Great had imposed on his conquered empire in the fourth century BCE. But as in Judaism, the monotheistic message of the original Christianity was not altogether inclusive. When in Galatians 3:28 (NKJV) Paul writes, "There is neither Jew nor Greek, there is neither slave nor free, there is neither male nor female; for you are all one in Christ Jesus," this idea extends only to those professing Christian beliefs. As Cyprian said in the third century, "Outside the Church there is no salvation."

Following the Reformation, Christianity was divided into Eastern Orthodox, Roman Catholic, and Protestant branches. In America, Protestant Christianity has been the dominant religion since its founding. Today, just under 50 percent of Americans are Protestant, 23 percent Catholic, and 2 percent Mormon. America's Protestants can be divided roughly into four major groups: Evangelicals—the Southern Baptists and many independent churches, including Pentecostal churches; Reformed—various Presbyterian churches including the Presbyterian Church in America; mainline churches— Episcopalians, Lutherans, Methodists, the Presbyterian Church (USA), the United Church of Christ, American Baptist Churches USA, and the Disciples of Christ; and the black churches.

Like Judaism, Christianity has seen consistent trends toward decreased observance. As a Pew study reveals: "In the past seven years, the percentage of adults who describe themselves as Christians has dropped from 78.4% to 70.6%. Once an overwhelmingly Protestant nation, the U.S. no longer has a Protestant majority. Today 46.5% of adults describe themselves as Protestants. The share of adults belonging to mainline churches dropped from 18.1% in 2007 to 14.7% in 2014. This is similar to the drop seen among U.S. Catholics, whose share of the population declined from 23.9% to 20.8% during the same seven-year period (Pew Research Center 2015)."

Diminished religious observance has been accompanied by efforts to attract a dwindling membership by appealing to trends in the popular culture. Large amphitheater-style churches, complete with upholstered seating and rock music, have replaced small churches with wooden pews and a church organ. But despite brief upticks in interest, these changes have not reversed the drift toward secularism.

To assume that this trend occurred spontaneously is to ignore evidence that Marxists have been attempting to infiltrate the clergy for years. In 1915, Marxist Antonio Gramsci wrote: "Socialism is precisely the religion that must overwhelm Christianity.... In the new order, Socialism will triumph by first capturing the culture via infiltration of schools, universities, *churches*, and the media by transforming the consciousness of society" (Coughlin and Higgins 2019, 44; emphasis in the original). To this end, the American League Against War and Fascism, a Communist-front organization, actively reached out to ministers, churches, and religious organizations with the goal of introducing Marxist ideology and undermining their core tenets.

As might be predicted, the trend toward embracing the "social justice" agenda of progressivism has been accompanied by diminished emphasis on Christian dogma. In its place, Marxist ideas, disguised as "liberal theology," have infiltrated churches. As pastor Lucas Miles writes in *The Christian Left*:

> Much like the infamous tactical device of the Ancient Greeks, the devil has "gifted" our modern-day society with Trojan Horses too: ideologies that appear to be valuable contributions to the faith but are instead full of morally subversive stratagems designed to unravel the very theological framework of the church. Slipping past the walls of Christian orthodoxy and sound doctrine, this barrage of intellectual and spiritual attacks has produced what is now being called the "Christian Left"—a growing constituency of "Christians" who have adopted (either knowingly or unknowingly) leftist, socialistic, and communistic thinking, ideals, values, and innovations (Miles 2021, 17).

Miles describes how this has been achieved:

These goals are often accomplished by the Left's use of spiritual sounding language and references to its good deeds plagiarized from true believers and adopted by the Left. See if you recognize these common lines of thought from the Christian Left:

+ Jesus accepts everyone.
+ Jesus would never get in the way of the love between two people.
+ Jesus was a refugee.
+ Jesus accepts foreigners and strangers.
+ God doesn't create walls that prevent us from coming to him.
+ People need to live their truth.
+ Some people are just born gay (or bi or transgender).
+ A real Christian accepts everyone.

As Miles argues, although Christianity teaches acceptance of the "other," what the Christian Left embraces is not Christian dogma. Jesus's message was not one of unlimited inclusivity or love. As he states in Matthew 10:34 (ESV), "Do not think that I have come to bring peace to the earth; I have not come to bring peace, but a sword." However, it is true that the universalist message of progressivism is more closely aligned with that of Christianity than that of Judaism, which may explain why it has been easier for the Christian churches to embrace it than it has been for Orthodox Jews.

The core tenets of Christian belief, including Jesus's death and resurrection, have in recent years been increasingly ignored by the Christian Left, as those doctrines require belief in miracles. Unfortunately, there are those today who are under the misimpression that people in the past believed in miracles only because they were incapable of reasoning properly, but that is decidedly not the case, as aspects of the Christian message were judged irrational even in antiquity. The ancient Greek philosophers were averse to believing in the incarnation and the resurrection, as is clear from their response when Paul addressed them on the Areopagus, as described in Acts 17:16–34.

But religious beliefs are not driven solely by reason. As the third-century Church Father Tertullian wrote, *Credo qui absurdum*, "I believe [in Christian doctrine on the Trinity and the Resurrection] because it is irrational." Elsewhere, he spurned philosophical rationality as the path to salvation by asking, "What has Athens to do with Jerusalem?" Tertullian was well versed in ancient philosophy but held that when rational thought opposes the faith required for salvation, it is to be disregarded. But this early emphasis on faith would over time be subordinated to the increased emphasis by Christian theologians on rationality and "natural law."

The current trend within mainline churches to marginalize faith amounts to an abandonment of the essential Christian *kerygma*. But it is an extension of trends in Christian theology. As Miles suggests, it is questionable as to whether what is being preached from the pulpits of Christian Left churches today qualifies as the Christianity preached by the early Church (Miles 2021).

The archetypal tensions between Judaism and Christianity arise from the particularism of Judaism versus the universalism of Christianity and from their different emphases on physicality versus spirituality, and law versus compassion. However, both are under attack by progressive ideology, and it is questionable whether the nonorthodox religious sects of either religion will survive the Godless Crusade to replace religion with secularism and atheism.

CHAPTER 6

The Origins of "Wokeism"

I saw the revolutionary destruction of society as the one and only solution to the cultural contradictions of the epoch.

—GEORGE LUKACS (COUGHLIN AND HIGGINS 2019, 61)

THE PROGRESSIVES' EXILE OF GOD from the public square has left a psychological void that must be filled. In recent times, the major secular alternative to the Judeo-Christian traditions has been Marxism. Marx's arguments for socialism and communism are not original to him; rather, Marxism is a modern expression of an ancient archetypal human impulse that aims at leveling society. But despite what Marxist ideologues choose to believe, the driving psychological motivation toward equity is not "fairness," it is envy of those perceived to have "more" (McMahon 2023).

Marx conceived of society as a Hegelian dialectical conflict between economic classes. In his vision of a future communist utopia—essentially a secularized restatement of the messianic end-time—the needs of workers were to initially be met by the state, and subsequently by the workers themselves without state interference. As Marx stated in his *Critique of the Gotha Program*, "From each according to his ability, to each according to his needs" (Marx 2023). But he was short on details as to how this utopia was to be achieved.

By most contemporaneous accounts, Marx was a self-absorbed ne'er-do-well who regularly took financial advantage of his friends and consistently failed to support his family (Johnson 1988). What is less well known is that Marx's earliest interest was not economics; rather, it was in replacing religion with an irreligious society. According to the educator Jennifer Hecht: "Between 1839 and 1841 Marx wrote his doctoral thesis. It was on Epicurus and Democritus.... Note that there is nothing here about communism; Marx was an old-school atheist before anything else. In the summer of 1841, he and Bauer began to edit a journal called the *Atheist Archives*.... In an 1844 paper Marx wrote: 'Religion is the sigh of the oppressed creatures; the heart of the heartless world, just as it is the spirit of a spiritless situation. It is the opium of the people. The abolition of religion as the illusory happiness of the people is required for their real happiness'" (Hecht 2003, 389–90).

Like Freud, Marx was a misotheist who viewed religion as an "illusion." But unlike Freud, he recognized the ontological existence of God and actively opposed it. His grandiose goal was to destroy God's influence, replacing it with himself as the ultimate authority. As he wrote: "With disdain I will throw my gauntlet full in the face of the world and see the collapse of the pygmy giant whose fall will not stifle my ardor. Then I will wander godlike and victorious through the ruins of the world and giving my words an active force, I will feel equal to the Creator" (Simpson 2021, 1). The megalomania of this statement is obvious, and its destructive implications should not be ignored. As an acquaintance witnessed, Marx was "a destructive spirit whose heart was filled with hatred rather than love of mankind.... Despite the communist egalitarianism which he preaches, he is the absolute ruler of his party...and he tolerates no opposition" (Simpson 2021, 3).

Marx was raised in a well-to-do family and spoiled by an overly generous father. By most accounts he was lazy and entitled and made little effort to obtain consistent gainful employment. His favored strategy for survival was parasitic—leaning on relatives and friends for financial support. Tragically, three of Marx's children died of malnutrition and two committed suicide. He had an illegitimate child with the family maid and insisted that his colleague Engels raise the child.

Disinclined to work, he condemned capitalism as the cause of all society's ills and concluded that its success was due to the exploitation of the laboring proletariat. He predicted that capitalism would meet its demise as the consequence of a workers' revolution, which would then set the stage for a utopian communist society. But as the historian Paul Johnson (1988) noted, "Marx never set foot in a mill, mine, or any other industrial workplace in the whole of his life," and his hostility toward capitalism was based on his own inability to succeed, rather than on solidarity with the working class. Marx's roots in the bourgeoisie and his self-aggrandizing motives would be shared by virtually all subsequent Marxist leaders, including Lenin, Mao, and Castro. Investigative journalist James Simpson has referred to them disparagingly as "entrepreneurial parasites" (Simpson 2021).

Marx insisted that the new utopian society must oppose religion, as it entices workers to accept capitalism's inequities. He accused religion of being "the opium of the people," numbing them to their present misery by distracting them with hope for a better future world rather than motivating them to act against their "oppressors" (Marx 1998). He dismissed the biblical social justice ideals of justice and truth as tools of the oppressor class, but as political scientist Heinrich Rommen noted: "Yet at the same time he thundered like an Old Testament prophet against the injustices and deceit of bourgeois society and philosophy. He therefore implicitly affirmed justice and truth as objective and transcendent, and not as merely relative and immanent in the conditions of socio-economics" (Rommen 1998, 128).

Socialism appeals primarily to the poor, to those who are neurotically guilty about their own success, and to those who feel compelled to signal their virtue by disingenuously registering concern for the disadvantaged (Le Bon 1899). Its promise of a better world is its primary weakness, as it is expected to deliver on that promise in *this* world, something it has repeatedly failed to do in practice. Austrian economist and political philosopher Friedrich Hayek (1988) attributed the failure of socialism to its excessive reliance on human reason and central planning. He argued that capitalism succeeds primarily as a result of unregulated transactions and the "invisible hand" of the market, which invariably outperforms the imposed rational designs of elite planners. According to Hayek, the ultimate success of capitalism is rooted in the Judeo-Christian ethic, and capitalism fails when its moral underpinnings are sacrificed to greed.

On the other hand, socialism fails because its conceptual basis is wrongminded. While capitalism allows for differences in human intelligence, industriousness, creativity, and competence, socialism's insistence on equity disincentivizes men from achieving their potential. Socialism requires a powerful central government to impose equitable outcomes, but history teaches that such governments invariably become corrupt and tyrannical, resulting in diminished standards of living for their citizens. Examples of failed Marxist experiments over the last century have included the Soviet Union, Communist China, Cuba, and various nations in Latin American and Asia. Yet Marxist fantasies persist, as they are motivated by irradicable human envy. Marxists target God and traditional values for somehow being responsible for their discontent. But while envy may be responsible for inciting revolutions, it never leads to the success of socialist society.

Before the 1960s, Marxism was widely rejected by Americans, who had thrived under capitalism. But in recent years, Marxist ideas have infiltrated America's institutions, in part due to increased income inequality, but primarily as the result of the "long march" through America's institutions—an idea attributed to Italian communist Antonio Gramsci and a phrase coined as a succinct mission statement by Marxist student activist Rudi Dutschke (Coughlin and Higgins 2019).

Socialism's successful infiltration into American society can be attributed largely to the efforts of the Frankfurt School of Marxist philosophers. Composed predominantly of Jewish philosophers who left Europe due to Nazi persecution, they were proponents of the "open society" described by the philosopher Karl Popper (1994) and viewed nationalism as a recipe for "fascism." Their goal was *Aufhaben der Kultur*, i.e., to "negate the culture," an idea they adopted from Hegel. As George Lukacs, a founder of the Frankfurt School, stated, "I saw the revolutionary destruction of society as the one and only solution to the cultural contradictions of the epoch" (Coughlin and Higgins 2019, 61).

Herbert Marcuse, a German Jew who trained under Heidegger, is generally viewed as the primary intellectual force behind American Marxism. Enamored with Gramsci's ideas, Marcuse taught at a series of American universities in the 1960s, using his positions to disseminate Marxist ideology to students. He viewed society as either "liberating" or "repressive" and argued that public tolerance should be extended only to those whose views conformed with his neo-Marxist perspective.

As Marx's ideas had little appeal for most Americans, Marcuse searched for a new strategy for transforming society and concluded that it might be possible to achieve this goal by combining Marxist ideas with the discontent of America's historically disenfranchised blacks. His ideas were adopted by his student Angela Davis and other black revolutionaries who dismissed the Reverend Martin

Luther King Jr.'s arguments for a merit-based society, in which blacks and whites could live together peacefully, and claimed that King's position tacitly endorsed racism by requiring blacks to adopt the values of whites in order to succeed. They insisted that blacks must remain separate from the white majority and continue to view themselves as an "oppressed" class with whites as "oppressors" who must be made to accept that they are morally bankrupt and legitimate targets for contempt.

Over the last sixty years, these ideas have been disseminated in the culture through the efforts of academia. Since the 1960s, liberal professors with Marxist leanings have displaced conservatives in the academy through a systematic strategy of ideologically based hiring rather than the traditional merit-based system, and they currently dominate the faculties of American universities. As *Inside Higher Ed* reported, a 2007 survey of 1,417 professors teaching at 927 institutions titled "The Social and Political Views of American Professors" found that 44 percent were liberal, 46 percent moderate, and 9 percent conservative. While only 3–18 percent openly identified as Marxists, the vast majority identified as "progressive" (Jaschik, 2017).

Recognizing racial difference as America's Achilles' heel, black civil rights activist and educator Derrick Bell developed Critical Race Theory (CRT), by adopting Marxist critical thought to the issue of race and by insisting that *all* societal issues be viewed through the prism of race. This approach targets blacks and other indigenous people of color (BIPOC) who have historically not prospered in America. But rather than examining the host of reasons that this might be the case, CRT invariably attributes poor outcomes to oppression by an "oppressive" white majority. According to CRT, "whiteness" is responsible for virtually everything that is wrong in society, and any aspect of the culture that BIPOC find offensive is a legitimate target for Marxist criticism. From this perspective, America is an incurably "racist" country that can only be redeemed by restructuring along progressive lines (Rufo 2023).

A high-profile example of CRT in action is *The 1619 Project*, the brainchild of "woke" *New York Times* journalists who claim that America's founding and subsequent success were due to the labor of black slaves. America's history is viewed entirely through the frame of race and oppression. When this assertion was sharply criticized by academic historians as a gross distortion of the truth, these journalists dismissed their critics as "excessively focused on facts." As the co-author of *The 1619 Project*, Nikole Hannah-Jones, a "woke" black woman, wrote in her response to her critics: "I've always said that *The 1619 Project* is not a history. It is a work of journalism that explicitly seeks to challenge the national narrative and therefore, the national memory. The project has always been as much about the present as it is the past" (Rindsberg, 2021).

Her response exposes three critical facts. The first is that *The 1619 Project* is not history, at least not as it has been conceived since Thucydides, i.e., as a recounting of the factual events of the past with consideration of the factors responsible for them. The second is that from the perspective of CRT, facts have no role in informing the present or guiding the future; instead, what matters is control of the present political narrative. Finally, from that "woke" perspective, truth is a subjective construct. The practitioners of CRT assume, in typical Marxist fashion, that the ends justify the means—the end in this case being the deconstruction of America's history. Progressive journalists like Hannah-Jones don't view it as their role to report facts accurately; rather, their concern is the preferred narrative that blacks were, are, and will always be oppressed, and that whites are their eternal "oppressors." From this radical dualistic perspective, one must conclude that all whites are irredeemably evil, and all blacks innocent victims.

The term "woke" was adopted from black vernacular English to denote, according to Webster's, someone who is "aware of and actively attentive to important societal facts and issues, especially issues of racial and social justice." Beginning in the 2010s, it came to encompass a broader awareness of social inequalities including racial injustice, sexism, and denial of LGBTQ+ rights.

The "woke" narrative is meant to stir anger, promote divisions, and ultimately collapse America's institutions, so that they can be replaced by a society constructed based on diversity, equity, and inclusion (DEI). *The 1619 Project* is a window into how progressive journalists currently view their role. They are no longer disinterested purveyors of fact; instead, they are political activists whose role is to help transform America.

Unfortunately, this perspective is not limited to America's journalists; rather, as Heather Mac Donald argues, it is true today for virtually all professions. Doctors, lawyers, corporate CEOs, musicians, artists, and so forth have, with few exceptions, accepted it as their role to serve as political activists, with the aims of countering racism and promoting DEI (Mac Donald 2018). This is a disturbing trend, as it undermines the traditional merit-based aims of these professionals and sacrifices the quality of professional services to a false ideology (Mac Donald 2023).

It has been said that America is as much a concept as it is a place—and that its history informs its national self-image. Progressives attack America's history because their goal is to challenge America's positive self-image. Columbus's discovery of America is reimagined by progressives as the beginning of the "oppression" of its indigenous peoples.[1] The Founding Fathers are denounced as "slaveholders." Abraham Lincoln's act of emancipating slaves is dismissed as an act of "white privilege." During the George Floyd riots in the summer of 2020, statues and monuments devoted to America's founders and

---

[1] The level of "virtue signaling" on this topic was recently highlighted by one of the co-owners of the ice-cream firm Ben & Jerry's. He was arrested protesting on July 4, America's Independence Day, insisting that the government return the land it had taken from the indigenous peoples. Shortly after his arrest, a local Vermont Native American chief suggested that the company might begin by returning its land to his tribe. To date, there has been no response or effort to do as suggested.

heroes were defaced, and torn down, with virtually no resistance from law enforcement officials ordered by progressive urban mayors not to intervene.[2] Government buildings were routinely attacked during "mostly peaceful" riots, as the progressive media termed them. The removal of the symbols of a society is a standard tactic Marxist-Leninists employ in their goal of erasing the history of a society.

Despite this, socialism is currently viewed positively by a substantial percentage of America's youth. As a 2019 Gallup poll showed: "Since 2010, young adults' positive ratings of socialism have hovered near 50%, while the rate has been consistently near 34% for Gen Xers and near 30% for baby boomers/traditionalists. At the same time, since 2010, young adults' overall opinion of capitalism has deteriorated to the point that capitalism and socialism are tied in popularity among this age group. This pattern was first observed in 2018 and remains the case today."

Progressives—who are currently essentially isomorphic with Democratic Party voters—favor an entitlement state that assures a basic standard of living (65 percent of respondents), whereas Republican voters continue to favor free-market capitalism (78 percent) (Saad 2019).

The Total State

The twentieth century witnessed the rise of totalitarianism, in which single parties and civic religion terrorized and murdered millions of citizens. In a magisterial exploration of these events, philosopher

---

[2] The progressive reporting around the death of George Floyd portrayed him as a martyr who was unjustly murdered by a white supremacist Minneapolis policeman. But like so many stories created by progressive journalists, it is not true. Floyd was a convicted felon and a drug addict who was resisting arrest on the day of his death. His autopsy showed that he had ingested a lethal amount of fentanyl and that there was no evidence he had been asphyxiated by pressure to his neck. The autopsy findings were not admitted into evidence at the trial of the policeman accused of murdering him, and the jury reported feeling intimidated by violent protesters prior to rendering a guilty verdict in the policeman's case.

Hannah Arendt argued that totalitarian states succeed primarily by exacerbating internecine racial and religious antagonisms. Hitler waged war against Jews, Poles, Slavs, and gypsies and threatened the German clergy. Stalin promoted tensions between Russians and Ukrainians while purging all expressions of religion in the USSR. Mao's Cultural Revolution in Communist China pitted ethnic groups against each other and expunged traditional religious expression. As Arendt wrote in *The Origins of Totalitarianism*:

> Few ideologies have won enough prominence to survive the hard competitive struggle of persuasion, and only two have come out on top and essentially defeated all others: the ideology which interprets history as an economic struggle of classes, and the other that interprets history as a *natural fight of races*. The appeal of both to large masses was so strong that they were able to enlist state support and establish themselves as official national doctrines. But far beyond the boundaries within which race-thinking and class-thinking have developed into obligatory patterns of thought, free public opinion has adopted them to such an extent that not only intellectuals, but great masses of people will no longer accept a presentation of past or present facts that is not in agreement with either of these views (Arendt 1976, 159; italics in the original).

It matters little whether the differences that are exacerbated have any basis in reality; what matters is that they be perceived as real by aggrieved elements within a society. In this vein, historically disenfranchised groups in America—blacks, women, LGBTQ+, the mentally and physically disabled—have all been manipulated by progressive politicians to foster discontent and division, while pressure has been placed on organized religion to shed traditional values and replace them with the values of 'woke" social justice.

Despite the empirical fact that the Judeo-Christian traditions contributed substantially to achieving equality and real social justice, "disenfranchised" groups are being taught that religion is an "oppressive" force that must be opposed. Students are indoctrinated to believe that the nuclear family, biological sex, limits on abortion, and so forth are antagonistic to DEI and freedom, and must be vigorously opposed.

In the past, the LGBTQ+ were marginalized by society for what was judged to be immoral behavior, but these groups now insist on imposing their values on society through a strategy of intimidation. Many are misotheists who scoff at religion and a traditional sense of decency (Gray 2018). They are enthusiastic foot soldiers in the Godless Crusade. With the support of progressive federal and state governments, as well as activist corporate CEOs, aberrant sexuality is currently on public display with the aims of undermining morality and disrupting society. Unfortunately, the morality of Americans has been so corrupted by progressive propaganda and pornography that exhibitionist behaviors now fail to register as offensive and are often viewed with amusement.

The corruption of morality is standard Marxist fare. The Bolsheviks in 1917 outlawed religious marriage and targeted the nuclear family as a means of uprooting "bourgeois" society and replacing theistic religion with an atheistic "civic religion." Mao's Cultural Revolution promoted intense hatred between groups in society, disrupted familial bonds, and purged China of its traditional beliefs. While totalitarian states have emerged historically from both the left and right of the political spectrum, they share in common hatred of religion and morality and a proclivity to promote ethnic and racial strife.

Those who doubt that there are organized Marxist forces behind what is transpiring in America today, and choose to label such claims as "right-wing conspiracy theories," might consider the following, selected from a list of forty-five communist goals published in the *Congressional Record* in 1963:

1. Emphasize the need to raise children away from the negative influences of parents.
2. Discredit the family as an institution.

3. Encourage promiscuity and easy divorce.
4. Present homosexuality, degeneracy, and promiscuity as "normal, natural, and healthy."
5. Infiltrate the churches and replace revealed religion with "social" religion.
6. Capture one or both of the political parties in the United States.
7. Get control of the schools and teachers' associations. Soften the curriculum.
8. Infiltrate the press.
9. Eliminate prayer on the grounds that it violates the separation of "church and state."
10. Belittle American culture and discourage the teaching of American history.
11. Grant recognition of Red China and its admission to the U.N. (Bruner 2023, 252).

These should sound familiar to anyone living in America today. Totalitarianism emerges from positivist philosophies that deny any role for divine or natural law. It rejects the virtues of truth, beauty, and goodness and insists that will and power should be the only guiding principles of the state. Writing about the history of the natural law in the postwar twentieth century, Rommen argued:

> We have recorded the victory of positivism. But this must not be taken to mean that positivism won a definitive and total victory on all intellectual, moral, and political fronts.... It is true that most university professors, and most practical jurists, to say nothing of the popularizers of shifting scientific fashions, spoke of natural law as a dead letter. Yet the idea of natural law once more found refuge in the *philosophia perennis*...whenever it was exiled from the secular universities and law schools. And the idea, divested of academic dress, went on living in common sense in the minds of ordinary men (Rommen 1998, 222).

112

The Madness of Crowds

Scholars have wondered how civilized nations, such as Germany in the 1930s, could fall prey to totalitarianism considering its hateful policies and destructive effects (Shirer 1960). The answer may be found in the psychology of the crowd. In the nineteenth century, psychologist Gustave Le Bon noted that when an aggrieved group perceives its cause as morally superior, it can act mercilessly against those whose views differ from their own (Le Bon 1899). Indeed, the psychology of revenge has been the driving factor of all totalitarian movements since the Jacobin Revolution in France, including the Russian, Chinese, and other Marxist revolutions.

While Nazism is often labeled a fascist movement of the Right, socialism was a core tenet of the movement, as evidenced by its unabbreviated name, *National Socialism*. The postwar consensus that Nazism resulted from unconstrained nationalism and authoritarianism misconstrues the truth, as the forces of envy are not limited to the right side of the political spectrum. The reflex identification of conservatism with "fascism" is a strategy of the Left that has largely succeeded since the mid-twentieth century, by purposefully blinding people to the imminent threat of totalitarianism posed by the Marxist-inspired Left.

Getting large numbers of people to accept false beliefs such as "systemic racism" requires cognitive conformity, and "woke" propaganda works most effectively on those who are excessively concerned with being judged negatively by others. How conformity of thought contributes to what is transpiring in the culture today has recently been addressed by educators Bethany Mandel and Karol Markowicz.

> Conformity is easier to achieve than it may seem. We all hope that we'd stand up for what is right, but generally people want to be accepted by their peers and will cover up their opinions to ensure they are. In the 1950s, a psychologist named Solomon Asch conducted the Asch conformity experiments. Each had

one real participant and several actors, who were all asked to match a line to another line of similar length. The actors would knowingly give the same wrong answer. About 5 percent of the participants always went with the group answer and around a quarter of the participants always gave the correct answer, unswayed by the answers of the actors. But the rest would sometimes go along and other times not (Mandel and Markowicz 2023, 27).

Herd mentality causes groups of people to behave in concert like a single organism. Due to social media, it is currently possible to create a herd mentality virtually, by reaching large numbers of people instantly with the same message and shaping their responses by registering "likes" and "dislikes." Those who do not conform to prevalent emotionally charged messages risk being shunned or "cancelled." The current surge in anti-Semitic sentiment is one result of this phenomenon. It is doubtful that most protesting the conflict comprehend its complexity. Controlling the beliefs of the culture is arguably the most effective strategy that progressives have for achieving their goal of transforming America.

Big Lies

The use of propaganda to control the thoughts of others has a long history in politics. In the *Gorgias*, Plato denigrates sophist rhetoric for its efforts at influencing others rather than being a reasoned approach to argument (Plato 2003). But propaganda became a formal topic of study in political science in the twentieth century. The term "propaganda" did not always carry the negative connotations that it does today, but its widespread use in totalitarian societies has made it virtually synonymous with false statements that are purposefully designed to mislead the public.

As the philosopher Jason Stanley (2015) notes in *How Propaganda Works*, propaganda is less problematic in totalitarian nations than in democracies because in the latter it is virtually always disguised as representing democratic values in order to make it more palatable for public consumption. It is virtually always rooted in a flawed ideology, with the purpose of benefiting society's elites. As Stanley suggests:

> Elites in civil society invariably acquire a flawed ideology to provide an apparently factual (in the best case apparently scientific) justification for the otherwise manifestly unjust distribution of society's goods.... As a mechanism of social control, the elite seek to instill the ideology in the negatively privileged groups. By this route the negatively privileged groups acquire the beliefs that justify the very structural features of the society that cause their oppression (Stanley 2015, 32).

As we shall see, corporate America's willingness to embrace "woke" ideas reflects a desire to obscure its role in causing much of the discontent of non-elite Americans.

CHAPTER 7

Discussing Religion and Politics

Politics and morality are inseparable. And as morality's foundation is religion, religion and politics are necessarily related. We need religion as a guide; we need it because we are imperfect. And our government needs the church because only those humble enough to admit they're sinners can bring to democracy the tolerance it requires in order to survive.

—RONALD REAGAN (THOMAS 1984)

I never considered a difference of opinion in politics, in religion, in philosophy, as cause for withdrawing from a friend.

—THOMAS JEFFERSON

HISTORIAN EDWARD GIBBON EXAMINED the factors that contributed to the decline of the Roman Empire (Gibbon 1993–1994). Although Gibbon's conclusions have been challenged, he remains a credible source on why civilizations fail (Heather and Rapley 2023). As empires rise and fall, there is no reason to believe that America will escape this fate. There are currently a variety of signs that augur

America's decline, including economic instability due to debt, large-scale immigration, and rampant corruption. Internal strife incited by aggrieved factions, loss of public trust in institutions, and a decline in religious sensibilities and morality are also contributing to America's instability.

Political transformations are often linked to religious ones. As an example, converting the Roman Empire from paganism to monotheism was undoubtedly a challenge, as the wholesale religious conversion of an empire cannot be the result of deep-seated convictions. Prior to the imperial-inspired conversion, those baptized into Christianity were motivated by sincere faith in its dogma. But the conversion of an emperor provided more pragmatic reasons to convert.

Large-scale religious transformations are generally accompanied by hostilities directed at old beliefs. In the fourth century, an ascendant Christianity directed its antagonism toward pagans, accusing them of immorality and labeling their sites of worship and rituals "evil." In *Confessions*, Augustine, who had converted from both paganism and Manicheism, attested to the immoral behaviors of pagans in his time (Augustine 1961). Although his criticisms are polemical, contemporaneous pagan writings confirm that adultery, homosexuality, and pedophilia were in fact widely practiced in the fourth century (Fox 2006).

Historian of religion Katherine Nixey describes how state-sponsored Christianity was characterized by the persecution of pagans by Christian zealots. Pagan priests and philosophers were exiled and killed, pagan temples desecrated and destroyed. Libraries that held the accumulated knowledge of the civilized world were burned, and their texts irretrievably lost to history. As Nixey suggests: "Today, the story of how Christianity came to conquer Rome is told in reassuringly secular terms, but this was a war. The struggle to convert the empire was nothing less than a battle between good and evil, between the forces of darkness and those of light. It was a battle between God and Satan himself" (Nixey 2017, 7–9). Indeed, the pagan horned satyr god Pan would be adopted by Christians as their image of the devil.

Nixey argues that in recent years secular historians have been inclined to downplay religious and metaphysical conflicts as the cause of societal strife, preferring instead to focus on contributing social and economic factors. In a similar vein, many Americans today are more inclined to frame the cultural revolution in nonreligious terms, reflecting resistance to accept the links between politics and religion.

The Terror

Like the fourth-century hostilities directed at pagan religion, attacks on the Church were a feature of the secular Jacobin Revolution of 1789 in France. The French experiment expressed an unconstrained moral vision based on the ideals of "liberty, equality, fraternity" and on the utopian fantasy of man's perfectibility. Unlike the American experiment of 1776, the French revolt was a misotheistic enterprise, directed as much against the Church, which had long been allied with the French monarchy, as it was against the aristocracy. The Revolution began with attacks on churches and clergy, and the revolutionary authorities removed the Catholic monarchy, nationalized church property, exiled thirty thousand priests, and killed hundreds more.

Launched in unfettered idealism, the Revolution devolved into a Reign of Terror. As historian Kim Holmes suggests: "The Jacobins who followed Robespierre in establishing the Reign of Terror shared...a philosophy of 'natural republicanism'; they believed that individuals who transgressed the laws of nature must be executed without judicial formalities. Anyone who stood against the republic stood against the people who were by right of their natural *goodness* above reproach. An enemy of the people became an enemy of the human race and thus guilty of treason" (Holmes 2016, 217–18; emphasis in the original). The Jacobin revolution would become a model for all leftist revolutions, including the current progressive cultural revolution in America.

Secular progressives blame religion for societal violence, while ignoring their own violence against religionists.

> The Family Research Council (FRC), a Christian public policy advocacy group, released a report last week numbering the hostile attacks against churches in the U.S. during the last four years at 420. The acts of hostility to churches included arson, bomb threats, gun-related incidents, assaults, and interruptions to worship. Some hostility fell into multiple categories....
> According to the report, violence against churches has been increasing. Fifty incidences of hostility against churches took place in 2018, but between January and September 2022, there were 137. Reports kept by the federal government reflect a similar trend. The Federal Bureau of Investigation (FBI) keeps track of hate crimes committed in the United States. In 2021, it reported 240 hate crimes motivated by anti-Christian bias. In 2018, that number was 172 (Turco 2023).

Most of these acts of violence were committed by militant progressives, although one would not guess that from the propagandist media.

Blacks, women, and members of the LGBTQ+ community are fearful that their newfound freedoms will be reversed by those clinging to traditional Judeo-Christian beliefs, and they view religious opposition to their ideas as an existential threat. Their exaggerated fears were heightened by the 2022 *Dobbs v. Jackson* ruling by the Supreme Court, which overturned the 1974 *Roe v. Wade* decision guaranteeing abortion "rights." Although widely unpopular among women, the *Dobbs* ruling was based on a point of law, not the repressive insistence of the "white patriarchy."

Claiming women's desire for abortion as a "right" is characteristic of progressive ideology, but it appears nowhere as such in the US Constitution, and not everything that a group might wish for constitutes a legal entitlement (Kirk 1953). Nor is the *Dobbs* ruling an abortion "ban," as progressives would have the public believe, falsely labeling it an attack by conservative Christians on a woman's "right to choose." In states governed by progressives, abortion laws will remain unchanged by the ruling, while the public in conservative states will be allowed to choose what restrictions they want to put on abortion via ballot initiatives and action by their legislatures.

Progressives consistently refuse to accept the increasing biological evidence that a fetus represents an identifiable human life, or to address whether the fetus might have the right to life. The positions progressives have adopted on abortion mimic those of ancient paganism. An article in *The Hill* addressed this issue.

> Abortion is an archaic practice. In Pagan Rome, abortion was commonplace, performed by a variety of surgical and medicinal methods and taken for granted by philosophers…. The ancient Pagans largely accepted infanticide as well, and the exposure of infants was common. The Greek father had an absolute right to expose his children. Exposure of infants, especially girls, was common and often linked to economic concerns about raising too many children. But even in large families "more than one daughter was practically never reared." Termination of female infants was so common as to contribute to a dramatically skewed sex ratio, estimated at "131 males per 100 females in the city of Rome, and 140 males per 100 females in Italy, Asia Minor, and North Africa" (Zorzi 2022).

Render unto Caesar

At different times in history, each of the monotheistic religions functioned as a theocracy in which political and religious aims were united, while at other times they were forced to coexist under antagonistic circumstances. *Ethics of the Fathers* (*Pirkei Avot*), a compendium of Jewish wisdom compiled in the first centuries CE, addresses how one should regard the ruling government. Avot 3:2 recounts how the deputy high priest Rabbi Chanina affirmed the government's role in maintaining social order: "Pray for the welfare of the government, for were it not for the fear of it, men would swallow one another alive. But Avot 2:3 warns: "Be careful in your relations with government officials; for they draw no man close to themselves except for their own interests. They appear as friends when it is to their advantage, but they do not stand by a man in his time of stress."

The question of how to coexist with Rome was posed to Jesus in Matthew 22:15–21: "The Pharisees went out and laid plans to trap [Jesus] in his words.... 'Tell us then, what is your opinion? Is it right to pay the imperial tax to Caesar or not?' But Jesus, knowing their evil intent, said...'Show me the coin used for paying the tax.' They brought him a denarius, and he asked them, 'Whose image is this? And whose inscription?' 'Caesar's,' they replied. Then he said to them, 'So give back to Caesar what is Caesar's, and to God what is God's.'" Jesus knew there were Jews who believed that paying taxes to the Roman government denied God's authority. Nevertheless, his response was that since religion and politics represent different magisteria, they should remain separate, and this became the template for how Church and state were to coexist. Then the Roman Empire converted to Christianity in the fourth century, and this conflict diminished—until Europe's emerging nations began to defy the authority of the Roman Church.

The Reformation produced a rupture in the Roman Catholic Church and gave rise to a variety of Protestant denominations, which were concentrated in Northern Europe, while Catholic dominance persisted in the South. The Reformation instigated armed violence between Catholics and Protestants that decimated much of Europe's population. In 1648, the Treaty of Westphalia ended the conflict, ruling that in the future, national sovereigns would determine the religion practiced in their domain. Scholars view the Reformation as a decisive step on the path toward secular modernity and credit it with the emergence of the nation-state, capitalism, and the Enlightenment (Eire 2016).

Whether the rise of the intolerant "woke" religion augurs the demise of the Judeo-Christian traditions—much as Christianity replaced paganism in the fourth century—remains to be seen. Those who continue to hold traditional religious beliefs must consider the possibility that in the future they will be harshly persecuted by "woke" zealots, with the support of a misotheistic progressive government. The current rise in violent hate crimes directed against Christians and the surge in overt anti-Semitism may represent the beginnings of progressive efforts to purge America of theistic religion. It is a situation that few would have imagined possible just a short time ago but one that must be recognized and confronted.

A New Religion

The psychology of "woke" activists is akin to that of fundamentalist religionists who are convinced that their beliefs are inerrant. As nineteenth-century psychologist Gustave Le Bon noted of socialism:

> Thanks to its promises of regeneration, thanks to the hope it flashes before all the disinherited of life, socialism is becoming a belief of a religious character rather than a doctrine. Now the great power of beliefs, when they tend to assume this religious form, of whose mechanism…lies in the fact that their propagation is independent of the proportion of truth or error that they may contain, for as soon as a belief has gained a lodging in the minds of men its absurdity no longer appears; reason cannot reach it and only time can impair it (Le Bon 1899, x).

As linguist John McWhorter suggests, it is not possible to engage in reasoned discourse with "woke" ideologues because they are inured to the influence of others. McWhorter, who is a successful black American, has suggested:

Language is always imprecise, and thus we have traditionally restricted the word religion to certain ideologies founded in creation myths, guided by ancient texts, and requiring that one subscribe to certain beliefs beyond the reach of empirical experience.... If we rolled the tape again, the word religion could easily apply as well to more recently emerged ways of thinking within which there is no explicit requirement to subscribe to unempirical beliefs, even if the school of thought does reveal itself to entail such beliefs upon analysis. One of them is this extremist version of antiracism today (McWhorter 2021, xx).

Chinese Americans who lived through the Cultural Revolution in the 1970s recognize "woke" ideology as virtually identical to what they experienced in Mao's China (Zhao 2022). This includes the "cancelling" of opponents by subjecting them to public humiliation and punishment for being members of the "oppressor" class, which often meant being only marginally economically better off than one's neighbor. The "politically correct" purging of speech was routinely employed in Communist China in its effort to undermine the expression of ideas that opposed the aims of the state.

As we have seen, "woke" progressive religion is based on neo-Marxist ideology and the Critical Theory version of social justice, whose tenets include diversity, equity, and inclusion. But while it is a truism in progressive society that diversity is a positive value, there is little empirical evidence to support this conclusion (Mac Donald 2018). Le Bon warned that immigration by groups that do not share the moral values or work ethic of Americans would eventually succeed in disrupting society. A similar argument was made in the late twentieth century by Harvard historian Samuel Huntington (1998), who argued in *Clash of Civilizations* that migration from Latin America would undermine America's future if Hispanic immigrants were not encouraged to adopt the dominant values of society. When Donald Trump made this argument in his 2016 campaign for president, he was labeled a "racist" by his progressive opponents.

When the late Secretary of State Henry Kissinger was asked about open-border immigration policies, he said, "It was a grave mistake to let in so many people of totally different cultural and religious concepts because it creates a pressure group inside each country that does that."

Progressives argue that assimilation is "racist" because it requires immigrants of color to accept the values of the white majority. From the perspective of multiculturalism and cultural relativism, assimilation is both unnecessary and inappropriate because no culture can be judged superior to another. But this is an ill-conceived cliche. And while cultural differences between immigrant groups can be maintained, and they often are in America, shared cultural values are absolutely necessary for a society to succeed. Unfortunately, many Americans fail to appreciate that the claim "diversity is good" is not axiomatic; rather, it has been accepted as the result of an effective propaganda campaign by progressives.

America's Founders recognized that governing a diverse society would be challenging if factional interests were not reconciled. For the first fifty years of the new republic, immigration was negligible, but in the nineteenth and early twentieth centuries, waves of immigrants arrived from Ireland, Western Europe, Southern and Eastern Europe, and Asia to meet the country's occupational needs in the Industrial Revolution. Prior to the 1960s, most immigrants were of European background, were acquainted with the Judeo-Christian ethic, and expressed a desire to be Americans. But today, many immigrants have different cultural and religious values from most Americans, and are being encouraged by progressives to resist assimilating into the dominant culture. This trend can be expected to lead to the fragmentation of society, which from the progressive perspective is welcome, because it will speed its transformation.

By favoring identity politics, progressives are insisting that people be evaluated based on immutable group characteristics rather than as individuals, much as socialism views the rights of the individual as subordinate to those of the collective. Identity politics has been used to justify affirmative actions for blacks—which discriminates against whites and Asian minorities in school admissions and job hiring[1] while ignoring individual merit. When merit is discounted in the workplace, corporate success suffers. When it is disregarded in the selection of physicians, lawyers, pilots, and other professionals, lives may be put at risk by incompetence[2] (MacDonald 2023).

The current insistence on "equity" is creating a topsy-turvy society. From the perspective of "woke" ideology, the only explanation for disparate outcomes in society is "racism," a patently absurd conclusion. Yet a large percentage of Americans accept this wrong-mindedness as true. Nonsensical arguments are offered on a number of fronts including that mathematics, the most abstract of topics, is "racist" because minorities do not score as well as whites in tests of math skills. According to an article in *Scientific American* entitled "Modern Mathematics Confronts Its White, Patriarchal Past," fewer than 1 percent of US doctorates in math are awarded to African-Americans, and fewer than 30 percent are awarded to women. Instead of considering the many other more likely reasons that might be the case, including innate differences in capacities to do math, the progressive author of the article concluded that these inequities are the result of "systemic racism" (Crowell 2021). When Harvard President Lawrence Summers suggested that women might not be as innately gifted as men for study in the physical sciences—an opinion with substantial evidence to support it—he was forced by enraged progressives to resign his position. The result of embracing this

---

[1] In a recent decision, *Students for Fair Admissions v. Harvard*, the US Supreme Court struck down affirmative action by universities, ruling that it is unconstitutional and reflects a form of racism. Progressive universities and the Biden Administration criticized the decision and vowed to oppose it.

[2] In this regard, the current Biden Administration's appointments, which have virtually all been made based on DEI factors rather than merit, have proven to be the most incompetent set of bureaucrats that the nation has ever witnessed.

simplistic thinking as truth will be a dumber America, one in which individuals are less likely to succeed and easier to manipulate.

In a recent move by the "woke" Biden administration, mortgage applicants with excellent credit scores were informed that they would be forced to pay higher mortgage rates to the benefit of those with poor credit, in order to achieve "equity." Penalizing those whose behavior would have been rewarded in the past disincentivizes achievement and favors those ill-prepared to assume financial risk, placing the economy at peril, as in the 2008 mortgage crisis. But when the desired goal is the deconstruction of society, such policies are seen as advantageous.

White Guilt

"Woke" ideology succeeds largely by intimidating whites who irrationally feel guilty about their "white privilege" and want to avoid being labeled "racist" (Steele 2007). Americans have grown excessively concerned with the opinions of others, likely because their opinions are currently more accessible to evaluation than in the past as the result of social media. A story is told about the first-century-CE sage Yochanan ben Zakkai, who on his deathbed was asked by his students for a blessing. He responded, "May it be God's will that your fear of heaven be like your fear of men." Dissatisfied, the students asked, "Is that all?" to which he replied, "If only it were so! Know that when a person transgresses, he says, 'May no man see me.'"

The current cultural revolution is supported by educated white progressives who confess to feeling guilty about America's "systemic racism"—for whose existence there is little evidence. They can be compared to individuals that one occasionally reads about who choose to confess to crimes they did not commit. Psychologists recognize that neurotic guilt is attributable to a harsh self-critical superego and is characteristic of obsessional personalities who regularly report irrational guilt and a fear of harming others.

The truth is that no one living today was engaged in America's slave trade, and few are old enough to have participated in the racism of Jim Crow. The notion of transgenerational guilt was dismissed in the sixth century BCE by the Hebrew prophets. As Ezekiel 18:20 insists, "The child will not share the guilt of the parent, nor will the parent share the guilt of the child." But "woke" activists ignore this moral principle. They argue that *all* white people, living and dead, are responsible for the ills of slavery, ignoring both the injustice and overt racism of this accusation and the fact that blacks and other people of color were—and in places in today's world still are—engaged in the slave trade.

Despite what progressive propaganda claims, overt expressions of racism are rarely seen in America today. White progressives' obsession with race reflects their unwillingness to accept that blacks and other minorities are capable of caring for themselves without assistance. Indeed, this progressive condescension is the only "systemic racism" that is widespread in America today.

CHAPTER 8

Religion in America

*It cannot be emphasized too strongly or too often that this great
nation was founded, not by religionists, but by Christians; not on
religions, but on the gospel of Jesus Christ. For this very reason
peoples of other faiths have been afforded asylum, prosperity, and
freedom of worship here.*

—ATTRIBUTED TO PATRICK HENRY

*Our Constitution was made only for a moral and religious people.
It is wholly inadequate to the government of any other.*

—JOHN ADAMS

IN 1620, A SMALL GROUP OF CALVINIST religionists seeking freedom
from the conformist pressures of the Anglican Church left Plymouth,
England, and landed on Cape Cod. These pilgrims imagined themselves as akin to the ancient Israelites who had left Egypt seeking
freedom in a new land. In time, America would become a refuge for
persecuted religionists from all over Europe.

By the eighteenth century, the Enlightenment was being commu-
nicated to America from Europe. But Christians were disturbed by

its disenchanting and anti-religious ideas and yearned for a return to the spirituality of the early religious settlers. In response, in the 1730s a religious movement known as the Great Awakening swept through America's colonies. It would profoundly influence the Founders' views on the relationship of religion and government (Wood 1990).

The idea of "separation of church and state"—a phrase from a letter by Thomas Jefferson, not in the First Amendment—has been used to minimize the influence of any organized church on the affairs of government. But in contrast to what progressives disingenuously argue today, the First Amendment was not intended to exclude religious values from the workings of government or from the public square. Instead, like Enlightenment thinkers on the Continent, the Founders recognized that the Judeo-Christian ethic played a critical role in maintaining societal cohesion, and they understandably assumed that these values would endure over time. But in recent years they have been undermined by progressives as part of their effort at transforming America—their Godless Crusade—and their propaganda has shrewdly adapted the Founders' own words to support ideas that the latter would never have embraced.

A prime example of this is Thomas Jefferson's preamble to the Declaration of Independence: "We hold these truths to be self-evident, that all men are created equal, that they are endowed by their Creator with certain unalienable Rights, that among these are Life, Liberty, and the pursuit of Happiness." Jefferson's preamble was crafted to serve as the rhetorical inspiration for justifying the independence of the new nation from the yoke of monarchical tyranny (Meacham 2012). But the "truths" set out in the document are not "self-evident." All men are *not* "created equal"; nothing in human biology or experience supports that notion. Indeed, that claim was challenged at the time by John Adams, who wrote: "That all men are born to *equal rights* is clear. But to teach that all men are born with equal powers, to equal influence in society, to equal property, and advantages, through life, is a gross fraud, as glaring an imposition on the credulity of the people as ever was practiced" (Kirk 1953, 94; emphasis in the original).

Jefferson was sympathetic to the egalitarian spirit; he supported the Jacobin revolution in France in 1789. But he would not have conceived of an American government based on the notion of equity. Nor would the possibility that men could somehow become women have entered his mind, as the Founders were both reasonable and commonsensical, disinclined to irrational ideas, and too skeptical to believe that technological progress could eradicate human nature. Instead, their notion of equality was as Adams argued, equality before the law, not a system that enforces equality of outcomes.[1] Like their Puritan ancestors, the Founders clearly valued merit and hard work. As Benjamin Franklin suggested, "God helps those who help themselves"—a notion at odds with progressive government that seeks power by providing entitlements.

Another idea in the Declaration of Independence that has been co-opted by progressives is the notion that liberty is an inalienable right. As conservative critic Russell Kirk noted: "Radicalism at the end of the eighteenth century expressed its case in terms of 'natural rights.' Ever since Paine's *Rights of Man* was published, the notion of inalienable rights has been embraced by the mass of men in a vague and belligerent form, ordinarily confounding 'rights' with desires" (Kirk 1953, 47). If one man claims for himself the "right" not to labor, another must support him. As Kirk pointed out, "If rights are confused thus with desires, the mass of men must feel that some vast,

---

[1] Much has been written about Jefferson as a slave holder. In this regard, he was not different from many of the Southern delegates. However, Jefferson was aware that slavery was wrong and envisioned a time when it would not be part of the American landscape. "Woke" progressives see this as mere hypocrisy, failing to consider the overall situation of slavery in the eighteenth century. The "three-fifths compromise," pertaining to the counting of slaves for purposes of representation, which they also deplore, was, as we shall see, critical to achieving a sufficient consensus to ratify the US Constitution. The Founders were imperfect, like all people then, and today. But they were sufficiently pragmatic and optimistic to see what needed to be done and to hope for a better future for the new nation.

Religion in America

intangible conspiracy thwarts their attainment of what they are told is their inalienable birthright" (Kirk 1953, 48).

As philosopher John Stuart Mill suggested in *On Liberty*, the rights of the individual are neither "unalienable" nor unlimited; instead, they are to be restrained if they infringe on the liberty of others (Mill 1946). The Founders believed, like John Locke, that freedom was best guaranteed by protecting individual and property rights, without which anarchy would ensue (Locke, Berkeley, and Hume 1990). Despite this, progressives justify their propaganda attacks by adopting the Founders' words out of context. In typical fashion, they work at undermining America's founding documents while adopting their own language to do so.

The Problem with Democracy

A standard charge by progressives is that those who disagree with their ideas are opposed to democracy. They fail to acknowledge that the United States is not a democracy, it is a republic. In their deliberations about what the new American government should be, the Founders searched antiquity to identify successful modes of governance. They were aware of the problems that can result from the cycle of timocracy, oligarchy, democracy, and tyranny, and in the end they chose to make the new nation a republic. Like Plato, they were wary of direct democratic majority rule because of its history of degenerating into a "tyranny of the majority." They determined that representative government would be best suited for a federation of individual colonies with different-sized populations and diverse interests.

The Founders recognized that compromise would be necessary if the colonies were to form a common bond. They adopted Montesquieu's idea of a tripartite government composed of executive, legislative, and judicial branches and imposed a system of checks and balances on them. They conceived of the Electoral College as a strategy that would give all states, big and small, a proportionate say in the election of a president.

Progressives object to all of this. Their anger at the current electoral system follows several presidential cycles in which progressive Democrats won the popular vote but lost to Republicans in the electoral college. They call for increased "democracy" in pursuit of a tyranny of the majority that would be led by progressive bicoastal urban elites. Their insistence on increased democracy has curiously been accompanied by calls for increased censorship, manipulation of social media platforms to block the dissemination of opinions opposed to their own, and the failure of the Democratic Party to allow primary challenges to incumbent progressive administrations.

When Benjamin Franklin was asked by a member of the public after the Constitutional Convention of 1787 what type of government the new country would have, he responded, "A republic, if you can keep it." The challenge of keeping the republic is substantial. It requires an informed electorate, adequate civic education, awareness of how government is meant to function, and shared moral values. As John Adams recognized, it requires the country to adhere to the Judeo-Christian ethic, which has been the basis of the social contract in America and the guide for how men are meant to behave in a free society, and which has been steadily undermined by the Godless Crusade to rid the world of religion. Unfortunately, since the progressive takeover of America's educational system, civic education in America has become dismally inadequate, and the Judeo-Christian ethic is under siege and for many no longer relevant. A 2016 study by the Annenberg Public Policy Center indicates the scope of the problem:

> Civic knowledge and public engagement are at all-time lows. A 2016 survey by the Annenberg Public Policy Center found that only 26 percent of Americans can name all three branches of government, which was a significant decline from previous years.

Not surprisingly, public trust in government is at only 18 percent and voter participation has reached its lowest point since 1996. Without an understanding of the structure of government; rights and responsibilities; and methods of public engagement, civic literacy and voter apathy will continue to plague American democracy. Educators and schools have a unique opportunity and responsibility to ensure that young people become engaged and knowledgeable citizens (Annenberg 2016).

The appalling state of civic engagement is reminiscent of ancient Rome prior to its collapse. In the twenty-first century, the American version of "bread and circus" includes social media, Netflix series, taking selfies, recreational drug use, pornography, and other hedonistic absorptions. When Alexis de Tocqueville visited America in the early nineteenth century to discover how the new nation had succeeded in creating a democratic republic, he found average Americans to be conversant with the activities of their government and concluded, "The health of a democratic society may be measured by the quality of functions performed by private citizens."

Sadly, the current health of America's educational system does not equip them to perform those functions: "When isolating the 64 countries that administered the test in both 2015 and 2018, US students ranked 30th in math, up from 35th in 2015, and eighth in reading, up from 15th in 2015. In science, US students ranked 11th, up from 17th in 2015" (Camera 2019). These results must be evaluated in light of the fact that America ranks fifth in the world in the amount of money it spends on education.

And the state of civic education is particularly bad. Few Americans can identify their political leaders, know how their government works, or can name the critical events in American history let alone realize their importance. They have little to no conception of how the Constitution divides government powers, or what each branch of government was designed to do.

A recent example of this was Joe Biden's claim that he would forgive student debt, a cynical effort at securing the youth vote before the midterm elections. Many young people with student debt voted for Democratic candidates because of this promise. But as the Constitution gives the power to legislate exclusively to the Congress, and confers no such power onto the president, and a recent Supreme Court decision ruled that Biden's offer was unconstitutional. An educated electorate would have recognized this as a political ploy.[2]

While the internet has made access to information widely available, civic education has been undermined by progressive propaganda. Education has been additionally compromised by the public's reduced attention spans. According to Wikipedia, the average attention span of an American in 2023 is *8.2 seconds*, hardly sufficient to ponder any complex matter, political or otherwise. Instead, education has been reduced to images and sound bites because of social media that foster ideological conformity by encouraging naïve individuals to accept "popular" ideas without regard for facts. As a result, American politics is no longer a serious deliberative process; it has devolved into a competitive sport, with each party cheering on its own team with little desire to communicate, compromise, or do what is in the best interests of citizens.

America's Original Sin

From its inception, America's future was tainted by the institution of slavery. The Founders recognized that slavery was a moral thorn in the side of the new nation but that it was critical to the economic success of the agrarian South. As a result, a compromise was struck at the Constitutional Convention that counted slaves as three-fifths of an individual for the purpose of representation. Without this compromise, the new nation would have been stillborn.

---

[2] The Biden administration ignored this ruling and devised a loophole to get around it.

"Woke" ideologues, unyielding in their criticisms and undeterred by historical or practical realities, refuse to accept the Founders' decision as anything except "racist." Claiming the moral high ground from their twenty-first-century perch, they condemn anyone who was even remotely involved in the slave trade, without acknowledging how widespread slavery was in the eighteenth century, or how unique the Founders were in their desire to address the issue. Common sense and humility might caution one not to condemn an eighteenth-century plantation owner for being a "racist," a term that had little relevance at that time. But progressives refuse to concede anything on the issue of "racism," as it is the defining feature of their narrative.

Although it is not widely recognized, in the years leading to the Civil War a second religious revival had occurred in America. During the 1830s and 1840s, a second Great Awakening promoted religious fervor on a variety of topics, including abolition. This movement can be credited with setting the stage for America's reckoning on slavery.

Abraham Lincoln, considered by many scholars to have been America's greatest president, was not a regular churchgoer, but he was skilled at adopting biblical ideas in his political speeches. Historians have credited Lincoln's popularity to his ability to capture the religious imagination of Americans and arouse them to patriotic fervor. The motto "In God We Trust" first appeared during the Civil War, testimony to the pervasive religious consciousness of the nation at that time.

Progress?

Following the Civil War, the size of the federal government grew substantially. Progressivism began as a late nineteenth-century political philosophy that maintained that a nation is best governed by a specialized managerial elite who set policy for the benefit of the people. John Dewey, an early leader of the movement, argued that government was best suited to determine the direction of education.

The roots of progressivism can be identified in Plato's *Republic*, which describes a utopian society ruled by an educated elite (Plato 1998).

Early modern progressivism included two approaches, one secular and a second based on Christian values. Rooted in Enlightenment thought, secular progressivism maintained that politics should be divested of religious values. But an equally powerful version of progressivism focused on the religious ideals of social justice, and that religious progressivism guided many of America's social movements in the early twentieth century. Religious values were adapted in the service of reducing the exploitation of workers and favoring the needs of community over those of the individual.

In the early 1900s, President Theodore Roosevelt, who served as a Republican president from 1901 to 1909 but ran as the Progressive Party candidate in 1912, instituted a series of progressive policies, but they blossomed in the administrations of Woodrow Wilson. Wilson was a Princeton academic who had championed the importance of political science and technical expertise in managing government. He was also a Virginian and an avowed racist who excluded blacks from Washington's federal bureaucracy.

Franklin D. Roosevelt served as assistant secretary of the Navy under Wilson. During his own four administrations, progressive programs such as the New Deal and Social Security were instituted, and the federal government grew enormously. Under FDR, religious progressivism increasingly took a back seat to progressivism opposed to a continued role for religion in politics.

John F. Kennedy was an anti-Communist who confronted the Soviet Union over its attempts to place nuclear-armed missiles in Cuba. He was assassinated in 1963 by Lee Harvey Oswald, a Marxist who denounced the United States, had lived for a time in Russia, and supported the Communist government in Cuba. Despite this, progressives were able to convince Americans that Kennedy had been the victim of a conspiracy led by right-wing extremists in America's security services. Kennedy was portrayed as a martyr who died for America's sin of racism and reactionary conservatism. But as journalist James Piereson has argued, other than innuendo there is no evidence that either conservatives or the American government participated in Kennedy's assassination (Piereson 2013).

The controversy surrounding Kennedy's assassination inspired a profound distrust in government institutions that Americans have never recovered from. It also allowed progressives to gain a strong foothold in the culture; it was in the aftermath of the assassination that "the long march through the institutions" began in earnest, allowing young radicals to become social activists who would counter the "evil" policies of conservatives.

Kennedy's successor, Lyndon Johnson, had worked in Franklin Roosevelt's administration and was a power player in Washington politics who used the opportunities afforded by Kennedy's untimely death to push a series of progressive policies, including the Civil Rights and Voting Acts. The profoundly cynical Johnson recognized that entitlement programs would make American blacks and other minorities dependent on progressive government and predisposed to vote for Democrats in perpetuity.

Revolution and Counterrevolution

The introduction of oral contraception in the 1960s profoundly changed America's attitudes toward sexual mores. Restraints on sexual behavior traditionally taught by religion were dismissed as antiquated and opposed to the freedom of the individual. Pop culture, with an insistent emphasis on "sex, drugs, and rock n roll," increasingly replaced religion as a more exciting alternative in the minds of many young people. In 1965, John Lennon was criticized for remarking that America's youth were more enthusiastic about the Beatles than about Jesus, but he was right.

The Nixon administration sought a return to conservative principles and law and order following the unrest of the '60s. Progressives viewed Nixon as an obstacle to their goal of capturing the reins of power. He was hounded by the progressive news media and forced to resign by the Watergate scandal. Since Nixon, all Republican presidents have routinely been vilified by progressives and the media.

With the Obama and Biden administrations, progressives pulled out the stops in their quest to secure one-party rule. Obama, a one-time community activist with strong Marxist ties that were carefully hidden from the public, campaigned on the platform of transforming America, but few recognized that he had a Marxist-style takeover of government in mind. Obama was the first black American president, prima facie evidence that America had moved past its history of racism. But while posing as a racial harmonizer, he reintroduced the divisive topic of race into American politics, and since his presidency race relations in America have soured.

The 2016 election of Donald Trump evoked a near hysterical reaction from progressives. Trump, a flamboyant businessman and newcomer to politics, was falsely and cynically accused of colluding with Russia in the election and impeached twice with little justification by a rogue partisan Democratic House of Representatives. After leaving office, he was hounded by frivolous prosecutions brought by the Biden administration's Department of Justice that were clearly politically motivated and aimed at thwarting his run for reelection in 2024. Under the Biden administration, America moved toward a soft totalitarianism, with increased censorship and punitive actions taken against those professing conservative political and religious values.

Progressives have been justifiably described as puritanical, perfectionistic, and intolerant. As journalist Noah Rothman notes in *The Rise of the New Puritans*:

> They deny that it is natural to have prejudices, that the assessment of difference is adaptive and promotes survival, psychological realities that cannot be expunged and should not be denied. "Woke" exercises designed to expunge "implicit bias" have been widely introduced into institutions and these serve no other objective purpose than to silence speech and promote unhealthy levels

of repression. Punitive actions taken against those who oppose "Woke" ideology may include reprimand, loss of employment, de-platforming on social media, and in some cases, imprisonment, behaviors that are routinely seen in totalitarian States, not in democratic government (Rothman 2022, 11).

The stated goal of "woke" ideology is ostensibly to correct the injustices of racism. Yet prior to the presidency of Barack Obama, racially motivated crime and discrimination had achieved their lowest reported levels in American history. Police brutality against minorities was also at record lows, and racially motivated hate crimes were rare. Right-wing fringe racist groups like the Aryan Brotherhood and Ku Klux Klan (KKK) were universally condemned by Americans. Nevertheless, thanks to progressive propaganda, a substantial percentage of Americans have been convinced that racism, police brutality, and hate crimes are currently rampant. A 2019 Pew poll about "Race in America" highlights the different perceptions about this topic held by progressive Democrats and Republicans:

White Democrats (64%) are far more likely than white Republicans (15%) to say the country hasn't gone far enough when it comes to giving black people equal rights with whites. About half of Republicans say it's been about right, while a sizable minority (31%) says the country has gone too far in this regard. Eight-in-ten white Democrats—vs. 40% of white Republicans—say the legacy of slavery continues to have an impact on black people's position in American society today. And when it comes to views about racial discrimination, 78% of white Democrats say the bigger problem is people not seeing it where it really does exist, while a similar share of white Republicans say people seeing racial discrimination where it really does not exist is the bigger problem (Horowitz, Brown, and Cox 2019).

Few topics today elicit more support from progressives than climate change. Yet despite what they insist, neither the rate of climate change nor its causes have been firmly established, and there is no compelling reason to embrace massive societal changes based on uncertain predictions. Whereas most Americans agree that efforts should be made to consider alternative forms of energy besides fossil fuels, enthusiasm for making this change tracks with political affiliation. In particular, America's youth have been convinced by progressive propaganda that climate change is currently at crisis levels, and they also blame conservatives for not taking their future seriously. According to a 2023 Pew poll:

> Nine-in-ten Democrats and Democratic-leaning independents say the U.S. should prioritize developing alternative energy sources to address America's energy supply. Among Republicans and Republican leaners, 42% support developing alternative energy sources, while 58% say the country should prioritize expanding exploration and production of oil, coal, and natural gas. There are important differences by age within the GOP. Two-thirds of Republicans under age 30 (67%) prioritize the development of alternative energy sources. By contrast, 75% of Republicans ages 65 and older prioritize expanding the production of oil, coal, and natural gas (Tyson, Funk, and Kennedy 2023).

As we shall see, the differences of opinion on issues of race and climate change track with where individuals are positioned with respect to concerns about taking risks and doing harm. These concerns can be excessive, particularly when they reflect features of an underlying mental disturbance.

CHAPTER 9

"Woke" as a Mental Disorder

Progressivism is a mental disorder which uses meaningless slogans to cover its emptiness. This tweet means absolutely nothing. Cancel rent? Ok, who is gonna build apartments for people to live in? Cancel mortgage? Ok, I can live in my house for free? Should've bought a mansion.

—DAVID RUBIN (2020) ON X, formerly known as Twitter

THE NOTION THAT A CULTURAL MOVEMENT is a mental disorder may sound extreme. In this case, however, it merits serious consideration.

Defining mental illness is notoriously difficult, especially as the definition has historically depended on different cultural norms (McNally 2011). Philosopher Michael Martin examined how conceptions of mental illness have changed over time as a result of progressive culture's increasing unwillingness to include moral values in the assessment of psychopathology.

Today we tend to blur morality and mental health. Alcoholics are sick, yet they are punished when their disease manifests itself as drunk driving or child abuse. Adults using illegal drugs are criminals. But their punishment is likely to be therapy supervised by a judge. Character faults have become "personality disorders," including most of the seven deadly sins: pride and envy are narcissism; gluttony is an eating disorder; sloth is a dependent personality disorder; acting out in anger is an impulse control disorder; greed is acquisitive desire disorder and, although lust is celebrated in our era of therapy-supported sexual liberation, misdirected lust is a psychosexual disorder (Martin 2006, 3).

Supreme Court Justice Potter Stewart famously opined, on the question of pornography, "I know it when I see it," and the same principle can be applied to mental illness. However, as the "experts" in the field have been co-opted by progressive ideology, it is currently necessary to rely primarily on commonsense criteria (Kradin 2021; Thomas 2023). These include 1) thoughts that are consistently divorced from reality, 2) behaviors that predictably create chaos, and 3) hostile projections that threaten society. Moral relativists might object that whole populations sometimes exhibit these symptoms. In answer, I might point out that entire societies—Nazi Germany, for example—have arguably exhibited time-limited mental disorder.

Freud avoided applying religious moral standards to psycho-analysis, as he viewed them as in part responsible for the repressed sexuality of Victorian society. But to suggest that Freud's psycho-analysis was amoral would be incorrect (Rieff 1979). Rather, Freud's ideas remained tethered to the Judeo-Christian ethic, and his definitions of psychopathology consistently included moral judgements. For example, he viewed excessive self-regard (narcissism) and manipulation of others for personal gain (secondary gain) as evidence of mental disorder. In *Civilization and Its Discontents*, he argued for a morally determined sublimation of the instincts in the service of sustaining a productive cohesive society (Freud 1930). The progressive notion of "nonjudgmentalism" would have been dismissed as naïve and dangerous by Freud and most psychoanalysts in the past.

Charting Our Divisions

In today's politically divided society one encounters polarized differences of opinion on the question of what values are most compatible with mental health. In *The Righteous Mind*, psychologist Jonathan Haidt (2012) examined differences between the moral stances of "liberals" and "conservatives," based on six dichotomous axes. He described the *Care/Harm* axis as how individuals assessed caring for others versus potentially harming them. Progressives claim to be highly attuned to caring for others and sensitive to what they perceive as harmful injustices, including the possibility of "injuring" someone physically or verbally; and they often refuse to distinguish between the effects of physical and verbal injuries. They forcefully condemn "strong" behaviors such as "racism," "hateful" speech, and aggressive "masculine" behaviors. Yet the same group will consistently ignore the obvious harm that results from the human and drug trafficking that has resulted from progressive open border policies.

By contrast, conservatives insist that it is wrong to coddle criminals and that empathy cannot be allowed to undermine law. As Rusty Reno (2016) argues, the "nonjudgmentalism" of progressive elites, meant to avoid harming the feelings of others, has allowed them to turn a blind eye to the harm being caused by the erosion of fixed moral standards in working-class neighborhoods, where divorce, drug use, and unemployment have been on the rise for decades.

Progressives approach the Fairness/Cheating axis by equating fairness with equity (Rawls 1971), whereas conservatives insist that it is cheating for the government to take money from working citizens and redistribute it to welfare recipients and noncitizen aliens.

On the Authority/Subversion axis progressives equate authority with hierarchy, inequality, and the oppressive exercise of power, whereas conservatives favor traditional moral values and the need to support society's institution.

Along the Loyalty/Betrayal axis, progressives deny American exceptionalism and claim that it is a false construct, while conservatives tend to be patriotic and view progressive positions as a betrayal of American values.

Progressives deny that anything is sacred—in fact they campaign ceaselessly to rid the world of religion—whereas conservatives rely on the Sanctity/Degradation axis, for example, to argue against abortion.

Finally, progressives rely on the Liberty/Oppression axis to critique "oppressor groups" and are willing to abandon personal freedoms for guarantees of government protection, whereas conservatives object to government interference with individual rights.

What is factually true is that America has witnessed an increase in chaos under progressive governance as a result of the positions they have chosen to take along these axes. Urban areas governed by progressive Democrats are in disarray, with violent crime on the rise and law enforcement ineffective. As a result, the majority of Americans believe that the country is moving in the wrong direction. According to a 2023 NBC News poll: "Representative of the deep dissatisfaction among Americans, 74% say the U.S. is headed in the wrong direction, 58% believe the country's best days are in the rearview mirror and 61% say they are so steamed they would be willing to march around for a day with a protest sign" (NBC News 2023).

Given what is transpiring, it is evident that progressive society has become maladaptive and chaotic and those who are promoting these ideas meet the criteria for mental illness listed above. But *why* are so many Americans willing to embrace progressive politics? What draws them to an ideology that is so obviously maladaptive? Examining some of the prevailing psychological trends in society may shed light on these questions.

Narcissus Among Us

In the 1970s, social critic Christopher Lasch noted the increased self-absorption of Americans and suggested that it was indicative of a "culture of narcissism." He wrote:

> After the political turmoil of the sixties, Americans have retreated to purely personal preoccupations. Having no hope of improving their lives in any of the ways that matter, people have convinced themselves that what matters is psychic self-improvement: getting in touch with their feelings, eating healthy food, taking lessons in ballet or belly dancing, immersing themselves in the wisdom of the East, jogging, learning how to "relate," overcoming the "fear of pleasure." Harmless by themselves, these pursuits, elevated to the program and wrapped in the rhetoric of authenticity and awareness, signify a retreat from politics and a repudiation of the recent past (Lasch, 1979, 5).

Unlike the Judeo-Christian ethic, which focuses on moral improvement, the culture of narcissism is preoccupied with "self-actualization," materialism, hedonism, and pop psychology. But labeling a society "narcissistic" does not convey its grave implications. Unfortunately, when psychological jargon diffuses into conventional discourse, serious mental disorders tend to be trivialized and are often glibly accepted as commonplace. For example, "neurosis"—a term often used in jest in societal discourse—was once likened by Jung to a cancer capable of destroying the quality of a person's life. As will be seen, narcissism is a serious disorder and by no means "benign."

Freud described the narcissist as incapable of forming genuine relationships, and narcissism as a psychopathology highly resistant to treatment (Freud 1914). Nevertheless, some narcissists can be charming and "high functioning" in sectors of their lives. They are frequently found in government, other high-power professions, the arts, and popular culture—that is, any occupation that tends to attract the attention and admiration of others.

Narcissists exhibit a complex of traits, including excessive self-reference, grandiosity, superficiality, entitlement, and a lack of empathy. They manipulate others for their own purposes and often exhibit sociopathic behaviors. As narcissists have difficulty evaluating their self-worth, they tend to oscillate between inflated and deflated states of self-esteem. Narcissistic character is structured as an ego defense against feeling envy and shame, and penetrating these defenses is likely to produce rageful reactions. Although the pathogenesis of narcissistic character is uncertain, inconsistent limit-setting and inappropriate attention by caretakers likely contribute to it.

The monotheistic religious traditions describe what Freud termed narcissism as pride, haughtiness, and arrogance and judge these traits as serious flaws. Moses is described as the "humblest of men" and Christ as "meek and lowly in heart." Religious teachings advise man to rid himself of an inflated sense of self-importance. These traditions suggest that only after curbing an inflated ego can one expect to enter into a heartfelt relationship with God and others. It is not surprising that the current rise in narcissism has been accompanied by a decrease in religious observance in society, as it is impossible to be genuinely religious and self-absorbed.

Child-Rearing for Dysfunction

As child development has been repeatedly shown to contribute to adult psychopathology, it is reasonable to question whether progressive child-rearing practices may be contributing to the widespread narcissism observed today. Jewish and Christian traditions provide guidelines for child-rearing based on generations of experience. They counsel that children require love and limit-setting. But progressive pedagogy has ignored this sound advice.

In the eighteenth century, Jacques Rousseau suggested that man is born in a state of innocence and subsequently corrupted by the institutions of society. He promoted the unsubstantiated fantasy of the "noble savage" based on his imaginings that primitive man was loving and peaceful. But anthropological studies have consistently failed to support this claim. Indeed, when such claims were made by progressive anthropologist Margaret Mead in *Coming of Age in Samoa*, subsequent critics exposed her findings as false.[1] Rousseau's idea gave rise to the mistaken belief that personality is determined by one's environment and that there is no such thing as an innately flawed human nature. It is perhaps noteworthy that Rousseau fathered several children and abandoned all of them to orphanages, raising doubts about his qualifications as a pedagogue (Johnson 1988).

Dr. Benjamin Spock was an American pediatrician generally accepted as the most influential progressive voice on how to raise a child.[2] *The Common Sense Book of Baby and Childcare*, first published in 1946, was one of the best-selling books of the twentieth century, selling 500,000 copies in the first six months after its publication and 50 million by the time of Spock's death in 1998. It served as the "Bible" for how to raise a child for parents of the Baby Boomer Generation. But what most parents did not know was that Spock was a progressive ideologue who emerged in the 1970s as an outspoken Marxist political activist.

Spock encouraged parents to be accepting and flexible and to treat children as reasoning beings, rather than setting clear limits on their behavior. At the time of publication, Spock's theories were criticized for relying on anecdotal evidence rather than actual research and for encouraging excessive permissiveness in child-rearing. His advice appealed to the inclinations of many mothers to protect and gratify their children while it opposed the father's

---

[1] Derek Freeman published *The Fateful Hoaxing of Margaret Mead*, in which he argued that Mead's misunderstandings of Samoan culture were due to her having been misled by Samoan women who had joked about sexual escapades they never had.

[2] Interestingly, he was personal pediatrician to Margaret Mead's children.

traditional role of enforcing limits and administering punishment. Corporal punishment—for any reason—was frowned upon, based on unsubstantiated evidence suggesting that it has no valuable role in child-rearing.

The last fifty years has seen an inexorable increase in permissive child-rearing, influenced by Spock and other progressive-minded physicians and psychologists. Parents wishing to appear "reasonable" will go to great lengths not to punish ill-behaved children. At the same time, there has been an increased trend of anxious parents insisting on involvement in all of their children's activities. As a result, children today are less likely to play freely with others.

> In a 2021 study led by Jelena Obradovic, an associate professor at Stanford Graduate School of Education, published in the *Journal of Family Psychology*, researchers observed parents' behavior when kindergarten-age children were actively engaged in playing, cleaning up toys, learning a new game and discussing a problem. The children of parents who more often stepped in to provide instructions, corrections, or suggestions or to ask questions—despite the children being appropriately on task—displayed more difficulty regulating their behavior and emotions at other times. These children also performed worse on tasks that measured delayed gratification and other executive functions, skills associated with impulse control and the ability to shift between competing demands for their attention (Crawford 2021).

As a result of these ideas on parenting, the relationship between parents and children has become vexed. Afraid of doing harm and disinclined to punish bad behaviors, parents are enabling young children to behave badly and allowing them to engage with social media, recreational drug use, and pornography without appropriate limit-setting. Parents have abandoned their role as guiding authorities, viewing the traditional parental role as too "strong," and instead choosing to be their child's "friend." But there are important differences between being a parent and a friend.

Children today routinely address their parents and other adults by their first names rather than acknowledging their proper roles and authority. This has led to increased disrespect for teachers, police, and adults in general. According to a survey conducted for the nonprofit Character.org, "Parents are significantly concerned about the poor behavior of today's school-age kids and are looking to schools for help nurturing better character traits, according to a recent study.

"A majority of parents said that, in general, children today don't treat others with respect, are dishonest, don't show gratitude, and are lazy, according to the nationally representative survey of 1,034 parents of children ages 6-18 conducted by market research company Ipsos between Aug. 31 and Sept. 16."[3] The influence of progressive psychology "experts" on child rearing has been nothing short of disastrous.

In *Positive Illusions: Creative Self-Deception and the Healthy Mind*, psychotherapist Shelley Taylor claimed that optimistic unrealistic assessments of self are required to promote the mental health of children and that fostering a child's illusions over truthful assessments of his or her capacities is beneficial. According to Taylor, "Increasingly, we must view a psychologically healthy person not as someone who sees things as they are but as someone who sees things as he or she would like them to be" (Martin 2006, 155).

In these statements one detects the influence of postmodern philosophy, in which narrative is viewed as more important than truth. It would appear that Taylor has no real evidence to support her claim, and in the past it would not have merited a serious reception. Yet today this approach has become mainstream. "Loving yourself unconditionally" may be a lovely sentiment, but unrealistically

---

[3] Lauraine Langreo, "Majority of Parents Say Kids Are Dishonest, Disrespectful, and Lazy," *Education Week*, January 24, 2023, https://www.edweek.org/leadership/majority-of-parents-say-kids-are-dishonest-disrespectful-and-lazy/2023/01.

inflated self-regard is the fast track to grandiosity and entitlement, the core features of the rising narcissism that society is witnessing.

Psychologist Jean Twenge (2014) offers the following example of the entitled expectations of young people in the workplace today: "Expectations for advancement and promotion are high. One young employee told a startled manager that he expected to be a vice president at the company in three years. When the manger told him that this was unrealistic (most vice presidents were in their sixties), the young man got angry and said, 'You should encourage me and help me fulfill my expectations.' Related to 'you can do anything' is 'follow your dreams' or 'never give up on your dreams'—like self-focus, a concept that *Gen-Me* speaks as a native language." Psychologists Greg Lukianoff and Jonathan Haidt have claimed in *Coddling of the American Mind* that the current generation may lack the mental fortitude required to confront real-world challenges, something that bodes poorly for the future of America (Lukianoff and Haidt 2018).

Corporations reinforce these unrealistic expectations in pursuit of financial gain. In a Nike sneaker advertisement, controversial football player Colin Kaepernick encourages young viewers to imagine a future without limits. In the ad, he declares: "Don't ask if your dreams are crazy. Ask if they're crazy enough!" If you can imagine a world in which everybody feels that their capacity is unlimited, then you are close to describing what is transpiring today. In the "woke" world, everyone is somehow magically endowed with the capacity to succeed at any task they choose to take on, and never has to accept physical or mental limitations. Social media offers the possibility of creating an online persona that exaggerates or frankly fabricates a story about who one is with no consequences. The honesty and humility that the Judeo-Christian ethic applauds has no place in today's narcissistic society.

Society today seems to be incapable of confronting bad behavior and taking steps to end it. Parents, teachers, universities, and governments are all reluctant to act forcefully to limit antisocial behaviors. The dictum of Proverbs 13:24 to "spare the rod, spoil the child" is judged excessively harsh, and corporal punishment is viewed as "regressive" by progressives and many conservatives alike. What is rarely questioned is whether it is in the best interests of a child to dismiss limit-setting and corporal punishment, or if it might be a misguided conclusion due to more than half a century of progressive propaganda.

Considering what is transpiring in society today, it should be clear to most honest observers that progressive ideas on child rearing have failed. Like so many ideological abstractions, they are divorced from a proper understanding of human nature, and immune to repeated failures in practice. After all, where is the *credible* evidence that reward without punishment, or bolstering self-esteem without genuine accomplishment, produces healthier children? It doesn't exist. But that children today are less respectful, more self-absorbed, more entitled, less empathic, and less inclined to help others than in the past, is unquestionably true and should not be ignored. Society should be seriously questioning the advisability of continuing to accept progressive pedagogy, especially as a recent article suggests that society is rearing a generation of sociopaths.

> Left-wing extremism is linked to toxic, psychopathic tendencies and narcissism, according to a new study published to the peer-reviewed journal *Current Psychology*. "Based on existing research, we expected individuals with higher levels of left-wing authoritarianism to also report higher levels of narcissism," the authors wrote. As result of the new data, study authors Ann Krispenz and Alex Bertrams have coined a new term for such psychological behavior: the "dark-ego-vehicle principle."
>
> "According to this principle, individuals with dark personalities—such as high narcissistic and psychopathic traits—are attracted to certain forms of political and social activism which they can use as a vehicle to satisfy their own ego-focused needs instead of actually aiming at social justice and equality," they told PsyPost.... "In particular, certain forms of activism might

provide them with opportunities for positive self-presentation and displays of moral superiority, to gain social status, to dominate others, and to engage in social conflicts and aggression to satisfy their need for thrill seeking" (Mitchell 2023).

Abandoning the traditional moral values of religion has had a negative effect on the fabric of society (Kradin 2021). The once cardinal virtues of prudence, justice, fortitude, and temperance are dismissed as "antiquated" and rarely considered by "experts" as goals worth promoting in a child's education.

Americans have recently watched the outbreak of anti-Semitism on college campuses following the Hamas terror attack on Israel. Angry students are seen marching in the streets and accosting their Jewish fellow students while chanting Hamas's terrorist slogans calling for the eradication of Israel and Jews. How intelligent young people can behave in such a vile manner is a question, and while the most commonly offered answer is the influence of progressive propaganda on college campuses, the conveniently ignored one is the failure of parents to inculcate moral values in their children from a young age, so that when they attend university, they have a clear moral compass. When children are instead provided with a "narcissistogenic" upbringing, it should come as little surprise that they lack empathy for others.

America's youth are currently guided by a progressive moral code based on the binary distinction between "oppressor" and "oppressed," one more concerned with abstract "identity groups" than individuals, and one that is incompatible with the tenets of the Judeo-Christian ethic. To ignore the unprovoked murder of civilians, the rape of women, and the slaughter of babies suggests a profound lack of empathy and a level of sociopathy that reflects the unbridled narcissism of today's progressive society.

The cultural trend toward "personal gratification"—once correctly recognized as "selfishness"—at the expense of establishing relationships with others is underscored by the results of a 2023 *Wall Street Journal* poll that showed that fewer than half of respondents viewed marriage as important. Only 30 percent said having children was desirable, compared with 59 percent in 1998. Thirty-eight percent of respondents said patriotism is important, compared with 70 percent in 1998. Marriage, children, family, and patriotism are key elements in ensuring societal cohesion, and these results suggest that society is on a path toward dissolution (Zitner 2023).

A narcissistic culture is necessarily superficial, preoccupied with appearances and acquisitiveness rather than relationships and the well-being of society. As could have been predicted, the *only* value that registered as increased in importance for the respondents was "money," named as the major concern for 43 percent of respondents, up from 31 percent less than a decade ago. In a progressive society that claims to be concerned with virtue and the ills of capitalism, it is telling to see what its real values are.

Entitlement is a cardinal feature of narcissism. Young people today insist that they are entitled to "safe spaces" where they can be shielded from criticism and unpleasantness. Some expect to be supported without having to work. When the progressive Biden administration announced student loan forgiveness, America's entitled youth cheered, neglecting to consider that it would mean that those who had never attended college and those who had conscientiously paid back their loans would be forced to foot the bill for debts they had not accrued.

Following the Covid pandemic, a substantial percentage of the workforce failed to return to gainful employment and was instead content to receive stipends from the US government, part of a progressive strategy designed to encourage public reliance on government support.

None of what I have described above is indicative of good mental health.

Obsessed

Although the culture of narcissism has been widely recognized, the accompanying uptick in obsessional behavior in society has received less attention. Obsessionality, paranoia, and narcissism are classified along a spectrum of what psychologists have termed "rigid character" (Shapiro 1981). Since the nineteenth century, obsessionality has been recognized as one of two major personality styles, the other being hysteria. As psychoanalyst David Shapiro notes:

> Two neurotic modes of volitional action—that of hysterical and impulsive characters and certain passive "weak" individuals, and that of rigid character serve to illustrate the forms of conscious self-direction. Among the former, aims are exceedingly vague and intentions are hardly articulated or self-conscious. Such a person may feel that he has no aims of his own, that his actions are entirely determined by force of circumstance or the expectations of others.... Among rigid characters on the other hand, there is an extraordinary degree of articulation and self-consciousness of aim and purpose, an often-excruciating consciousness of choice and decision, and great deliberateness of action (Shapiro 1981, 18).

The cardinal features of obsessionality are familiar to most. They include perfectionism, a propensity toward control of self and others, and excessive and often irrational feelings of guilt. Obsessionals intellectualize their experience and tend to show restricted affect, that is, difficulty identifying (*alexithymia*) and expressing their feelings. Obsessionals also suffer from ambivalence, pervasive feelings of doubt, and difficulty making decisions. Consequently, they tend to avoid commitments and are inclined to "undo" their decisions. Freud recognized that the obsessional defends against repressed hostility, and disguises it as politeness, considerateness, and kindness.

These personality traits have been attributed to excessive reliance on the activity of the left cerebral cortex, which favors intellectualization, resulting in difficulties in identifying feelings. Neurobiologist Anthony Damasio (2000) has suggested that feelings are necessary to motivate choice and that the obsessionals' difficulties in identifying their feelings may explain their difficulties in making decisions. Neuropsychiatrist Iain McGilchrist (2018) has opined that the increased emphasis on left-brain activities in modern society, at the expense of right-brain activities, is producing an "ungrounded" society, one that is predisposed to abstractions and ideologies with little connection to reality. One-sided left-brained activity diminishes imagination and the capacity to appreciate metaphor and myth, elements that are critical to religious experience.

Because of their reliance on sensation and a propensity to doubt, left-brained obsessionals are less likely to believe in an immaterial God. This absence of faith is portrayed in John 20:25, which describes the apostle Thomas's refusal to believe that Jesus was resurrected unless he could see and feel his wounds, to which Jesus responded, "Because you have seen me, you have believed; blessed are those who have not seen and yet have believed." (John 20:29) Doubt is the antithesis of faith, something that eludes obsessionals.

Curiously, as we saw earlier, hyperrationality can paradoxically yield irrational ideas and behaviors in a phenomenon Heraclitus described as "*enantiodromia*." As McGilchrist notes: "Once the theoretical mind is untethered from the body and community, in which it is grounded, and from which it receives its intuitions, there simply is no longer any solid basis for discriminating truth from untruth. And once again one sees parallels in some kinds of contemporary philosophy, and some kinds of belief systems driven by the irrationality of identity politics, which leads subjects to doubt everything except the validity of a bizarre conclusion which they feel driven to accept by formal rules. But never doubting the rules" (McGilchrist 2021, 369).

Safety First—and Second, and Third

Extreme and irrational risk avoidance is prominent among obsessional personalities, who are phobic about harm. As they are unable to evaluate risk properly, they tend either to exaggerate or to minimize it. This phobic response to risk permeates "progressive" culture, taking the form of innumerable safety regulations and disdain for those who do not share the fear, as was recently exhibited in the excessive concern displayed by young, healthy obsessional progressives with contracting Coronavirus. Instead of accepting the extremely small risk of dying from complications of the virus—death was limited almost exclusively to the elderly and those who were already medically compromised—they opted for extreme and scientifically unsound precautions against contracting infection, supporting the decisions of progressive bureaucrats to lockdown the public and to restrict personal liberties.

Despite the fact that the emerging scientific data demonstrated that lockdowns, masks, and vaccines were ineffective at protecting against the virus, these obsessionals insisted on wearing masks even when alone and outside, and on opting for multiple vaccinations at frequent intervals without supporting evidence (Kradin 2022). These behaviors are consistent with Freud's early observation that obsessionals are prone to "magical thinking." But they also indicate the lack of faith and trust that religionists testify to.

The truth is that obsessionals suffer from free-floating anxiety. They are easily frightened but ashamed to admit it to themselves or others. Rather than recognizing that their compulsive thoughts and behaviors are motivated by irrational anxiety, they choose to rationalize their fears, by insisting that the source of their fear is located in their environment and making efforts to control it. When challenged, they insist that their concerns and behaviors are justified and that *no* risk is worth taking if it can be avoided. Hypersensitive to criticism, obsessionals are unlikely to admit to making mistakes and inclined to demand "nonjudgmental" behaviors by others.

In *Escape from Freedom*, social psychologist Erich Fromm explained that obsessionals are ambivalent about authority. While harboring hostility toward those who hold power over them, they are also quick to defer to authority if they assess that they are powerless to resist it. In such cases, they exert their autonomy through passive aggression, which allows them to thwart others covertly. How the obsessional perceives power is key, as Fromm suggests:

> Returning now to the discussion of the authoritarian character [the obsessional], the most important feature to be mentioned is its attitude toward power. For the authoritarian character there exists, so to speak, two sexes: the powerful ones and the powerless ones. His love, admiration, and readiness for submission are automatically aroused by power, whether of a person or an institution. Power fascinates him, not for any values for which a specific power may stand, but just because it is power. Just as his "love" is automatically aroused by power, so powerless people or institutions automatically arouse his contempt. The very sight of a powerless person makes him want to attack, dominate, humiliate him (Fromm 1960, 167).

Ironically, the division of people into "two sexes: the powerful ones and the powerless" closely mimics the "woke" classification of groups into "oppressors" versus "oppressed." And interestingly, Fromm was part of the neo-Marxist Frankfurt School, whose ideas were seminal to the "woke" ideology.

As Fromm suggests, obsessionals are uncomfortable with freedom. They prefer to have others make decisions for them, as it absolves them from taking responsibility and possibly making mistakes. They favor the protection of government over personal freedom. But they may also resist being told what to do when it suits them to.

Freud recognized that obsessionals harbor substantial hostility toward others (Freud 1953–1974a) This repressed hostility can erupt in destructive acts, as with progressives during the 2020 George Floyd protests. While obsessionals profess a concern for the well-being of others, they can concomitantly spew hated. As McGilchrist warns, "It is a matter of observation that those who espouse grand theories supposedly based on love of mankind are by no means the kindest people one meets; and those that are innately suspicious of such schemes often surpass them in generosity and kindly warmth toward actual human individuals" (McGilchrist 2021, 358). In a similar vein, Shapiro notes that "virtue signaling" is invariably a neurotic behavior that rarely represents the genuine feelings of the obsessional: "When the [obsessive] compulsive person reminds himself that he should do something because it is the right thing, the nice thing, or the generous thing, he is prompted not by kindness, generosity, or concern for justice but by a sense of rules and duties to do something kind, generous, or nice" (Shapiro 1981, 80).

Obsessionals have an abhorrence of "chaos." They insist on imposing order. They also have a distaste for what they perceive as "waste," be it material waste or wasting time. They are enamored with the notion of efficiency, which justifies them in imposing bureaucratic rules and limitations on others. Indeed, the obsessional is the ideal bureaucrat, preoccupied with detail and order while missing the forest for the trees. The net result of their efforts is to limit the degree of freedom of a society until it becomes stifled by rules and regulations. These are the ideas that pervade our present technological society. But they are the result of a neurotic flawed ideology driven by irrational anxiety, not by the concern for the public good. But from unresolved feelings of anger, the same "orderly" obsessives are capable of being dangerously destructive, especially when their defenses are challenged.

America's youth are exhibiting increased evidence of obsessionality. They insist on being cared for and report feeling irrationally vulnerable to harm. The reasons are multi-determinate and include the tone of progressive culture, permissive child-rearing with insufficient boundaries, a society that glibly accepts divorce and family disruption, social media that promotes anxieties about a host of issues including body image, and the loss of God and meaning in society. But whatever the cause, the phenomenon is real, and it has created a generation that is phobic about accepting even minimal risk and ill-prepared to confront the challenges of everyday life with confidence.

It should be clear that narcissistic and obsessional personality styles contribute to the ideas and behaviors exhibited by progressives. The neurotic basis of progressives' behavior is betrayed by their animosity toward those holding differing beliefs. Most healthy people can tolerate the differing beliefs of others without attacking them. Thomas Jefferson once remarked that he never let a difference of opinion interfere with his friendships. But progressives have little insight into their own hostility and instead project it onto others. Consequently, it should come as no surprise that they are quick to accuse those who question their ideas and actions of being "haters," "bigots," and "racists."

The Paranoid Style in "Woke" Politics

Paranoid ideation is frequently observed together with narcissism and obsessionality, as these rigid personality styles overlap. Paranoid psychology is a typical feature of those who govern totalitarian societies and is commonly seen in zealots ascribing to either theistic or secular religion (Berger 2010). In *Thought Reform and the Psychology of Totalism*, psychiatrist Robert Lifton illustrated the paranoia of Chinese Communist bureaucrats with a quotation from a party activist: "The evil ideology and evil habits left behind by the old society calling for the injuring of others for self-profit and seeking enjoyment without labor still remain in the minds of other people to a marked degree. Thus, if we are to wipe out all crimes from their root in addition to inflicting upon the criminal the punishment due, we must also carry out various effective measures to transform the various evil ideological conceptions in the minds of the people so that they can be educated and reformed into new people" (Lifton 2014, 14).

From this extreme perspective, the new society can only prevail if the old "evil" and dangerous traditional ways have been expunged. According to this rigid black-and-white thinking, the "other" cannot be tolerated.

Paranoia is characterized by an excessive degree of "projection," which has multiple purposes in the psychic economy. It is normally used to "fill in the blanks" when there is a lack of information in an effort to construe meaning in a previously never encountered situation (Kradin 2007). But in psychopathology it serves as a primitive defense of the ego, one in which repressed "negative emotions" are misattributed to others. Evidence of projection can be identified in the biblical literature. In Numbers 13:33 (NKJV), the spies sent by Moses to investigate the land of Canaan reported encountering giants in the land and concluded, "We were like grasshoppers in our own sight, and *so we were in their sight.*" Obviously, the spies had no idea what the Canaanites *actually* thought of them; they were projecting their own inadequacy. In Matthew 7:5 (ESV), Jesus criticizes those who do not recognize their projections: "You hypocrite, first take the log out of your own eye, and then you will see clearly to take the speck out of your brother's eye." Jesus refers to this as "hypocrisy," and projections can have that appearance, but most projections are at best vaguely conscious, whereas hypocrisy implies a conscious choice.

Although "woke" ideology is often described as a racially obsessed variant of Marxism, this does not capture its psychological underpinnings. The intensity of hatred expressed by "woke" ideologues toward those who disagree with them, and those they label "ultra-MAGA Republicans," "fascists," "Nazis," or "white supremacists," is indicative of a projective psychology. Their claims that conservatives are planning to attack them represents a projection of their own wish to harm others, and the intensity of their projections qualifies as clinically paranoid and dangerous.

LGBTQ+ groups routinely make paranoid claims, such as the following on a Human Rights website that caters to their issues: "Their [conservatives'] words rile up far-right extremists resulting in more stigma, discrimination, and violence against LGBTQ+ people. The rights and very existence of trans people is not up for debate. We will keep fighting back until we are all treated equally, with dignity and respect" (Luneau 2023).

Mental health professionals who have treated transgendered patients know—or should know—that members of the LGBTQ+ community frequently suffer from pathological levels of anxiety, depression, paranoia, and narcissistic and borderline character disorders that require psychiatric intervention.

As psychoanalyst Marie-Louise von Franz (1985) explained, projections require a "hook" to hang themselves on, and transgenders are correct in perceiving that many conservative Americans do not approve of their values, but this does not mean that conservatives harbor violent intentions against the LGBTQ+ community. The majority of conservatives are tolerant of private sexual choices, but they do not wish to see them publicly displayed or to be forced by progressive legislation to celebrate them. When officials from the "woke" Biden administration issued statements that parents who object to their children being exposed to pornography at school are a threat to public safety, made outrageous unsupported claims that "white supremacy" is the greatest danger facing the country, or claimed that conservatives are threatening the LGBTQ+ community, they were either cynically fostering dangerous paranoid ideation for political gain or paranoid themselves.

Psychiatrists and law enforcement officials are well aware of the dangers that paranoid individuals potentially pose to others. When they attribute their own unrecognized hostility to others, they may also perceive a need to act against them in "self-defense." Most of us have known paranoid individuals. They are suspicious, appear uncomfortable around others, and are easily threatened. It is impossible to convince them that their perceptions are incorrect, and they interpret attempts to do so as an effort to deceive them. Instead of questioning their delusions, they view themselves as highly perceptive and capable of penetrating the underlying motives of others where other people do not. While there is invariably a kernel of truth to their perceptions, their assessments are exaggerated. Trump Derangement Syndrome, in which the president is accused of being a "dictator" and a "fascist" and equated with "Hitler," is an example of paranoid ideation that has reached delusional and therefore psychotic proportions, yet it is a paranoid delusion that perhaps half the country suffers from.

It is evident that there is considerable overlap between the psychological predispositions of progressives and the rigid character disorders of narcissism, obsessionality, and paranoia. These disorders exhibit overlapping features, any of which may predominate at any given time. The ideology of many "woke" progressives is a rationalized guise for these underlying neurotic predispositions. Unfortunately, the psychopathologies that underly the "woke" ideology are receiving inadequate attention, as social critics tend to primarily focus on political issues while ignoring their underlying psychological motivations.

CHAPTER 10

"Woke" Psychotherapy

Critical Social Justice (CSJ)-driven therapy is a completely different practice to traditional counselling and psychotherapy.... The worldview informing CSJ is turning counselling and psychotherapy into practices that weaken the client.

—VAL THOMAS (2022)

HOW ARE PROGRESSIVE IDEAS BEING DISSEMINATED? The broad answer is through virtually all institutions of the culture, but a largely underexamined source is the mental health profession (Kradin 2021; Thomas 2023). In 1966, social critic Philip Rieff (1966) suggested in *Triumph of the Therapeutic* that America was becoming a culture of therapy, with a propensity to imagine moral failings as mental disorders.

In the past, religion was the primary source of "therapy" for those in mental distress. The religious "cure of the soul" included introspection and the understanding that confession and repentance for sins can promote psychological well-being. Freudian psychoanalysis incorporated many of these ideas but eschewed the metaphysical notion of "sin." And yet it can be demonstrated that many of the complaints that patients bring to secular psychotherapy have their roots in perceived sins. Jung, who was more favorably disposed toward religion, argued that therapeutic change was impossible to achieve without an acceptance of a forgiving "power" greater than oneself. He opined that most of his adult patients were troubled by the absence of meaning in their life that could be found only through religion. According to Jung: "I have treated many hundreds of patients. Among those in the second half of life—that is to say, over 35—there has not been one whose problem in the last resort was not that of finding a religious outlook on life. It is safe to say that every one of them fell ill because he had lost that which the living religions of every age have given their followers, and none of them has really been healed who did not regain his religious outlook" (Jung 1950, 26). Jung's ideas were adopted by Alcoholics Anonymous and other "twelve-step" programs, which focus on combating addictive behaviors by seeking the assistance of a "higher power."

Therapy as the New Religion

Most psychotherapeutic approaches today eschew religious beliefs and reject the notion of sin. Freud did not reject the Judeo-Christian ethic, but he did think that it was the product of a secular "natural law" rather than a revealed morality. Viktor Frankl, an Austrian psychologist and Holocaust survivor, developed a therapeutic approach that he termed "logotherapy," which was based on the idea that man can take control of his situation by rationally adopting the Judeo-Christian ethic as the guide to a moral and meaningful life (Frankl 1992).

Most secular philosophers and anthropologists, however, insist that there is no universal right and wrong, and in recent years moral relativism and nonjudgmentalism have increasingly replaced the Judeo-Christian ethic for the psychotherapeutic community, with profound effects on how mental illness is defined and approached. In the absence of consent to a shared moral code, it is impossible to judge any behavior undesirable or to characterize it as a "psychopa-thology." Thus, as might be expected, "woke" psychotherapists reject the idea of psychopathology as judgmental, created by an "oppressor" class to stigmatize the less fortunate in society by labelling them "mentally ill" (Kradin 2021). This analysis ignores the fact that some behaviors are predictably deleterious to the well-being of both the individual and society. The idea that mental distress can be alleviated by identifying oneself as a victim of "oppression" runs counter to the Judeo-Christian ethic and simply affirms the neurotic complaints of patients.

Historically, the psychoanalytic movement has included a number of prominent members who have espoused Marxist ideas and an "open society." These include Erich Fromm, Wilhelm Reich, and Karen Horney, to name but a few. It is no surprise that in the present cultural climate, many therapists have embraced neo-Marxist "woke" ideology. In *Cynical Therapies: Perspectives on the Anti-Therapeutic Nature of Critical Social Justice*, several British and American psycho-therapists and counselors discuss the disturbing changes they have witnessed within the mental health profession and conclude that therapy today is increasingly no longer client-centered or politically neutral. Rather, it is being shaped by critical "social justice" ideology focusing on innate "identity" and hierarchies of "oppression" instead of treating patients as individuals. Therapists are being trained to understand patients as representatives of their race or gender and as either "oppressed" or "privileged" (Thomas 2023).

Viewing mental illness through the prism of class conflict rather than as a personal psychodynamic has led to a number of misguided ideas. Progressive psychotherapists believe that mental hospitals are places where the mentally ill are "oppressed," ignoring the positive effects that long-term hospitalization can have for the chronically mentally ill. Anyone who has treated the severely mentally ill knows that for their own safety, as well as that of their families and society, there can be a need for long-term institutionalization, until the patient has made sufficient progress to be able to rejoin society safely. Estimates suggest that 30 percent of the urban homeless are severely mentally ill and in need of long-term institutional care, yet the progressive mental health profession favors their being allowed to remain on the streets, where they represent a danger to themselves and others (Gutwinski et al. 2021).

Freud's psychoanalysis emphasized the importance of "working through" the patient's resistance by breaking down ego defenses. His approach was comparable to that of the religious cure of the soul, which saw repentance and a "contrite heart" as the road to recovery. But progressive influences have skewed the balance of the mental health profession toward empathy rather than interpretation, although the latter is required to penetrate the resistance of ego defenses. While some psychotherapists continue to pay lip service to the importance of "interpretation," in practice it is often judged as potentially "harmful" by therapists who have not been adequately analyzed and who unconsciously collude with the resistances of their patients. By embracing the progressive attitude toward the Care/ Harm axis, they inappropriately judge their patients as too fragile to tolerate criticism and therefore fail to confront their resistance to change. As a result, many psychotherapy treatments today are ineffective and allow deep issues to remain unanalyzed.

There is arguably no field in America that has contributed more to the "woke" phenomenon than the mental health profession through its encouragement of overly protective caretaking and victimization. Journalist Greg Lukianoff and psychologist Jonathan Haidt have suggested in *Coddling of the American Mind* that "something strange is happening at America's colleges and universities. A movement is arising, undirected and driven largely by students, to scrub campuses clean of words, ideas, and subjects that might cause discomfort or give offense. In December 2014, Jeannie Suk wrote an online article for *The New Yorker* about law students asking her professors at Harvard not to teach rape law—or, in one case, even use the word "violate" (as in "that violates the law") lest it cause students distress" (Lukianoff and Haidt, 1).

Gender Gap

Women currently make up the majority of those working in the mental health profession, including psychiatrists, psychotherapists, and social workers—resulting in a feminization of how therapy is both conceived and delivered, with a primary focus on empathy to the exclusion of critical interpretation. The nexus between feminine psychology and "woke" ideology has not received sufficient attention, particularly as it is currently frowned upon to accept possible distinctions between the psychologies of men and women. But studies suggest there are important sex-based differences in how men and women identify with progressive ideas. According to a 2022 University of Michigan study, "Monitoring the Future":

> In the early 2000s both boys and girls leaned liberal, with only around 17–20% identifying as conservative. In 2014, however, conservative 12th-grade boys jumped up to 22%, and then up to 26% in 2020. In contrast, in 2020, only 13% of boys identified as liberal, a number which has stayed constant for the past three years…[but] among 12th-grade girls, there is a growing trend to identify as liberal. In 2012, only 19% of 12th-grade girls considered themselves liberal—in 2022, 30% of the girls self-identified as liberal, compared to only 12% of whom called themselves conservative" (University of Michigan 2024).

According to a 2024 Gallup poll, more women than men support leftist issues, including gay and lesbian parenting and notions of "toxic masculinity." The survey showed that 44 percent of young women ages 18–29 identified as liberal in 2021, while only 25 percent of men did. A decade before, roughly the same number of men and women had identified as liberal (Saad 2024). Although issues including abortion and misogyny account for part of this trend, innate differences in the psychology of men and women should be considered.

"Woke" ideology seeks to expand the aggrieved factions in society, and the psychotherapy profession has assisted in this regard. By exaggerating the emotional consequences of normal developmental events, modern psychotherapeutic and "self-help" notions are encouraging indoctrinated individuals to identify as "oppressed" and to feel justified in attributing their unhappiness to others.

For many people today, anyone who criticizes character flaws or offers realistic assessments that are not "supportive" is judged as "mean-spirited." Compare this attitude to that of Leviticus 19:17, essentially: "Don't hold grudges. On the other hand, it's wrong not to correct someone who needs correcting." Reared to avoid challenges and reinforced in this belief by the psychotherapeutic community and "political correctness," many young people today think they are entitled to act out angrily when not indulged or that they are in the right to insist on not being challenged by ideas they do not agree with. Rather than rejecting these infantile displays as inappropriate, parents, teachers, and therapists either ignore or appease them, further enabling bad behavior.

Sanctioning psychological hypersensitivity runs contrary to the Judeo-Christian ethic. In the Jewish text *Ethics of the Fathers*, Avot 2:5 suggests that the overly sensitive "cannot learn." That being too sensitive to criticism might be detrimental is dismissed by "woke" progressives; instead, it is encouraged to protest criticism as "microaggressions." The conversations of young people today are excessively self-referential and peppered liberally with allusions to their anxieties, depression, and "traumas." Trauma, a term once reserved for serious mental or physical injuries, has been reimagined to include virtually anything that may have made one uncomfortable in the past. While it is admirable that people today are more psychologically attuned than in the past, when sensitivity is emphasized at the expense of adaptability, the value of psychotherapy is questionable, as Harvard psychiatrist George Valiant elucidated in *Adaptation to Life* (Vaillant 1977).

Hypersensitivity has resulted in many young people being unable (unwilling?) to function effectively in the workplace, as a recent survey suggests:

> The fact that the youngest people in the workplace are struggling to keep their heads above water should alarm everyone.
>
> In the short term, Gen Z's stress is leading to ambivalence and withdrawal in their professional lives. According to 2022 data from Gallup, they are the most disengaged group at work. They also report more overall stress and work-related burnout than other cohorts. "We found that during the pandemic, a good portion of Gen Zers admitted to not giving a full effort at work, which is a symptom of burnout and other workplace behaviors like disengagement, unclear communication, lack of manager support and loneliness," says Nishizaki.
>
> …In the US, for instance, 61% of US workers who responded to the December 2022 LinkedIn survey are considering leaving their jobs in 2023, leaping to 72% among Gen Zers, by far the most significant group. Globally, McKinsey's research showed 77% of Gen Zers are looking for a new job—almost double the rate of other respondents.
>
> By 2025, Gen Z will make up 27% of the workforce in OECD countries, and one-third of the global population. If the majority are too stressed to work, Nishizaki believes it would be "devastating—economically, socially and much more" (Carnegie 2023).

Numerous factors are contributing to this problem, but there is increasing evidence that the widespread use of social media has had a profound negative effect on the mental fortitude of young people. As psychologist Jean Twenge (2023) discusses in *Generations*, the addictive and otherwise deleterious effects of social media on Gen Z have been profound and in some cases crippling. And those effects were compounded by the social isolation brought on by the lockdowns during the Covid-19 pandemic.

From Diagnosis to Affirmation

What in the past were judged psychopathologies, including homosexuality and transgenderism, have been normalized by progressive mental health professionals, with little resistance from society. To suggest that alternative sexual lifestyles might represent psychopathology is condemned by progressive society as the homophobic result of antiquated religious beliefs. The cultural change in attitude on this topic has been rapid and dramatic, as a 2017 Pew report indicates: "Seven-in-ten now say homosexuality should be accepted by society, compared with just 24% who say it should be discouraged by society. The share saying homosexuality should be accepted by society is up 7 percentage points in the past year and up 19 points from 11 years ago. Growing acceptance of homosexuality has paralleled an increase in public support for same-sex marriage. About six-in-ten Americans (62%) now say they favor allowing gays and lesbians to marry legally" (Pew Research Center 2017).

This shift in public opinion is attributable to progressive insistence that alternate lifestyles expressing the increased freedom that results from moral relativism and inclusiveness must not be judged. That the psychological problems—including anxiety, depression, narcissism, borderline personality, and addictions—of individuals in the LGBTQ+ community are substantial and cannot be attributed solely to "stigma" cannot be debated due to a censorious "political correctness." As a consequence, well-intentioned mental health professionals are inhibited from discussing the mental health issues seen in this population for fear of being condemned and punished by progressive professional societies.

But compassionate psychological concern for those who suffer should not be silenced by *ad hominem* ideological attacks. All would agree that people should not be stigmatized or inappropriately labeled "abnormal," but proper diagnosis, uninfluenced by political philosophies, is required for effective treatment. Society must not be forced to relinquish moral concern for those in need in order to accommodate ideological narratives that ignore unpleasant truths.

Studies have repeatedly shown that an increased percentage of homosexuals suffer from narcissistic and borderline personalities. As psychotherapist Gidi Rubinstein points out:

> According to orthodox psychoanalytical theory, narcissism and homosexuality are strongly associated. This association played a major role in pathologizing homosexuality. The present study compared self-esteem and two measures of narcissism among 90 homosexual and 109 heterosexual male students, who filled in a demographic questionnaire, Rosenberg's Self-Esteem Scale, the Narcissistic Personality Inventory, and the Pathological Narcissism Inventory, which addresses both grandiose and vulnerable subtypes of narcissism. The hypothesis, which is based on the Freudian connection between narcissism and homosexuality, is supported by the results, indicating that the homosexual students score higher in both measures of narcissism and lower on the self-esteem measure, compared to their heterosexual counterparts (Rubinstein 2010).

Homosexual men also exhibit a higher incidence of promiscuity and addictive behaviors. According to the Addiction Center website, an estimated 20 to 30 percent of the male homosexual community abuse substances, compared to about 9 percent the general population. A larger than average percentage of homosexuals and transsexuals are exhibitionists and are compulsively inclined to transgress the mores of society. One witnesses this behavior regularly at Pride Parades that celebrate the LGBTQ+ community. Transsexuals invited by the Biden White House to celebrate Pride Month in 2023 chose to expose themselves in the presence of young children, although they later apologized after facing widespread public criticism. Homosexual transvestites have taken to making a show of themselves at library events with the approval of progressive administrators. The public needs to understand that there currently are a substantial number of LGBTQ+ members in positions of power in government, corporations, the press, and other cultural institutions who view themselves as activists with the goal of setting policies that normalize and popularize the behaviors of the LGBTQ+ community. As might be expected, they insist that their "freedoms" should not be undermined by Judeo-Christian religionists who may oppose their behaviors in public.

Disruptive exhibitionist behaviors are part of a pattern of narcissistic sociopathic behavior that is being purposefully ignored because it serves the political aims of progressivism. The LGBTQ+ community and groups such as Black Lives Matter and Antifa are anarchic forces in society. Progressives support their disruptive behavior specifically because that behavior undermines religious values and the fabric of society. But as a result, the mental health problems of the LGBTQ+ community are purposefully left unaddressed.

An example of sociopathic behavior by a member of the LGBTQ+ community was actor Jussie Smollett's claim that he had been attacked by MAGA racists in Chicago because he was a black homosexual man. Smollett is an apparent narcissist who sought attention, sympathy, and a pay raise via the intense media outrage. Unfortunately for him, the Chicago police quickly recognized his story had been fabricated, a fact that was confirmed when two paid coconspirators in the hoax confessed. Despite overwhelming evidence that the "hate crime" was a lie, and even after being found guilty in a Chicago courtroom, Smollett continued to insist that his story was true, and he received unqualified support from progressive ideologues in the media. As he met the "woke" intersectional criteria of being black, homosexual, and a friend of Michelle Obama, his crime went unpunished.

Psychoanalyzing Religion

Discerning mental illness in devout religionists can be a difficult challenge for mental health professionals. Freud suggested that the thoughts and behaviors of traditional religionists shared features with obsessional neurosis, and others have noted that religious visionaries may have suffered from psychosis (Freud 1953–1974b; Hancock and Kreisberg 2010). What may appear as mental illness to the secular atheist can be interpreted as virtue by the religionist. Unless an individual specifically requests therapeutic relief from scrupulous religiosity, where to draw the line between these two perspectives can be challenging.

Nevertheless, it may be evident to members of a religious community that a coreligionist's thoughts and behaviors have become maladaptive and disturbing. British psychoanalyst Donald Winnicott was once asked how to distinguish between someone with mental illness and someone who is simply diligently observing the tenets of his or her religion. After pondering the question, Winnicott suggested that the answer is in whether one feels "bored" by the speech and actions of the individual; if so, that individual is likely mentally ill. Winnicott argued that most people will be bored by those whose conversation and behavior is out of touch with their true feelings and will sense that their actions reflect an "as if" false personality construct (Meissner 2013). This criterion can be applied to those who espouse rigid secular "woke" ideas, as well. If upon listening to the rigid puritanical rants of a "woke" ideologue, one feels bored—not by the content, but because the person is experienced as "false" and simply mimicking ideas heard from others, then that person is likely mentally ill.

CHAPTER 11

Gnosticism Redux

*The divinity is there, within you; have faith that it is so
and entrust yourself to it.*

—PAUL BRUNTON (2024)

*Rather than a cognitive procedure of the intellect alone,
Gnostic knowledge is experience, a lived experience of spiritual
regeneration. It is a transforming knowledge, whose immediate
effect is salvation.*

—GIOVANNI FILORAMO (2024)

THE PROGRESSIVE AGENDA HAS BEEN CHAMPIONED primarily by America's elites, who have expressed disdain for both the working class and political conservatives. As Plato recognized, condescending impulses emerge in all societal endeavors, and religion is no exception. In his insightful *Coming Apart*, Charles Murray provides evidence that the discrepancies in American society are not only economic but also reflect the cultural dominance of progressive ideas being propagated by urban elites (Murray 2012). On the basis of Murray's data, Rusty Reno has argued that while the tenets of progressivism—including moral relativism; diversity, equity, and inclusion; and nonjudgmentalism—have had little effect on the bourgeois stability of elite culture, they have devastated the lives of the working class, and he harshly criticizes the elites for their lack of concern in this regard. In this respect, America's elites share features with the Gnostics of the second century.

Gnosticism was a spiritualized mode of Christianity that gained popularity among Christian elites and threatened to undermine the authority of the "proto-orthodox" Church. *Gnosis* means "knowledge," and Gnostics believed they were privy to spiritual truths that were unavailable to the average man. In other words, the Gnostics were "woke."

The New Gnostics

In *The Gnostic Religion*, philosopher Hans Jonas (1958) elucidated the tenets of Gnosticism and compared it to what is occurring in modern culture. Like the philosophers, Gnostics believed in a transcendent God but formulated their beliefs in mythic terms. They viewed the God of Judaism as a benighted demiurge who was responsible for the "evil" material world and unaware of the presence of a "higher god."[1] They argued in Neoplatonic terms that the "sparks" of the supreme transcendent god, including the human spirit, had fallen into the world where they had been trapped in matter and the body, respectively. The imprisoned spirit of man had forgotten its true origin. In Gnosticism, Jesus was viewed as a messenger sent to earth to wake man from his slumber and to arouse the soul to return to its rightful place with the transcendent god. Although there were different variants of Gnostics, they all agreed that salvation could only be obtained via direct knowledge of the divine rather than through faith (Pagels 1981).

---

[1] In one Gnostic myth, this god was called Yaldabaoth, which roughly translates in Hebrew to a "childish" uninformed deity.

According to Gnosticism, each person consists of a body, a soul, and a spirit, but only the spirit is derived from the supernal realm. They envisioned mankind as comprising three groups based on their "spiritual" potentials. At the lowest end were the *sarkikoi*, the "fleshy ones," individuals trapped in their physical bodies and lacking the capacity to attain salvation. The *psychikoi* made up an intermediate group who had the potential to achieve *gnosis*, but only if guided by a spiritual adept, and only if they were to make concerted efforts. Finally, there were the *pneumatikoi*, that is, the true Gnostics, innately gifted and best positioned to attain salvation and to lead others to the truth. Gnosticism was an elitist belief system that denied most the possibility of salvation.

The "woke" Gnostics viewed themselves as nearer to this god than their fellow man. They embraced the serpent's words about the Tree of Knowledge in Genesis 3:5 (ESV): "For God knows that when you eat of it your eyes will be opened, and you will be like God, knowing good and evil," and viewed the notion of "original sin" as an effort on the part of proto-orthodox religion to suppress freedom.[2] But knowledge was a prelude to the ultimate goal of eating from the Tree of Life, so that they might achieve immortality and literally become as gods. Yuval Harari, the Israeli historian Rabbi Sacks called a "twenty-first-century Gnostic," hints that through the creation of a bionic transhuman race the wealthiest technocrats will at some point in the future achieve immortality, while the unwoke will continue to live and die according to the natural order (Harari 2015). One can imagine what such a division in society would lead to.

Gnosticism was an effort by elites to achieve greater individual freedom and to distinguish themselves from other early Christians,

[2] In the second century, Christian orthodoxy, which had not yet achieved authority, accepted the God of Judaism and the Hebrew Bible as authoritative. On the basis of Genesis, it accepted that the world was "good," that authority lay with apostolic succession, and that anyone who professed faith in Christ's resurrection could be saved regardless of "knowledge."

many of whom were freed slaves, much as today's progressives aspire to distinguish themselves from "deplorable" Trump supporters. In this vein, linguist John McWhorter (2021) has argued that "woke" ideology is the equivalent of modern-day Gnostic religion. Like their forebears in the second century, today's "woke" Gnostics hold perfectionistic ideas concerning what one must believe and are convinced that they are best positioned, like Plato's philosopher king, to guide the direction of society. They value academic credentials and "expert" status above common sense and insist on imposing their ideas on society.

Consider Barack Obama's criticism of America's unwoke conservative working class during his campaign for the Democratic presidential nomination in 2008: "And it's not surprising then that they get bitter, they cling to guns or religion or antipathy to people who aren't like them or anti-immigrant sentiment or anti-trade sentiment as a way to explain their frustrations" (Krugman 2008). Or ponder Hillary Clinton's statement—which may have cost her the presidential election in 2016: "You know, to just be grossly generalistic [sic], you could put half of Trump's supporters into what I call the basket of deplorables. Right? The racist, sexist, homophobic, xenophobic, Islamophobic—you name it. And unfortunately, there are people like that. And he has lifted them up" (Reilly 2016).

For today's progressive Gnostic, the *sarkikoi* are Hillary Clinton's "deplorables," too "ignorant" to merit redemption; the *psychikoi*, independent voters who with effort can be persuaded to see the correctness of the "woke" agenda; and the "woke" *pneumatikoi*, those right-thinking Democrat bicoastal elites who by virtue of their ideology are entitled to rule over others.

Not surprisingly, many corporate leaders in America embrace "woke" ideas and collude with progressive politicians to pressure Americans to accept their imaginings for the future. Consider the statement by Larry Fink, a UCLA-trained progressive financier who heads BlackRock, the largest investment firm in America: "You have to force behaviors. If you don't force behaviors, whether it's gender or race or just any way you want to say the composition of your team, you're going to be impacted. That not just recruiting, it's development. We're going to have to force change" (@EndWokeness 2023).

Of course, one might wonder why a corporate executive feels it his duty to force behaviors on others, but clearly he feels it is his right to do so. In some instances, the efforts of "woke" corporatists have had substantial negative economic consequences for the businesses they are supposed to be stewarding for shareholders.[3] In recent months, "woke" corporations including Anheuser-Busch, Disney, and Target, to name a few, have cumulatively lost *billions* of dollars on account of CEOs who, like Fink, chose to take "woke" positions that have offended their customer base. But these negative effects on their bottom lines have had little effect to date on their insistence that society must change in the direction that they choose for it.

What Moves Them

The underlying motives of these modern-day Gnostics are to some extent obscure. It is evident that they enjoy exerting control over others, but this does not fully explain their behavior. Some are likely sincerely drawn to the "woke" agenda, having been indoctrinated into it at progressive elite universities. Many are narcissists who enjoy the attention that they receive from "woke" organizations that honor them with banquets and public citations for their activism. Some are members of the LGBTQ+ community who see it as their role to promote alternative lifestyles. Many have financial incentives, and as globalists they believe that by adopting the "woke" cultural line they will find it easier to do business with Communist China and other countries that are large potential markets for their goods. Indeed,

---

[3] As part of the war on language, "woke" CEOs routinely refer to "stakeholders" rather than "shareholders," indicating that investors are not only concerned with making a profit but have a "stake" in the future of society. This allows them to justify decisions that result in financial losses for a "good cause."

profit may be the leading motivation, but one that CEOs are reticent about, as they fear the backlash from non-elites, and so they tend to mystify their motives. As the writer and director David Mamet recently stated in an interview, the Hollywood "woke" see themselves as members of an elite group with "godlike" powers (Prager 2023).

Nevertheless, it is difficult to comprehend how educated individuals can justify embracing the often blatantly irrational and simplistic stances of "woke" ideology. The sad truth is that it is eminently possible to be intelligent, educated, and well-meaning, yet lack common sense and as a result repeatedly make poor assessments and bad decisions. A surprisingly large number of highly educated elites fall into this category, something that I can attest to, based on my own experience on the Harvard faculty. Indeed, the recent inability of three Ivy League university presidents to condemn genocide when testifying before Congress is indicative of not only their broken moral compass but also a profound lack of common sense—all three were unable to field what should be easy questions artfully, and unable to recognize that flatfooted testimony would inevitably evoke widespread condemnation.

It is difficult to grasp how these "woke" elites fail to see the problems that result from uncontrolled immigration, diminished law enforcement, explicit sexual education to grade school students, and so forth. The leading explanation is that America's progressive elites include psychologically immature narcissistic individuals whose lives are largely insulated from their bad choices and who lack sufficient empathy to appreciate the hardships their bad ideas are imposing on their fellow Americans.

As cultural critic John Gray argues, the notion that knowledge is the path to salvation is a distinctly Western phenomenon that began with early Christianity. As he suggests: "If you want to understand modern politics, you must set aside the idea that secular and religious movements are opposite. Since they aimed to extinguish the influence of religion in society, Jacobinism and Bolshevism were secularizing forces; but both were channels for the millenarian myths of apocalyptic Christianity.... A mix of Christian notions of redemption with a Gnostic belief in the salvific power of knowledge has propelled the project of salvation through politics" (Gray 2018, 74.

Hans Jonas (1958) perceptively recognized that the Gnostics of the second century and the "woke" ideologues of today share a sense of alienation from this world. But while the second-century Gnostic denied the physical world, the "woke" Gnostic denies the spiritual one. Yet both have sought increased personal freedom based on knowledge and viewed the structures of law and morality as unduly limiting. In the end what they truly share is an antinomian iconoclasm and the fantasy of breaking out of a physical body that is fated to die. As Reno writes: "None of this should come as a surprise. Unchecked by loyalty to God, nature, and custom, the American dream of freedom cannot help but become militant. The future is mine to make! I can be anything! There is nothing about being born into Western culture that can control my future. I'm even free from the maleness or femaleness of my body. The promise of life without limits intoxicates. If I can dismiss my body, then perhaps I can be free of the reality of death" (Reno 2016, 30).

In the second century, the response to Gnosticism from the conservative forces of the Church was both negative and harsh. What would become the orthodox Christian Church rejected the Gnostics' view of the world and their denial of the God of the Hebrew Bible as its Creator. They condemned the elitist impulses that sought to exclude others from salvation. The Gnostic movement was expunged, and except for a few Mandeans in Iraq, it no longer exists. But the archetypal self-serving impulse that inspired Gnosticism persists in the human psyche and will not be eradicated. It remains to be seen what the future of today's "woke" Gnostics will be. But conservative forces will continue to oppose them, as they did in the second century.

CHAPTER 12

"Woke" Capitalism

*A man who has never gone to school may steal from
a freight car; but if he has a university education, he may steal
the whole railroad.*

—ATTRIBUTED TO THEODORE ROOSEVELT

*Forget the politicians. The politicians are put there to give you
the idea that you have freedom of choice. You don't. You have no
choice. You have owners. They own you. They own everything.*

—GEORGE CARLIN (2024)

THE SOCIETAL CHANGES THAT AMERICANS are witnessing are
confusing and purposefully designed to be so. Wealthy elites are
reticent about advertising what their goals for America are, as most
citizens would find them objectionable. To understand what is transpiring, one must look to see who benefits.

The government of America has been increasingly anti-demo-
cratic since the twentieth century, and today the interests of Americans
are only nominally represented. The prevailing cultural ethos is

best described as "corporate." Progressivism provided the basis for a managerial culture by calling for a government run by "experts." This corporate ethos is best exemplified today by the European Union, but increasingly America's government ascribes to it as well.

Rule by Corporation

In 1941, James Burnham published *The Managerial Revolution*, in which he argued that the future would not see capitalism pitted against socialism but instead would be a society in which heads of corporations would set policy for the state. Burnham wrote: "The economic structure of managerial society seems to raise obstacles for democracy. There is no democracy without opposition groups. Opposition groups cannot, however, depend for their existence merely on the good will of those who are in power. But since in the managerial society of the future all major parts of the economy will be planned and controlled by the single integrated set of institutions which will be the managerial state there is no independent foundation for genuine oppositional political groups" (Burnham 1966, 169).

The society that Burnham imagined overlaps with both socialism and fascism and stands in opposition to the government imagined by America's Founders. It is a top-down form of governance that removes power from the hands of the people and transfers it to an oligarchy of corporate CEOs—and it is happening in America today. However, global corporatists are aware that Americans, laboring under the misimpression that they are living in a democratic republic, are likely to react badly to the realization that they no longer have anything meaningful to say about how they are governed. As philosopher Jason Stanley (2015) suggests, the answer to this dilemma for corporatists has been to disguise what is occurring with propaganda and distractions that adopt the language of democracy so that Americans will not see what is transpiring. The endless intense criticism of Trump and "ultra-MAGA" conservatives coming from corporate media and the Democrat progressives is meant to ensure that non-globalist, America-first populism does not interfere with the corporatist plans for the country. That is why Congress, funded by these corporations through hefty campaign contributions, increasingly votes like a "uniparty."

It has been apparent for some time now that America's elites have been contemplating how best to benefit financially from the global economy. The digital age afforded them potent new opportunities to bypass the impediments of nationalism, party factionalism, and laissez-faire free-market capitalism. American notions of privacy and personal freedom, which traditionally were opposed to state control, were substantially changed by the terrorist attacks of 9/11, when Americans opted to allow government to infringe on their privacy and freedom in exchange for the promise that it would keep them safe. Government and corporations both realized that they could benefit from access to information about American citizens in a massive way by monitoring their behaviors online and in the digital economy, and as a result, the nation was increasingly transformed into a surveillance state in which virtually every aspect of a citizen's life could be observed, and Constitutional safeguards ignored. This transformation took a quantum leap during the coronavirus epidemic, as the crisis gave government and corporations carte blanche to restrict the activities of both small businesses and private citizens in a manner previously unimaginable. As Americans are discovering, once privacy and freedoms are sacrificed, they are difficult to reclaim.

Globalists in America and Europe were planning for a pandemic prior to Covid-19 and understood that it would be an opportunity to impose global control over the world's populations. The "Great Reset," the brainchild of the German technocrat Klaus Schwab, founder of the World Economic Forum (WEF), calls for a new global economy headed by sympathetic politicians and technocrats. These globalists share an atheistic technological vision for the future and expect to benefit handsomely from the decline of free-market capitalism and America's hegemonic leadership in the world. In their place they plan to force a transformation toward *managed capitalism* and the related political goal of *managed democracy.*

Managed capitalism opposes the cardinal rule of Adam Smith's (2015) laissez-faire capitalism, as it imposes top-down market regulation rather than allowing the "invisible hand" of the free market to determine trade. Managed capitalism undermines the market's self-regulation, replacing it with the policies of elite managers who may have little to no proven experience in the business sector. Managed capitalism resembles Marxism, but rather than aspiring to an equitable utopia for workers, it aims at maximizing profits for corporate elites.

Globalism Gets Going

Progressive corporate and political elites are working to strip Americans of their ability to resist globalist policies. To achieve this, they must distract Americans sufficiently so that they do not protest the loss of their liberties. For this purpose, corporate leaders have embraced "woke" progressivism in an attempt to divert attention away from how the current economy disadvantages the average American, and from the corruption that drives it (Ramaswamy 2021). Money management firms such as BlackRock, State Street, and Vanguard pressure corporations to embrace the "woke" sociopolitical agenda, and since the George Floyd riots in 2020, corporate America has embraced the false claim of "systemic racism," as well as an unpopular LGTBQ+ agenda, often at the cost of shareholder profits—although diminished shareholder profits have not reduced the compensation of CEOs and other senior managers. Corporations favor divesting Americans of any loyalties that compete with the managed state, including belief in God, adherence to the Judeo-Christian ethic, and patriotism. They have become very effective allies in the progressives' Godless Crusade.

In 1961, at the end of his last term in office, President Dwight Eisenhower delivered a warning to the public concerning the American "military-industrial complex." America had just defeated totalitarianism and was now the world's leading power. But Eisenhower warned that the war had created new avenues for greed and power and that forces within the corporate world and in politics, working together and left unchecked, would eventually corrupt democracy:

> In the councils of government, we must guard against the acquisition of unwarranted influence, whether sought or unsought, by the military-industrial complex. The potential for the disastrous rise of misplaced power exists and will persist" (Eisenhower 1961).

In *Democracy, Inc.*, his examination of American exploitation, the political scientist Sheldon Wolin (2017) discussed how corporations have been a corrupting influence on democracy since their inception. He describes "inverted totalitarianism"—a state in which citizens are gradually divested of their power by corporate influences. In this scenario, government officials, increasingly dependent on donations to finance their elections and on bribes to augment their personal wealth, can be counted on to make governing decisions based on the wishes of corporations, and to become less responsive to the citizens who elected them. The "electorate" takes on importance only in the run-up elections and can be ignored in the interim. Indeed, free and fair elections are risky as they can potentially undermine corporate plans, and one can easily imagine scenarios in which the outcomes of elections might be assured without the public being able to identify outright fraud. There are good reasons to believe that this may have happened in America's 2020 presidential election, which removed the anti-globalist candidate from office.

Stop the Steal

The greatest sin, according to the Biden administration and the "woke" corporate media, is to question the outcome of the 2020 presidential election in which Donald Trump, despite registering seventy-five million votes, lost to a lackluster Joe Biden. But the following is only a partial list of the irregularities that occurred in that election: 1) widespread mail-in voting occurred for the first time, 2) election rules were changed just prior to the election in a manner not prescribed by state laws and constitutions, 3) Donald Trump was banned from the major social media platforms, 4) information concerning Joe Biden's corrupt business dealings was kept from the public, and 5) claims of ballot harvesting and voting irregularities in Democrat urban areas were ignored.

One can easily imagine that these types of quasi-legal interventions could sway an election result without being exposed as blatant election fraud. Those who question the election are referred to as "conspiracy theorists," and those who chose to protest the conduct of the election on January 6, 2021, were persecuted by the Biden Justice Department. A female protester was killed without cause, with no inquiry or consequences for the Capitol policeman responsible for her death, who was instead commended and promoted. The road to "soft" totalitarianism does not require force, it simply requires citizens to remain uninformed and docile.

The public ignorance required to sustain this charade has been promoted by lies pedaled by progressive media and politicians. As political scientist Sheldon Wolin suggests, "Lying is more than deception; the liar wants the unreal to be accepted as actuality, so he sets about to establish as true what is not actually the case, not really real. A lie by a public authority is meant to be accepted by the public as an 'official' truth concerning the real world. At bottom, lying is the expression of a will to power" (Wolin 2017, 263).

Today Americans tacitly accept that politicians lie, but when lies are exposed, trust is degraded, and without trust, government cannot function.

Wolin focused on the events following September 11, 2001, and described how the last Bush administration lied to Americans by adopting surveillance mechanisms ostensibly meant to safeguard the homeland but then used them to spy on Americans. But this pales in comparison to the steady stream of lies told to the public by the Biden administration: that the southern border was secure; that one was protected from Covid-19 by masks and vaccines; that inflation was transient; that the economy was prospering, that "white supremacy" was the greatest threat to democracy, that January 6, 2021, was the greatest insurrection since the Civil War—and the list goes on. With the assistance of corporate leaders, Big Tech, and corporate media, the Biden administration and the "intelligence community" continued to surveil Americans and censor anyone who dared to expose the truth.

Two of the biggest lies fed to the American people were that President Biden 1) was not cognitively impaired[1] and 2) not a corrupt politician. Progressive propaganda convinced many Americans to ignore these facts or to make excuses for Biden. Nevertheless, his popularity reached historic lows—suggesting that Americans are beginning to recognize that they are being repeatedly "gaslighted" and they do not like it. Mr. Biden's cognitive impairment was obvious to anyone who watched his performance in public, and despite what supporters of his administration argued, one did not need to possess a medical degree or conduct a detailed cognitive examination to recognize the obvious signs of serious cognitive decline. Yet with flagrant disingenuity, the progressive news media continued to insist that Biden was doing an outstanding job, assuming as usual that their viewing audiences would dismiss the evidence of their "lying eyes." It was like watching the movie *Weekend at Bernie's*.

The corruption of the Biden family is also obvious. The Bidens may be elites, but they are apparently morally bankrupt. Joe's father was an alcoholic; Joe ogles women and sniffs young girls; he is a confirmed plagiarist and a compulsive liar who routinely took showers with his young daughter and swims in the nude in front

---

[1] The first Biden-Trump debate, in June 2024, clearly demonstrated the impaired cognitive faculties of Mr. Biden and undermined the efforts of the Democratic Party and the mainstream press to hide this fact.

of female Secret Service officers. Joe's son Hunter and his daughter were both addicted to drugs. Hunter openly cavorted with his brother's widow with his father's approval, and his brother Jim has never held an honest job. Only a society that lacks both common sense and a moral compass could judge Mr. Biden and his family favorably.

That Mr. Biden and his family are steeped in corruption is beyond any reasonable doubt. The amount of circumstantial evidence indicating it is overwhelming, and endless investigations to establish a "smoking gun" are not required to prove it. As President Harry Truman once said, "No man can get rich in politics unless he's a crook." The Biden family has accrued millions of dollars for reasons that they are unable and unwilling to explain. But as corruption is rampant throughout American government, members of Congress can be expected to circle the wagons around Biden rather than invite exposure into their own dealings (Schweitzer 2021).

Corruption explains the proclivity of America to entangle itself in foreign wars that enrich the military-industrial complex and politicians of both parties, who are supported by its campaign contributions. The current war in Ukraine is ostensibly being fought to combat Russian aggression and to reinforce Ukrainian democracy. Whereas the former reason may be valid, to claim that Ukraine, a country ruled by a strongman who has cancelled future elections, is a "democracy" is a stretch. Ukraine is widely recognized as one of the most corrupt countries on the planet, it has financial ties to the Biden family, and large sums of financial aid from the US have apparently made their way into the Swiss bank accounts of Ukrainian oligarchs and into the accounts of arms manufacturers in the United States. Instead of making efforts to negotiate an end to the war, the Biden administration and its supporters in Congress insisted on continuing it, without a realistically achievable goal or endpoint in sight, while the military-industrial complex continued to rake in the profits.

Never Let a Crisis Go to Waste

Wars provide good opportunities for the government to incite fear and anxiety. As Hobbes (2021) argued, a citizenry at war will be inclined to cede its freedoms in return for protection by the state. But epidemics can also serve this purpose. The Covid-19 pandemic was an example of how existential fears stoked by government propaganda encouraged citizens to sacrifice their freedoms in return for policies that they falsely believed would protect them. To consolidate power in the midst of the pandemic, progressive government at all levels enlisted the mainstream media and the medical profession to endorse a stream of lies that sowed fear among the public (Kradin 2022). Silicon Valley technology platforms were enlisted to censor opinions that differed with progressive government policies by falsely labeling them "misinformation," which is an infringement of the First Amendment.

Topics deemed out of bounds by the unholy alliance between government and Big Tech include 1) China as the source of a manufactured virus, 2) the NIH's funding of gain-of-function research in China, 3) the failure of masks to prevent the spread of infection, 4) that the vaccines were experimental with unknown short and long-term complications, 5) that they were largely ineffective and had serious side effects, and 6) that children were not at substantial risk of developing life-threatening disease. Experienced and academically reputable physicians who took exception to the positions of the government on the basis of the emerging scientific findings were threatened with loss of their medical licensure and had their reputations tarnished (Kradin 2022).

The Covid pandemic drove Pfizer Corporation's 2022 revenue to a record $100 billion; it made $37.8 billion from Covid vaccine sales in 2021. But Pfizer and other large pharmaceutical companies were not alone. As an article in *The Washington Post* suggests, "The majority of the largest American corporations have prospered in the coronavirus economy. Millions of consumers spent more time and money online during government-mandated lockdowns, watching Netflix, viewing ads on Google and Facebook pages, filling Amazon shopping carts and turning the video game business into a bonanza for Nvidia, Microsoft and others."

Who suffered from the pandemic? The answer is small businesses that were unable to remain open due to government-enforced lockdowns and the American public that was encouraged to live in fear and sacrifice their freedom and their children's education to unnecessary lockdowns and school closures.

Globalist corporatists and Marxists share in having no national loyalties. They favor one-party government rule and managed economies, which reduce economic uncertainties (Heather and Rapley 2023). Ultimately, their desired goal is to replace national governance with planetary governance that benefits corporate elites. The biggest winner on the world stage will be China, as it plans to replace the US as the world's hegemonic power by 2030 and is well on its way to doing so thanks to the assistance of the Biden administration and its progressive policies, which are destroying America's economy, its borders, and its morality.

The history of how China came to be a world power is worth reviewing. In 1979, the World Economic Forum played a major role in strategizing China's transformation from a communist country to one with a managed capitalist economy. The result was hugely successful from an economic perspective, and it won China the admiration of many globalist technocrats. A young Justin Trudeau commented that he was impressed that China's "basic dictatorship is allowing them to actually turn their economy around on a dime," and Klaus Schwab remarked that China would become a "role model for many countries" (Bruner 2023, 255).

The cooperation between corporations, the Biden Administration, and the Chinese Communist Party (CCP) is noteworthy. That the Biden family managed to reap millions of dollars from Chinese firms linked to the CCP, very possibly for favorable policy treatment in return, is routinely glossed over by progressives and Democratic party apparatchiks. But it's not just the Biden family. As investigative journalist Sean Bruner remarks, concerning events surrounding the coronavirus pandemic:

> The evidence that capitalist Controligarchs were in bed with the Chinese Communists was everywhere. It was not merely that they had both covered up the coronavirus origins—that was to be expected. It was that the entire Western establishment— from Big Tech to Big Academia to Big Finance to Big Media, to especially Big Pharma and even its personification, Dr. Anthony Fauci, who claimed to embody science itself—endorsed the CCP's coverup. Everyone from Klaus Schwab to billionaires such as Bill Gates was praising the authoritarian lockdowns happening in China. They seemed to love the tyrannical CCP system (Bruner 2023, 261).

Hayek (1988) argued that the moral underpinnings required to govern markets successfully are lost in a managed economy. While capitalist markets are driven by self-interest, they fail when honesty and fairness are ignored, as they were during the global financial crisis of 2008. Like other successful human transactions, capitalism requires trust; when it is lost and transactions are based solely on self-interest, economic systems become corrupt and fail. Recognizing the causes and results of corruption, the Hebrew Bible insists that merchants must transact business honestly because not to do so is equivalent to theft. As Deuteronomy 25:15–16 (ESV) states, "A full and fair weight you shall have, a full and fair measure you shall have, that your days may be long in the land that the Lord your God is giving you. For all who do such things, all who act dishonestly, are an abomination to the Lord your God."

When capitalism is underpinned by the Judeo-Christian ethic, people prosper. But this is not the case today.

Woke Capitalists

In the past, when corporations grew large and greedy, as they did in America during the Gilded Age at the turn of the nineteenth century, government exercised its power to promote fair trade by breaking up monopolies. But that strategy is rarely considered today. Instead, government colludes with global corporations to further the latter's expansion at the expense of small businesses and the middle class, in return for political contributions and graft.

As the quotation at the beginning of this chapter suggests, greed and corruption are not new. Civilizations in the past have declined as a result of them. America will not survive as the world's preeminent economic power in the face of globalist collusion with progressive politicians, rampant corruption, and efforts to undermine its position relative to Communist China. It will not flourish when citizens are consistently lied to by a news media that is owned and controlled by global corporations.

The sociopathic narcissism of America's elites—their greed, pride, and lust for power—are all antithetical to religious values and to the values that America was founded on.[2] The Judeo-Christian ethic insists that man must consider the interests of others. It insists that business be conducted ethically, that judges not take bribes or be unduly influenced by either wealth or the lack of it, and that rulers act righteously and wield power for the benefit of those they serve. In the past, elites embraced the concept of *noblesse oblige*, but that is no longer the case. Instead, corruption is now rampant, often visible, and widely sanctioned by the progressive ruling class. Uprooting corruption requires the cooperation of government, institutions, and citizenry; when they are mired in it together, the demise of a free society is all but guaranteed.

Corruption is a sign of moral decay. It severs the relationship between God and man, the bonds between men, and perhaps most

---

[2] The seven cardinal sins are pride, greed, gluttony, sloth, envy, lust, and wrath.

critically the relationship of man to himself. Corruption is contagious, and it spreads like a miasma through society. Unfortunately, it has been little improved by human "progress." Despite the Panglossian musings of progressives such as Harvard psychologist Steven Pinker, who argues that man has grown more civilized with time, the truth is that greed, sexual desire, and the lust for power have not changed, and they are alive and well in America today. Americans are addicted to their possessions, pleasures, and comforts, and new technologies have not satiated their desires; instead, they have led them into even greater excesses.

Pinker's conclusions are in line with what most people today assume about "progress"—and with the progressives' promotion of progress as an end in itself. In contrast, recall early twentieth-century Christian social critic G. K. Chesterton, who argued that the assessment of progress must involve a decision as to what is "good," and insisted that the evaluation of technological progress should include consideration of whether it is likely to promote well-being for the individual and society. But Chesterton's belief that progress should be judged on the basis of traditional religion and morality—on the "old moral standards"—is precisely the principle that the Godless Crusade is bent on tearing up, root and branch. Progressivism and the Judeo-Christian ethic are incompatible.

CHAPTER 13

Lies My Culture Told Me

A harmful truth is better than a useful lie.

—THOMAS MANN

A lie would have no sense unless the truth were felt dangerous.

—ALFRED ADLER

LIKE FISH THAT EXIST IN A WATERY MEDIUM without recognizing the possibility of a nonaqueous world, man is immersed in the ambient culture of his time. And much of the present culture is the result of propaganda based on the flawed ideology of society's elites and designed to mislead the public. But as the film *The Matrix* suggests, one can take the "red pill" and penetrate misleading ideas to arrive at the truth. The Judeo-Christian traditions and the ancient philosophers both viewed the truth as the highest value and recognized that without it, societies lapse into dystopias. Postmodern thought has promoted the nihilistic idea that there is no universal truth—that individuals are free to choose whatever truth suits them. Even if that were theoretically the case, this mindset is incompatible with the values necessary to maintain a viable society. The claims made by progressives are destabilizing America; it is possible to recognize that and reject them.

Progressive perspectives on education, feminism, race, and sex have become sacred cows in our culture, making it difficult to discuss these topics without being criticized as opposing the American ideal of freedom. But the current notion of freedom is skewed, and virtually every idea that emanates from it is twisted as well. In the past, individual freedom was limited by the Judeo-Christian ethic, which acknowledged the authority of a power greater than the individual and insisted on the need to consider the welfare of others. Today, the notion of moral authority is under attack, and in its absence, freedom devolves into chaos. It is critical to recognize that those who are promoting progressive ideas are positioned to remain immune from their consequences. Their lives are largely unscathed by the absurdities of "woke" ideas, but much of America is suffering from them. If America is to survive without descending into chaos and class warfare, the current cultural milieu must be reassessed, and values that promote the general welfare of society must be reinstated. What follows is an examination of some of the areas that have suffered from the flawed ideology of progressivism.

Miseducation

The coronavirus epidemic lockdowns forced parents to attend to what their children were being taught in school. They were surprised to learn that children were no longer being taught in a traditional manner but instead were being indoctrinated into progressive ideas and Critical Race Theory. Education prior to the 1960s had focused on reading, math, and history, all presented in a classroom milieu that was generally patriotic. But following the social unrest of the '60s, young political activists entered the teaching profession with the goal of transforming America by indoctrinating young minds into Marxist ideas (Bork 2003). Rusty Reno has argued that conservatives are inclined to see what is transpiring in America as the result of a Marxist plot to undo its institutions, and that while such a plot unquestionably exists, there are also other forces in society that are primarily concerned with rejecting any restrictions on individual freedom (Reno 2016). Both movements seek to rid society of its dependence on the Judeo-Christian ethic, a project that ultimately will end in the unraveling of society.

Higher education was the initial target of these activists, and over time they succeeded in convincing universities to abandon the classical Western canon and replace it with courses—including feminist theory, Afro-American studies, queer theory, and other sundry subjects of little intellectual or practical merit—designed to promote identity-based divisions. The goal was to eliminate the influence of the classics by white European males on the culture and to institute a focus on multiculturalism and equity rather than merit—the latter viewed as a Western value that promotes the hierarchical structuring of society (Mac Donald 2023).

The faculties of American universities are currently populated by progressive educators, with few conservatives represented. The diversity of thought on campuses has been sacrificed, and universities have become training grounds for progressive activists who share perspectives on the culture and politics. "Politically correct" speech has become the rule on campuses, and the classical liberal goal of encouraging free speech and discourse has been replaced by targeted censorship.

At the same time, a focus on individual freedom and subjectivity has encouraged students to accept the panoply of imagined gender orientations promoted by the LGBTQ+ community and to reject gender as biologically determined. As psychologist Jean Twenge writes:

> These new attitudes around gender are the logical conclusion of rising individualism in at least two different ways. First, Gen Z's

gender fluidity takes previous decades'"different is good" and "be who you are" attitudes around race and LGB identification and applies them to gender identity. If people are all unique then it follows that gender is an individual choice—and perhaps people should not be limited to just two choices.... Second, Gen Z's attitudes put a new twist on the individualism of the post-1960s gender equality revolution which argued that being male or female should not restrict opportunities (Twenge 2023, 350).

The university has become a breeding ground for narcissism and a place where objective truth is routinely denied.

One might expect progressive education to be limited to politically sympathetic urban areas, but it is not. Instead, because of the outsized influence of the progressive teachers' unions and training institutes, progressive educators are now everywhere, and virtually no part of America has been spared their influence. Students and parents are hard-pressed to identify a university or college in America where "woke" ideas do not dominate the campus milieu.

But while the progressive transformation of higher education has been recognized for some time, parents were surprised to discover that "woke" ideas were also being taught to grade-school students from kindergarten up. Religious traditions have long known that early education is key to sculpting future adult beliefs. Ignatius of Loyola, the founder of the Jesuits, famously remarked, "Give me a child until he is seven, and I will give you the man." In this vein, the progressive philosopher-educator John Dewey argued that children should be educated by the state so they will grow into citizens holding beliefs that the government approves of, and it is to this end that progressive grade schoolteachers have been indoctrinating young minds. The progressive teachers' unions and local and federal governments insist that children be more responsive to the state than to their families, and oppose sharing school curricula with parents who might disapprove of what their children are being taught and offer up resistance.

Domestic Terrorists

That is exactly what happened in Virginia in 2021. When parents began to recognize that their children were being indoctrinated into Critical Race Theory and early sex education, many objected and protested. In Loudoun County, the Department of Justice, with the assistance of the FBI, sought to have protesting parents labeled "domestic terrorists" at the behest of the teachers' unions in an effort to stifle their protests. Despite that, disgruntled parents fought back and were successful in removing the local school board, and Virginians elected a new conservative governor who had campaigned on reversing what was transpiring in the public schools.

Most progressive activists are nonviolent; they seek to transform society through propaganda and by exerting pressure to conform. The majority of supporters of progressive ideology are neither ideologues nor activists; rather, they are what Lenin termed "useful idiots" who simply accept the lies that the progressive media tell them and seek to avoid confrontation. They passively accept, without ever questioning the veracity of these claims, that America is an oppressive "systemically racist" nation and that those who adhere to religious values are "bigots." They accept that criticizing the antisocial behavior of minorities or questioning the gender of mentally ill transexuals is never permitted. The "useful idiot" is a product of the strategic "dumbing down" of Americans and widespread social pressure to achieve conformity. They are often referred to by politicians as "low-information" voters, and they make up a substantial number of the progressive base. As a Wikipedia article on "low-information voters" suggests:

> A 1992 study found that in the absence of other information, voters used candidates' physical attractiveness to draw inferences about their personal qualities and political ideology. A study...found that low-information voters tend to assume female and black candidates are more liberal than male and

white candidates of the same party. A 2003 study...found that the placement of candidates' names on the ballot was a point of influence for low-information voters. An analysis...found that less-informed voters were significantly more likely to vote for incumbents accused of corruption than were their better-informed counterparts, presumably because they did not know about the allegations.

While it is hard to believe, a substantial number of Americans do not know that 1) Trump did not collude with Russia to win the 2016 election; 2) there is overwhelming evidence that Joe Biden and his family engaged in an influence peddling operation for years; 3) over eight million aliens crossed the border since Joe Biden was elected; 4) America has been funding Iran, the world's greatest sponsor of terrorism; 5) the war in Ukraine is unwinnable; 6) crime is on the rise in most urban areas governed by progressive mayors; 7) there is no nationwide abortion "ban." These voters cannot be expected to respond to these issues unless they are properly informed—and the propaganda driven media is disinclined to inform them.

As a result of progressive education and parenting, America's youth have become a disruptive force in society. Like students in the past, they are idealistic and inclined to protest perceived injustices, but they are more self-absorbed, less knowledgeable, more focused on unrestricted freedoms, and less religiously observant than in the past. For at least two generations, parents—too distracted to recognize what has been transpiring around them—have ignored what their children were being taught at school. Unfortunately, there is no greater threat to America's future than the progressive indoctrination of its youth.

I'll Never Grow Up

In the past, liberal youth were expected to moderate their naïve idealism when confronted with adult obligations. Winston Churchill is credited with saying, "If you're not a liberal when you're twenty-five, you have no heart. If you're not a conservative by the time you're thirty-five, you have no brain." But the cumulative effects of propaganda on young minds virtually guarantee that America's youth will not easily shed their progressive ideas, especially as more are shunning the responsibilities that traditionally were part of adult life (Twenge 2023). Yet America cannot afford to tolerate the entitled emotional outbursts and destructive behaviors of its youth who wreaked havoc during the 2020 George Floyd riots and following the Supreme Court's *Dobbs* decision and the terrorist attacks on Israel. Society cannot continue to permit "woke" students to obstruct the affairs of daily life or of government whenever they object to a political decision or an election result. Many young people see protests as amusing distractions from everyday life, and they are encouraged by activist teachers to "take to the streets" to protest. But disrupting society is not a game, and if society is to avoid devolving into anarchy, there must be consequences for bad behaviors. Parents need to appreciate that it is in no one's best interest—not theirs, their children's, or society's—to tolerate constant threats of violence from ill-behaved, entitled children. Unless this behavior is confronted and appropriately punished, the future of America is bleak. Those who object, by insisting that these protests are protected by the First Amendment, are wrong. When protests grow violent and threaten a nation's stability, they must be quelled.

The prospect of confronting and punishing one's children holds little appeal for most parents, especially those who have been taught to eschew punishment as "regressive." But these ideas about child-rearing are wrong. The entitled behavior of today's youth can be traced to parents who have consistently enabled bad behaviors in an effort to avoid meting out punishment. Reasoning with children is a luxury that elites can afford, but the rest of society is suffering from the unwillingness to set limits and enforce punishments. Progressive pedagogy has failed to produce productive citizens and should be rejected as a failed experiment, with thought given as to how to deprogram America's youth from the insidious indoctrination they have received.

Preemptive Surrender

God and religion are the traditional opposition of the Left. This is true for the entire spectrum of liberalism, from its inception in the Enlightenment to its current neoliberal, progressive, Marxist, and "woke" incarnations. America's spiritual leaders are naïve in believing that they can accommodate progressive ideas while maintaining the core tenets of religious dogma. Today many leaders in churches and synagogues have abandoned core beliefs and instead chosen to embrace progressive "social justice" as the basis of their "religious" practices. But progressivism today is a secularizing movement opposed to religious beliefs even when they may appear to share areas of overlap, as the ultimate goal of progressivism is the elimination of God and religion from society.

Those American church and synagogue leaders who believe that embracing progressive ideas will bring more congregants into the fold are misguided; there is no evidence this has been the case (Miles 2021). Pope Francis, unlike his predecessor, Benedict XVI, has consistently aligned himself with progressive causes, appearing to believe that diversity, equity, and inclusion are core Christian values. Francis has called on Catholics to embrace a greater role in the Church for women, approved blessing those in same-sex unions, and criticized dissenting conservative clerics and removed them from their positions. This has led conservative Catholics to question whether he has confused Christianity with socialism, as his positions appear to contradict centuries of Catholic dogma. As political philosopher Daniel Mahoney suggests:

> When progressivists, whether Christian or secular, equate dogmatic egalitarianism, a "social justice" that is coextensive with

collectivism, and glib talk about achieving "global fraternity" with the demands of the Gospel, they engage in the sloppy thinking and lazy sentimentality that characterizes the softer forms of the religion of Humanity. Sadly, we've come to expect such talk from bishops and clerics who barely speak of Jesus Christ, who confuse good intentions with good judgements and who are more concerned with "social justice" and "global fraternity" than the salvation of souls. No matter who espouses it, the religion of Humanity is a corrupting falsification of true faith and reason. The fact that many believe it is compatible or even co-extensive with Christianity is a sign of the depth of the crisis that confronts us in and outside the Church (Manent 2022, viii).

Unfortunately, this problem is not limited to the Catholic Church. The mainline Protestant churches and Reform synagogues routinely support progressive ideas at the expense of normative religious ideas. Having abandoned traditional beliefs and practices, they are vulnerable to the erosive antireligious influences of progressivism. While some imagine there can be a syncretism between religion and progressive ideas, as currently configured the latter are incompatible with belief in God. If this trend is not reversed, it is likely that only traditional orthodox modes of belief will survive, while "reform" movements will be absorbed by an atheistic secular humanism.

Believing the Lies

Americans are a trusting people who find it hard to believe that they are being lied to routinely and purposefully by institutions they have been taught to trust. They dismiss the possibility that the American mainstream news media is currently replete with journalists who are more indebted to the agendas of their corporate masters than they are interested in reporting facts. But the truth is that today many journalists have been trained as political activists and view it as their proper role to support progressive narratives depicting the policies of the ruling elites favorably. They fill the airwaves with lies of commission and of omission, all the while disingenuously insisting that they are impartial purveyors of "facts."

This is obviously not the case, as, when examined, the "facts" they report have repeatedly proved to be false—virtually always in a direction that benefits progressive causes and undermines those of conservatives. According to a 2022 Pew Research Center poll, "More than nine-in-ten journalists surveyed (94%) say made-up news and information is a significant problem in America today, with 71% identifying it as a very big problem and 23% seeing it as a moderately big problem; 6% say it is a small problem or not a problem at all" (Gottfried et al. 2022).

Mainstream journalism reports falsehoods daily. Journalists from the once prestigious *New York Times* have received Pulitzer Prizes for their false reporting[1] yet have refused to retract their errors or to return the prizes. Instead, the progressive media routinely denounces politically inconvenient truths as "misinformation" and seeks to censor the truth—a far cry from how journalists in the past viewed their role of "speaking truth to power," corruption, and abuse. In recent years journalists have misled the public concerning the origins of Covid-19, the efficacy of masks and vaccinations, the collusion of President Trump with the Russians, the provenance of Hunter Biden's laptop, and the general tenor of the Biden administration, to name but a few stories.

Journalism schools and other professional training institutions, including medical and law schools, currently consider it to be their purpose to train progressive social activists. Merit and professional competence are deemed less important—and even frequently denigrated as signs of "white privilege" that detract from the goals of diversity, equity, and inclusion (Kradin 2022; Mac Donald 2023).

---

[1] Any lingering doubts concerning the facts of the Trump collusion reporting were dispelled by the report of Special Counsel John Durham in 2023. He concluded that it had been a hoax perpetrated by the Clinton campaign with the assistance of the FBI and the media.

Fluent in Newspeak

Progressives have corrupted the English language to further their goals and to silence opposition. They modify words with the goal of transforming public opinion. Cognitive psychologists have long recognized that modifying language affects how people think and feel (Beck and Beck 2011). New progressive-friendly terms are frequently introduced into the public domain, and pressures are then exerted to have them adopted by the public. Once this has occurred, it can be difficult to reverse the untoward effects, as Orwell described in his description of Newspeak (Orwell 1983). When one adopts terms like "systemic racism," or refers to illegal aliens as "undocumented migrants," or uses "preferred pronouns," one has surrendered to collective lies and is assisting in the corruption of truth.

Armed with the neo-Marxist notion of "social justice," progressive ideologues stoke racial divisions for political gain by encouraging society to define women, homosexuals, transexuals, the mentally ill, and the physically disabled, as "oppressed," and by pushing the notion of "intersectionality"—that is, overlapping sectors of oppression—to promote victimhood as a desirable goal (Ramaswamy 2022). By attacking "white privilege" and promoting equity of outcomes (in contrast to equality under the law), they deny the importance of merit and lower the standards of society (Mac Donald 2023).

When the US Supreme Court recently ruled that affirmative action in university admissions was racist and unconstitutional, progressive politicians sharply criticized the justices and accused them of participating in a "rogue court." Indeed, progressives have decided that the democratic legislative process is too slow and burdensome, and therefore they increasingly rely on progressive-friendly courts to accomplish their goals via lawfare. The current conservative majority on the Supreme Court has repeatedly been criticized by progressives for standing in the way of "progress" by its upholding of the US Constitution.

Diversity Is Our Weakness

The notions of diversity and inclusiveness were first widely promulgated in antiquity by Alexander the Great as part of an enlightened vision for his new empire. Today, the idea that diversity is a public "good" is rarely seriously questioned in progressive society (MacDonald 2018). It is simply assumed that we are all enriched by interacting with as many different types of people as possible. But what is the evidence to support this claim? Might the cohesiveness of a society suffer from diversity?

America's Founders were concerned that factionalism might impede the ability to govern the new nation. In the *Federalist Papers,* James Madison favored limited diversity as a bulwark against the "tyranny of the majority," but he feared that excessive diversity might result in problematic divisions and preclude national coherence (Wood 1990). Ultimately, the Founders opted for a republic with limited diversity, but they could not have imagined the diverse interests that are currently vying for representation in America. It stands to reason that it will be difficult to reach consensus in a country composed of groups with many divergent interests. This is especially true if these groups are being encouraged, as they currently are by progressives, to maintain their identity rather than to assimilate the dominant values of the country. Progressives are not interested in making America more "interesting," they are intent on destroying its social fabric as too "restrictive."

Fostering the identity of groups diminishes the affective bonds between people and leads to heightened factional tensions, exactly what the Founders feared. As Madison wrote in *Federalist* 10: "By a faction, I understand a number of citizens, whether amounting to a majority or a minority of the whole, who are united and actuated by some common impulse of passion, or of interest, adverse to the rights of other citizens, or to the permanent and aggregate interests of the community. There are two methods of curing the mischiefs of faction: the one, by removing its causes; the other, by controlling its effects."

Factionalism makes it hard to "love your neighbor," the cardinal tenet of the Judeo-Christian ethic, and not incidentally the basis of a cohesive society. There is no compelling evidence that diversity promotes tolerance. Instead, it denies the natural inclination of individuals to bond with those with whom they share kinship bonds and common values. Adages like "birds of a feather flock together" are neither bigoted nor "racist"; instead, they recognize deep and likely biologically determined truths about human nature that should not be ignored. As Rabbi Jonathan Sacks points out in *Morality*: "Sharing a common identity builds support for inclusion; bringing differences of ethnic and religious identity to the fore evokes the very exclusionary reactions it is meant to avoid. Identity politics deepens the fragmentation caused by multiculturalism, adding to it not just culture and ethnicity but also other forms of identity based on gender and sexual orientation. There is a real danger here of the splitting of society into self-segregating, noncommunicating ghettos" (Sacks 2020, 137).

Efforts at creating harmonious relationships between distinct groups by political enactment are doomed to fail, as was demonstrated when a few years after the dictator of Yugoslavia died, the once artificially unified ethnically and religiously diverse country dissolved into bloody civil war.

What's a Racist? Someone Winning an Argument with a Progressive

"Woke" ideologues cynically manipulate racial antagonisms for political purposes. The politics of black identity has been percolating in society since the 1960s. It is based on Afro-pessimism, which holds that blacks can never expect to assimilate into American culture because of its "systemic racism"; consequently, black identity can only be safeguarded by remaining separate from white society, in what amounts to neo-segregation.

According to Critical Race Theory (CRT), all issues in society are to be interpreted "structurally," based on the "oppressive" nature of "whiteness." From this unquestionably racist point of view, whites are expected to acknowledge and apologize for their "privilege," but can do nothing to change it. Blacks are to be accorded considerations not afforded to others in society, Asians, for example, who are also considered to be "white," and therefore to share responsibility for the wrongs of slavery and "white oppression." "White" is merely a euphemism for anyone who achieves success in America's merit-based capitalist society. That talent and hard work might explain discrepancies in outcome is dismissed as "racist" because of the obvious inequity of that conclusion.

Progressives insist on affirmative action policies in education and the workplace with no regard for the adverse effects these policies have historically had on blacks. As the black economist and social critic Thomas Sowell (1975) has suggested, accepting less-qualified black students to Ivy League universities, only to have them fail to maintain expected standards and be forced to drop out, is neither commonsensical nor compassionate, particularly as the same students likely would have fared better at less prestigious schools where they would not have been forced to compete with intellectual elites.

"Woke" activists argue for reparations for the wrongs of slavery while discounting the substantial advances in civil rights over the last 150 years. They dismiss both the problems of determining who historically was wronged by slavery and the negative feelings that such policies inspire. Should a black person who immigrated to America from Ghana in the 1990s receive reparations for the wrongs of American slavery that ended in 1865? Should a white American whose family immigrated to New York from Eastern Europe in the early twentieth century be forced to pay those reparations? No rational person would think so, as those outcomes are unreasonable and unjust. But this is the divisive policy that progressives in "woke" America believe to be justified.

It should be clear to anyone with a sense of fairness and moral clarity that "woke" ideology is perverse, destructive, and antithetical to common sense and religious values. It is irrational, unscientific, and unquestionably racist, as it targets people for criticism and penalties based solely on the color of their skin. It is a flawed ideology and must be repeatedly called out as such. Yet despite all this, many whites in America, motivated by neurotic guilt, accept these "woke" insults to their intelligence and character. "Woke" ideology is so wrongminded that one must conclude that those who promote it and those who accept it share in being morally bankrupt.

The claim that America's legal system is "systemically racist" is irrefutably untrue. Statistics show that blacks are less likely to be killed by police during the commission of a crime than whites (Mac Donald 2016). By falsely claiming rampant bias against blacks by law enforcement, "woke" district attorneys justify their refusal to investigate or prosecute serious crimes when an offender is black. Black repeat offenders who should be serving lengthy jail sentences are allowed to go free, or given inappropriately light sentences, while bail requirements are waived for a host of crimes. Progressive judges arbitrarily rule that crimes committed by blacks are "minor," thereby contributing to society's moral decay. How very different this is from the biblical commandment of Deuteronomy 16:20, which insists that judges be dispassionate: "Justice, justice alone shall you pursue."

What is virtually never reported by the mainstream progressive media is the fact that a disproportionate percentage of the serious crimes in America are perpetrated by blacks, as it apparently contributes to negative stereotypes. But it is true; stereotypes, although overly general, are often earned. Nevertheless, whenever this fact is raised, it is dismissed by progressives as "racist" and as a reactionary effort to restore "white supremacy." Rather than address this fact, the progressive legal system has created a program of biased preferential treatment for criminals based on race, an idea that would be inconceivable in a society guided by the Judeo-Christian ethic. By forgiving black criminal behavior, progressives are putting society at danger, as well as insulating the black community from taking responsibility for its behavior. This is the ugly "racism" of progressive condescension. But race has been the progressives' primary tool in their goal of transforming America, and this approach will continue to be used as long as it is succeeding.

Martin Luther King's argument that America should aspire to becoming a color-blind society is met with hostility by "woke" progressives, as it rejects Afro-pessimism. A lucrative cottage industry has sprung up around promoting racial division, in which whites who deny the accusation of racism are accused of "white fragility" that somehow keeps them from acknowledging the "truth" about their racism. This can be likened to the medieval practice of subjecting "witches" to trial by water—those who floated were confirmed as witches, while those who drowned were cleared of the charge.

The Scientific Explanation

The topic of "racism" is best approached through what is currently known about how the human brain evaluates difference. The notion of unconscious racial bias is valid, but it is also *normal* and cannot be altered. To understand why this is, one must recognize how the human nervous system reacts to difference. The central nervous system is designed to make rapid subliminal distinctions between people and things in order to evaluate them as possible threats. These responses occur automatically and unconsciously within milliseconds. After a brief interval, the reasoning neocortex decides how to respond to perceived differences based on learned experience, and only this part of the response to difference can be learned and reconfigured (Sapolsky 2017). The progressive claim that anyone can be divested of bias is both ungrounded and unsubstantiated.

Consequently, the only response that can justifiably be deemed "racist" is a conscious choice to disadvantage another based on his or her race. No one should be condemned for making distinctions, despite claims to the contrary by opportunistic race hucksters such as Robin DiAngelo (2018) and Ibram X. Kendi (2023). What is unquestionably "racist" is refusing to condemn the defamatory statements made against whites and other groups by "woke" activists. The notion that blacks or other "oppressed" groups cannot be racist is utter nonsense that should be soundly condemned by all decent intelligent people.

Corporations participate in "woke" propaganda either because of misguided belief, out of fear of public criticism by activists, or for financial incentives. In the recent past they have provided financial backing for groups such as Black Lives Matter, an openly Marxist organization that failed to use the huge donations it received following the George Floyd riots of 2020 to benefit the black community in any substantive way, and instead used the funds to buy new homes for its corrupt leaders. Those who work for "woke" corporations are routinely and unjustly forced to accept accusations of "racism" that they know are untrue with little recourse and to undergo "sensitivity" training programs designed to disseminate "woke" propaganda.

Social scientist Charles Murray has spent his career studying ethnographic differences in America in the hope of identifying issues that can be addressed to produce positive change. For his efforts, he has been harshly attacked as a "racist." According to Murray, numerous well-designed studies have repeatedly yielded two findings. The first is that:

> American Whites, Blacks, Latinos, and Asians, *as groups*, have different means and distributions of cognitive ability. The second is that American Whites, Blacks, Latinos, and Asians, *as groups*, have different rates of violent crime. Allegations of systemic racism in policing, education and the workplace cannot be answered without dealing with the reality of group differences.

... The two facts make people excruciatingly uncomfortable. To raise them is to be considered a racist and hateful person. What's more, these facts have been distorted and exploited for malign purposes by racist and hateful people (Murray 2021, x).

These studies have shown that blacks in this country *as a group* have a significantly lower mean intelligence quotient (IQ). Substantial evidence indicates that IQ is the primary predictor of one's ability to succeed academically and at cognitively demanding occupations. Blacks consistently fare less well in these areas compared to whites and Asians, and to a lesser extent to Latinos, again not as individuals but as a *group*.

Ideologically inclined to assume that this deficit *must* be acquired rather than innate, progressives directed efforts at improving the quality of predominantly black schools in the 1970s and '80s, and as a result, IQ scores rose modestly but then leveled off with no additional improvement. This was a disturbing result that progressives have refused to accept, although it does indicate that continuing to throw money at the problem is not likely to solve it.

Progressives simply choose to deny the implications of these studies and accuse Murray of being a "racist" for suggesting the possibility that innate inequalities may exist. Murray acknowledges that there are highly intelligent and competent blacks at all levels of society and notes that America has had a black president and black Supreme Court justices, senators, mayors, and cultural heroes, none of whom could have been promoted to positions of prominence in a genuinely "systemically racist" country. When judged solely on merit, individual blacks succeed to the same extent as others. But *as a group* they do not, and there is no basis for ascribing that result to the persistent negative effects of slavery or Jim Crow. Other groups in society—Irish, Italians, Jews, and so forth—and specifically people of color—Chinese, Vietnamese, and so forth—have suffered traumas in the past but have managed to overcome their effects within a generation or two. The truth is never "racist" or "bigoted," it is simply the truth, and failure to accept it precludes ever doing anything productive about it.

Black Crime

The amount of violent crime perpetrated by blacks is disproportionately higher than that committed by other groups in society. It is spurious to blame this on economic disadvantage, as other groups in America have been poor without having perpetrated an excess of violent crime. Progressive initiatives to transform the legal system to reduce artificially the culpability of black criminals only endangers public safety and enables more crime. Wherever the ill-conceived idea that defunding the police will reduce "bias" against blacks and help control crime has been implemented, crime has increased.

The vast majority of homicides in America today are black-on-black crimes (Masterton 2022). According to Chicago Police Department numbers, in 2022, 3,016 people were shot in 2,441 separate incidents, almost all related to black-on-black crime. But as this does not fit the progressive narrative, these statistics are routinely suppressed by the media. Instead, liberal journalists leap to defend the notion of "systemic racism," despite a lack of evidence; and when the topic of black crime is broached, accusations of "racism" are used to shut down debate. But in a genuinely moral society, as the Hebrew Bible suggests, no group is to be accorded special privileges above another, not blacks, whites, women, men, straights, or LGBTQ+, etc. If justice is to be restored, whites and other groups need to become inured to accusations of "privilege" and "racism" by progressives and vigorously reject these false accusations. It is immoral not to treat people on the basis of their behavior: "To be liberal cannot mean that one condescends to other people. All men are equal, but they should be truly equal—for good and for bad. If a man is good, he is surely good regardless of his origins; if he is bad, he should be handled with equality and labeled evil no matter what or who he is. To do less than that…is racism of the worse kind and will be met by the black man himself with the contempt that it deserves" (Kahane 1972, 102).

The Black Family

Progressives are loath to acknowledge that the breakdown of the nuclear family, in large measure instigated by progressive welfare programs, has succeeded in eroding the moral fabric of the black community and is actively contributing to its dysfunction. Today fewer than 40 percent of black households include a father (Ross 2018). Eroding family values is part of the progressive strategy to diminish the relevance of the Judeo-Christian ethic, which finds its optimal expression in the nuclear family. In *How the West Really Lost God*, social critic Mary Eberstadt (2022) provides evidence that disruption of the nuclear family has also resulted in diminished religious affiliation. She argues that religion and family are codependent variables and that a decline in one necessarily results in a decline in the other. The absence of fathers, the instability of the nuclear family due to divorce, cohabitation outside of marriage, and diminished childbearing have all been linked to reduced religious participation, and all are common within the black community.

In the past, black churches played an important role in stabilizing the black community. The Reverend Martin Luther King Jr. was the pastor of a Baptist Church, and black churches were at the forefront of the Civil Rights Movement. According to the Pew Research Center, 47 percent of blacks attend church at least once weekly, a significantly higher percentage than the 36 percent of whites. But among urban black youth, where single-parent households, gang membership, and hip-hop culture are prevalent, these numbers are reversed, and 75 percent of black millennials no longer attend church, compared to 65 percent of whites.

America's white mainline churches contribute to the problems of the black community by adopting ill-conceived "compassionate" stances. Churches that drape themselves in Black Lives Matter banners to signal virtue benefit nobody. In fact, it is condescending and racist to do so. Serious problems call for serious solutions, not window dressing, and it is never compassionate to allow them to fester unaddressed. Churches must learn this lesson if organized religion is to have a viable future in America.

The truth is that virtue-signaling whites born after 1960 have likely never witnessed brutal racism and must be encouraged to stop displaying their ignorance by decrying imaginary "racism." America's youth need to learn the true history of race in America, not the skewed or fabricated "woke" version. There was slavery and Jim Crow in America, but there was also a Civil War and a Civil Rights Movement, and no other country can claim that honor. Prior to the Obama administration, most Americans believed rightly that race was a disappearing issue in America. And today, the only active and pernicious form of racism in America is progressivism's condescension toward blacks and other peoples of color. Unfortunately, when conservative blacks attempt to speak the truth about racism in America or address what ails the black community, they are routinely denounced as Uncle Toms, and even as "white supremacists" by black race-baiting hucksters and white progressives who benefit from maintaining the status quo.

Progressive Democrats cynically manipulate the black community in order to guarantee its vote in elections but do nothing to improve the situation of that community. "Afro-pessimism" based on an immutable identity as an "oppressed" group may have short-term political benefits for progressives, but it is an untenable long-term strategy. If blacks are to succeed in America, they will need to abandon the politics of grievance, reject the enervating assistance of progressive Democrat government, and take responsibility for their own lives. Whites in turn must stop accepting the accusation of racism and cease trying to appease those blacks who seek to intimidate them. Whites should reconsider the notion of multiculturalism and proudly embrace the West for its role in creating philosophy, mathematics, science, art, and history that we have all benefited from, rather than emulating degenerate cultural expressions such as hip-hop.

They're Not Sending Their Best

America is a nation of laws, and when they are not enforced, chaos ensues. Lawlessness has been encouraged by progressives, and the compassionate stance of the Judeo-Christian ethic has cynically been used to justify it. Consider the following statement by Nancy Pelosi, the progressive former Democratic Speaker of the House of Representatives, as to why Christians should support unlimited illegal migration through the southern border.

According to the *Catholic World Report*, Pelosi urged Catholic bishops "to tell people in the pews that opening the borders 'is a manifestation of our living the gospels.' Our patron saint of San Francisco, St. Francis of Assisi, said, "Preach the gospel. Sometimes use words." We need the words to be said because it isn't being picked up just automatically." The same article pointed out that "Pelosi, who claims to be a 'good Catholic,' is at odds with much of the dogma of the Roman Catholic church, including its stand on abortion, and has been denied communion by the Archbishop of San Francisco because of her anti-Catholic stances" (Higgins 2011).

This argument from the former Speaker is a good example of the strategy of eliciting guilt that is often used by progressive politicians to justify lawlessness and to stifle honest opposition.

Despite what some prominent progressives claim, it is not possible to believe in God *and* support progressivism, as their goals are antithetical. When Joe Biden and Nancy Pelosi proudly refer to their observance of Roman Catholicism, they are engaging in political theater, even if they choose not to recognize it. Like the Devil, progressives will quote scripture when it furthers their goals, while at the same time criticizing Christians for their "antiquated" retrograde beliefs. In a recent example of such hypocrisy, Congresswoman

Alexandria Ocasio-Cortez, a self-described socialist, criticized a young Christian ex-Marine who had intervened to stop a black felon from committing a crime on a New York subway, insisting that he needed to "read his Bible!" as, according to her, he lacked Christian compassion.

The recent influx of immigrants at the southern border amounts to nothing less than an invasion inspired by the progressive Biden administration for political advantage. It has led to increased crime, illegal drug importation, the death of hundreds of thousands of Americans from fentanyl, and the heightened risk of terrorist attacks. The apparent plan is to import an immigrant underclass that will support the needs of America's elites, serve as a source of cheap labor for businesses, and provide a new voter bloc for the Democratic Party, as part of the latter's quest to remain in power in perpetuity. Criticisms of this strategy are invariably dismissed as right-wing "conspiracy theories." But whatever the rationale for this policy might be, what is certain is that no country can exist without borders.

Progressives show no genuine interest in improving the lives of these aliens. When immigrants enter the country legally and apply for citizenship, they must undergo a process that includes learning the English language and how the American government works. They must provide evidence that they are prepared to work and will not be financially dependent on the state. When they enter America illegally by seeking asylum—falsely, in over 80 percent of cases—they bypass these critical steps and as a consequence are relegated to work at low-paying jobs with little future opportunity for advancement. As a result, they become a permanent underclass fated to mow the lawns and clean the houses of America's elites in perpetuity. The progressive Democrats' immigration policy is nothing less than a soft form of politically sanctioned slavery.

Compounding the problem of massive illegal immigration is the establishment of sanctuary cities by progressives who refuse to assist law enforcement in returning criminal illegals to their countries of origin. These city governments ignore crimes committed by aliens and put law-abiding American citizens at risk. But when migrants began to pour into sanctuary New York City, its mayor, Eric Adams, insisted that the Biden administration close the border because the city could not afford the economic burden of supporting them. When immigrants were transported to the wealthy progressive sanctuary enclave of Martha's Vineyard, the elite residents called in the US Army to remove them, a response emblematic of their virtue-signaling hypocrisy.

Sex Matters

Religious morality calls for limits on sexual "freedom." Judaism encourages sex for procreative purposes and places no proscriptions on sexual behaviors within marriage. Abortion is permitted only if a pregnancy endangers a woman's life. As the Law in Tohoroth indicates, "If a woman is in hard labor (and her life cannot otherwise be saved), one cuts up the child within her womb and extracts it member by member, because her life comes before that of the child. But if the greater part (or the head) was delivered, one may not touch it, for one may not set aside one person's life for the sake of another." Jewish Law was conceived when infant mortality was high, and it does not attribute all the benefits of personhood to a full-term infant until it has survived a month outside the womb (Schenker 2008).

Christianity has a less favorable perspective on human sexuality, in part because of Gnostic influences that denigrated the "fleshy" body and the physical world. Paul recognized the need to marry but thought it preferable to remain celibate while awaiting the imminent arrival of the Kingdom of God. Contraception and abortion are both proscribed by Roman Catholicism, which holds that life begins at conception. Protestant attitudes toward contraception and abortion, which vary with the many Protestant denominations, cannot be rehearsed here, but in general they are more lenient than those of Catholicism.

In general, the Judeo-Christian traditions discourage sexual activity outside of marriage. They reject homosexual behavior and do not condone same-sex marriages. There is no notion of subjective gender, and transgenderism is viewed as unnatural and not considered to be an option.

The modern history of homosexuality is complex. Until the late twentieth century, the public's opinion of homosexuality paralleled that of the Judeo-Christian religious traditions. In 1952, when the American Psychiatric Association published its first *Diagnostic and Statistical Manual of Mental Disorders* (DSM), homosexuality was listed as a mental disorder. However, that decision was soon criticized by progressive mental health professionals. The American Psychiatric Association stopped listing homosexuality as a mental disorder in 1973, stating that "homosexuality per se implies no impairment in judgment, stability, reliability, or general social or vocational capabilities" (Davies 2017). The American Psychological Association adopted the same position in 1975 and urged mental health professionals to combat the "stigma" of mental illness associated with homosexual orientation. Increasingly, homosexuals were portrayed as a marginalized "oppressed" group that had been wrongly discriminated against (Mac Donald 2023). The Royal College of Psychiatrists in the United Kingdom wrote:

> There is now a large body of research evidence that indicates that being gay, lesbian, or bisexual is compatible with normal mental health and social adjustment. However, the experiences of discrimination in society and possible rejection by friends, families, and others, such as employers, means that some LGB people experience a greater than expected prevalence of mental health difficulties and substance misuse problems. Although there have been claims by conservative political groups in the USA that this higher prevalence of mental health difficulties is confirmation that homosexuality is itself a mental disorder,

there is no evidence whatever to substantiate such a claim (Royal College of Psychiatrists 2014).

But reading between the lines of the Royal College's statement, one detects a tacit admission that homosexuals do exhibit an increased incidence of mental health issues, including drug addiction. As is their inclination, progressives attribute this to societal stigma, which allows homosexuals to be framed as an "oppressed" group. The possibility that mental disturbances may inhere in the homosexual personality is dismissed as inconvenient. Rather, critics are disparaged as members of "conservative political groups"—a euphemism for Republicans, conservative Catholics, Evangelical Protestants, and Orthodox Jews. Because of the pressure from progressives and gay activists, those who voice concerns about homosexuality are condemned as dangers to modern "compassionate" society and to the freedom of the individual to choose his or her sexual orientation.

The secular mental health profession has been aligned with the progressive movement since its inception. So it should have come as no surprise when it ruled that homosexuality was no longer a mental disorder, but the science underlying its decision was at best vague. Indeed, the DSM conferences that determine what is a mental disorder are as much culturally and politically motivated as they are scientifically motivated.

Data indicate that Task Force votes played a central role in the making of DSM-III, from establishing diagnostic criteria and diagnostic definitions to settling questions about the inclusion or removal of diagnostic categories.... While the APA represented DSM-III, and the return to descriptive psychiatry it inaugurated, as a triumph of *empirically based decision-making, the evidence presented here fails to support that view.* Since the DSM is a cumulative project, and as DSM-III lives on through subsequent editions, this paper calls for a more socio-historically informed understanding of DSM's construction to be deployed in how the DSM is taught and implemented in training and clinical settings (Davies 2017; emphasis in the original).

Indeed, like so many stances taken by our institutions these days, the decisions of the American Psychiatric and the American Psychological Associations are less scientific findings than they are statements of progressive ideological bias (Mac Donald 2023).

No one knows what causes homosexuality (Sheldon et al. 2007). Studies suggest that it typically occurs in a small percentage of men and women, but whether it is genetically determined, environmentally driven, or a combination of both is uncertain. However, it is noteworthy that the same mental health professionals who insist that there is no such thing as a biological man or woman accept that homosexuality is biologically determined. The hypocrisy of that position should be obvious.

In the past, one of the concerns with homosexual behavior was a propensity for promiscuity. This became a public health concern during the AIDS epidemic of the 1980s. But progressives argued that many homosexuals were engaged in monogamous relationships and that the claims of promiscuous behavior were greatly exaggerated. While some homosexuals do enter stable monogamous relationships—and in 2015 they were given the right to marry legally—evidence suggests that homosexuals typically have difficulties with monogamy. According to a 2013 article in *Slate*:

> The dirty little secret about gay marriage: Most gay couples are not monogamous.... The thorny part of the gay marriage experiment is sex, and more precisely, monogamous sex. Mundy writes about an old study from the '80s that found that gay couples were extremely likely to have had sex outside their relationship—82 percent did. That was before AIDS and the great matrimony craze in the gay community. She also tells the story of Dan Savage, who started out wanting to be monogamous until he and his partner had kids, and then they loosened up on

that in order to make their union last. "Monogamish" is what he calls his new model. But as Mundy asks, can anyone out there imagine a husband proposing that same deal to his pregnant wife.... A long *Gawker* study last week explored this problem in greater detail. In the fight for marriage equality, the gay rights movement has put forth couples that look like straight ones, together forever, loyal, sharing assets. But what no one wants to talk about is that they don't necessarily represent the norm: "The *Gay Couples Study* out of San Francisco State University— which, in following over 500 gay couples over many years is the largest ongoing study of its kind—has found that about half of all couples have sex with someone other than their partner, with their *partner knowing*" (Rosin 2013; emphasis in the original).

Of course, it can be argued that extramarital affairs are also common among heterosexuals, but what is unusual is that homosexual affairs appear to be sanctioned by both partners, which suggests that promiscuity inheres to the culture of homosexuality and is accepted as such. It is impossible to reconcile homosexuality with the morality of the normative Judeo-Christian traditions, and there are good reasons why religious leaders frown on homosexuality.

The book of Genesis commands man to "be fruitful and multiply" as part of nature's plan. Homosexuality obviously falls outside that plan. Homosexual behaviors were commonplace in pagan culture, and monotheistic religion sought to discourage them. But progressives no longer place credence on divine commands or nature. They are not content that homosexuality has been destigmatized and legally sanctioned; instead, they insist that Americans "celebrate" homosexuality, as well as other variant sexualities, including transvestism, transgenderism, and transhumanism, as part of their effort at divesting America of traditional religious values.

Not very long ago, most Americans would not have accepted homosexuality as "normal" behavior. Even Barack Obama expressed objections to the idea of homosexual marriage and to homosexuals serving in the military. But through a concerted campaign of propaganda and invective against those who continue to express reservations, progressives have managed to convince Americans that homosexuality is not only acceptable but praiseworthy as a manifestation of freedom to do whatever one pleases without restrictive rules.

Today, as a heated controversy concerning the role of transgenderism in society is ongoing, it has become commonplace for its critics to begin their arguments by confessing that while they object to the rise in transgenderism, they do support homosexuality, signaling that they are not biased against all alternative sexual lifestyles. But this is not virtue; rather, it is evidence of the slippery slope that one embarks upon when one accepts any of the notions promulgated by the insidious progressive culture. There is no need to apologize for holding negative views about homosexual behavior—not to do so is simply symptomatic of the continuing surrender to immoral behaviors that are on the rise in America. Although most Americans today will rightly or wrongly tolerate virtually any behavior that takes place in private, they do not wish to be forced to accept public displays of aberrant sexuality as normal or be pressured to embrace them as praiseworthy by LGBTQ+ activists in the community. The question that is not asked is the pragmatic one: Have homosexuality and transgenderism had a positive influence on society? Obviously, some maintain that they have, but others will not agree, and the question should be debated, not shut down. Underlying those questions are more fundamental ones: How is freedom being defined? Are all behaviors acceptable expressions of individual freedom?

One standard response by progressives to criticism of alternative sexuality is that "no one has the right to discourage the love between two people," as though that is a genuine religious value. It is not. Neither Judaism nor Christianity accepts homosexual behavior as an acceptable expression of love. Indeed, even Plato and Aristotle were critical of homosexual relationships between free adult men, and as Plato discussed in his dialogues, homosexual love should not be focused on lust or promiscuity. "Love" that takes place in a group hot tub, or through a hole in a wall, or is intense but short-lived, falls short of how most people would define "love" even in today's increasingly nonjudgmental society. Recently a gay Congressional staffer released a pornographic video of himself engaging in sex in the Capitol building. Although it is only an anecdote, it typifies the degrading effect that homosexuality is having on the culture. Of course, in response to being fired, the staffer complained that he had been "victimized."

Having achieved widespread tolerance of homosexuality within the culture, progressive activists now insist on forcing acceptance of other aberrant sexual behaviors. Private shop owners who have refused to create wedding cakes for homosexual couples have been shunned and sued, rather than being treated as neighbors who simply hold opinions that do not agree with those of the LGBTQ+ community. Churches that advertise a welcoming and accepting stance for practicing homosexuals are not supporting "love," they are simply betraying their own orthodoxies. LGBTQ+ members who currently support the Palestinian cause should be forced to recognize that fundamentalist Islamists have executed and will continue to execute homosexuals without compunction for what they judge as abhorrent behavior.

Misgendered

"Woke" activists have attempted to replace the physiological facts of biological sex with subjective notions of gender. Sex is a universal aspect of nature rooted in biology. It includes the anatomical differences of primary sex organs, endocrinological differences, and other secondary sexual characteristics. In the past, psychological constructs of gender were considered normal when they concorded with biological sex. All other possibilities were judged a departure from reality and therefore delusional.

Postmodern philosophy has parted ways with nature and adopted an abstract perspective that views all reality as a mental construct, allowing concepts to be fully dissociated from nature. Indeed, transgenderism is merely a subset of the larger idea of "transhumanism," which seeks to deconstruct the limits of nature, with the ultimate hope of achieving personal immortality. These abstractions are supported by the narcissistic grandiosity of today's youth, who have been taught to reject limitations and to believe that one can be anything one chooses. These ideas are antithetical to the Judeo-Christian traditions that view nature as God's handiwork and man's capacities as limited by it.

Until recently, psychiatrists knew that gender dysphoria was rare and virtually always accompanied by pathological levels of anxiety, depression, narcissism, borderline personality disorder, and addiction. The mental health profession agreed that persistent gender dysphoria was a serious psychopathology requiring psychotherapy. Only in rare intractable cases were surgical interventions sanctioned to "affirm" a subjective gender choice.

But this position has changed in recent years due to the infiltration of progressive ideology into both the mental health and medical professions (Kradin 2021; Kradin 2022). Professionals have embraced hormonal and "gender-affirming" surgeries as primary treatments, downplayed mental health interventions, and thus discounted the complex psychological problems of the gender-dysphoric patient—which, as in the case of homosexuality, are misattributed to "stigma."

As a result of the insistent call for inclusion and acceptance of transgenderism as a variant of normal gender—and following the road map created by homosexual activists—there has been a marked increase in the number of young people claiming to be transgender or other variants of nonnormative gender. Most evidence suggests that this change is being driven by "woke" cultural pressures to identify as "other" than heterosexual and by a narcissistic desire to distinguish oneself as different and more "interesting" than one's peers (Twenge 2023). The incidence of transsexuality is greatest in progressive urban areas and a recent study reported that 40 percent of students at Ivy League Brown University now claim to have "non-binary" genders (Monroe-Hamilton 2023).

Views concerning transsexuality differ markedly between the political parties, as a Pew poll shows: "While eight-in-ten Republicans and Republican-leaning independents say that whether someone is a man or a woman is determined by the sex they were assigned at birth, most Democrats and Democratic leaners (64%) take the opposite view and say a person's gender can be different from the sex they were assigned at birth" (Brown 2017).

There is good reason to be concerned that young children are being prematurely labeled "transgender" and as a result being subjected to irreversible hormonal and surgical treatments. Whereas in the past it was widely recognized that young children may express gender fantasies that do not persist into adulthood, today "woke" parents, teachers, and medical professionals have chosen to deny this, and to insist instead that medical and surgical interventions are called for. Some narcissistically disturbed mothers will encourage their young children to believe that they are transgender and push them toward gender-affirming surgeries in order to create an abnormal and potentially harmful bond with their children—a phenomenon that comes under the diagnosis of "Munchausen by proxy," a serious mental disorder that can do great harm to children (Kradin 2022).

Intervening at prepubertal ages with what amounts to experimental hormonal and surgical treatments sentences children to irreversible changes, including sterility, osteoporosis, and the inability to reverse the effects of gender-affirming care. The insistent claims made by the LGBTQ+ community that transgenderism must be normalized and, like homosexuality celebrated, aim at undermining the influence of religion and the understanding of sexuality that the human race has shared since creation.

Another recent controversy involves "transgender women" who wish to breastfeed. In yet another linguistic sleight of hand, "woke" activists have created the term "chestfeed" to describe this bizarre request. While it may be possible for men artificially to secrete small amounts of milk from male glands hyperstimulated through pharmaceutical interventions, there is virtually no data to indicate that it is safe, either for the biologically male transsexual or for the feeding baby. The progressive medical profession doesn't appear to be disturbed by this trend, or by the lack of scientific evidence for its safety. However, when lawsuits related to this and other questionable medical practices begin to mount, they may sing a different tune, as an article in *The Economist* suggests:

> On February 22nd a lawsuit was filed that could mark the start of a backlash. Chloe Cole, an 18-year-old who has become a voice for detransitioners in America, is suing Kaiser Permanente, a large American medical provider, for medical negligence. Ms. Cole decided at the age of 12 that she was a boy, was put on puberty blockers and testosterone at 13 and underwent a double mastectomy at 15, before changing her mind and detransitioning at 16" (*The Economist* 2023).

Sadly, physicians as a group have a long history of participating in unethical behaviors (Kradin 2022). They have a propensity to conform with cultural trends in a desire to please and gain approval and have colluded with totalitarian governments when it was popular to do so, as Robert Lifton (2000) discusses in *Nazi Doctors*. By doing so they violate their Hippocratic oath to "first do no harm." During the Covid-19 pandemic, physicians repeatedly took inappropriate scientific and ethical stances for political reasons, resulting in widespread skepticism and loss of confidence in the medical profession (Kradin 2022). According to a recent study by Symphony RM, 41 percent of Americans say that they lost trust in their doctors as a result of their advice during the pandemic.

Women's Lib

When the current cultural revolution began in the 1960s, a primary focus was improving the position of women in society. In the mid-twentieth century, oral contraceptives dissociated sexual activity from pregnancy, which freed women from the institution of marriage unless they opted for it. While it may have been liberating for women to deny the need to marry, their new "freedom" was based on self-interest and failed to consider the traditional relational role of women. Leaders of the Feminist Movement in the '60s, including Betty Friedan and Gloria Steinham, were Marxist sympathizers, and this undoubtedly contributed to their calls for women to leave the "strong authoritarian" influences of the family and to pursue careers outside the home.

But as Suzanne Venker and Phyllis Schlafly argued, "Many don't realize that the entire women's movement was predicated on a Marxist view of the world. Feminism is a branch of socialism, or collectivism, which draws on a socio-political movement that attempts to create a stateless society in which policy decisions are pursued in the (supposed) best interests of society. Feminism like Communism depends on hypothesizing an oppressed class.... Breaking up the family was not incidental but central to its ideology" (Venker and Schafly 2011, 28).

As a result of the influence of feminism, many women have chosen to pursue what had been traditional male career options rather than to prioritize motherhood and child-rearing, so that today the majority of women work outside the home. Indeed, progressive societies have consistently encouraged women to participate in the workforce, as women leaving the home undermines the coherence of the nuclear family and promotes the interests of both business and government. Feminists argued that raising a family is "boring" and stunts the unrealized capacities of women. As a result of factors including the feminist campaign to "liberate" women, the birth rate in America has declined to below sustaining levels. Compared with earlier eras, people today start having their children later and have less time to meet their childbearing goals before they reach the biological limits for having children.

Biblical tradition views men and women as the heads of the nuclear family and suggests that they play different roles. Women's role was to bear and raise children, while men were viewed as the primary providers. As a result of progressive propaganda, no one can state this today without risking scathing criticism for being a "sexist." But the fact is, being in the workforce full time is a challenge for women who also wish to raise a family. Women today report being anxious and exhausted from trying to balance the demands of the workplace with those of family. A recent article noted that when 276 physicians were studied during the Covid-19 pandemic, doctors who were also mothers were likely to be responsible for childcare, schooling, and household tasks, and to report symptoms of anxiety and depression (Davies 2017; Frank, Zhao, and Fang 2021).

Recall Chesterton's point that pushing "progress" can be a way to avoid asking whether or not a given change is actually "good." Today the "liberation" of women is looked back on as "progress" by nearly everyone. Certainly, anyone who dares to suggest that it may not have been entirely "good" is frowned upon. But there are reasons to suggest this is the case. In addition to the increased stress placed on women, there is the harm potentially being done to children. As nearly 60 percent of women over the age of sixteen work outside the home, most young children today are being reared in daycare centers and have reduced maternal-child interactions. To be exact, "58% of working parents with children five years old and younger—or about 6.38 million parents across the nation—use center-based childcare options, according to estimates from the 2019 National Household Education Survey. The survey also found that of the 11 million working parents in the US, 31% of them do not rely on any outside childcare, 25% of them rely on nonrelatives for childcare, and 47% rely on relatives for childcare" (Jackson et al. 2021).

Think of the Children

Progressives conveniently argue that sending young children to daycare has no deleterious effects on young minds; to admit otherwise would be a serious impediment to the goals of progressive ideology. But the deteriorating mental health of today's youth suggests this may not be the case. A 2021 review on the topic, "The Deal with Daycare: What Do the Data Denote?," in *Psychology Today* suggests that daycare may be harmful to the mental health of children.

> Research has, however, found that some infants—particularly those who began daycare in the first year of life, who spent more than 10 hours a week in daycare, and whose mothers provided less sensitive care—had an increased risk of developing insecure infant-mother attachments.... In particular, children who experience formal daycare center care for long periods of time in early childhood are more likely to manifest behavior problems later on, although these increases do not rise to the level of clinical diagnosis. These effects are stronger in low quality care arrangements and when group size is larger. These externalizing effects do not show up consistently, and are sometimes contradicted, in studies of high-quality daycare (Shpancer 2020).

Insecure maternal-infant attachment has been linked to the adult development of narcissism: "Results indicated that those high in pathological narcissistic vulnerability reported greater insecurity in attachment, negative trait emotional reactivity and experienced a more negative and intense emotional reaction to rejection. Grandiose narcissism was related to a more deactivated pattern of emotional reactivity, and less positive (rather than more negative) emotional reactions. Findings have important implications for therapy, particularly regarding communication of emotions for individuals high in vulnerable and grandiose narcissism" (Reis 2021).

The perceived benefits of "self-actualization" for women, or the need to maintain an economic standard of living for the family, have led women to seek substitutes for rearing their children. Although many factors undoubtedly contribute to how children who attend daycare centers will ultimately fare, it is reasonable to question whether diminished early maternal-child interactions may be contributing to the mental health issues that we are witnessing in America's youth today. Whereas the roots of narcissism are complex, it would be foolhardy to dismiss daycare as contributory, despite what progressive forces in the culture would have us believe. As we have seen, narcissism and obsessionality are prevalent in society today, and sociopathy is on the rise—and the prevalence of those pathologies would appear to explain the sudden dominance of the "woke" ideology now poised to destroy America and Western culture. A large percentage of America's youth are suffering from anxiety and depression. When psychological research finds that early maternal-infant interactions are a prelude to adult psychological well-being, can the society-wide reduction in interactions of this type be safely ignored?

Feminism has undergone several transformations since the 1960s. The goal of first-wave feminism was to achieve political equality with men, and women now have the right to vote. Second-wave feminism aimed at equality in society and particularly in their jobs and careers, and this has largely been achieved. But it is questionable whether women have grown happier competing with men in the workplace. Some mothers are opting to remain at home to raise their children, recognizing the psychological and spiritual importance of direct mothering. A 2013 *Atlantic* article describes a woman who left her job to raise her daughter.

> I was missing out on key moments in my daughter's life, and I was an exhausted, nervous wreck. It would be an easy story to say that my consulting firm pushed me out—but it was the opposite. They tried hard to keep me. They let me work from home often and take time off for appointments. "Just get the job

done," they said. That was the problem, though, getting the job done was all about giving everything to the job, and that wasn't sustainable for me once I had a child. I don't fault my firm at all. They are a scrappy service business that needs to consistently deliver high value to their clients by working better and harder. I was good at my job, which was why they were willing to accommodate me—but it was also why, after having my second child, I had to leave (Fondas 2013).

This is becoming a common story.

Despite what progressives would have us believe, biology is a factor in determining "destiny." As we have free choice, we can choose to ignore this, but invariably there will be a price to pay. The Judeo-Christian traditions do not limit man's potential, but they do recognize that nature does, and that true happiness depends on accepting that fact and not struggling against it.

When women choose to live like men, they will pay a price for that choice, as young mothers are recognizing. When a person denies his or her biological sex and opts to "transition" to another, he or she will pay a price, as those who have had undergone unsuccessful gender-affirming surgeries are beginning to admit publicly. And when people conclude that reality is a "mental construct," all of society will pay the price.

Aborting America

In recent years, science has made strides in its study of the early phases of human gestation. The union of sperm and ova represents the moment of conception. In most instances the fertilized egg has the potential and capacity if undisturbed to grow to become a viable fetus. Ultrasound and other physiological monitoring have demonstrated that the fetal heartbeat can be detected by six weeks into the first trimester and that the fetus is capable of feeling pain. Abortion is the termination of a human life, and the later it is performed, the less ethical justification there is for the procedure.

Obviously, only a woman can bear a child, but this does not disqualify men from having opinions on the topic, as some radical feminists argue. Many pregnant women will acknowledge that if they have experienced sensations in their womb indicating the presence of another life, they have regrets about terminating it. As with so many progressive ideas, it is easy for men and women to protest for abortion rights without ever considering the other side of the story—in this case, the life of the fetus. While it is understandable that women do not want men or the government to tell them how to deal with an unwanted pregnancy, it is a topic that requires discussion, not strident protest.

America is currently one of the few countries that allows abortions beyond the second trimester, and one must question why any ethical human being of either sex would insist on the freedom to kill a fetus that has reached the stage of viability. Perhaps women of any age who insist on the right to abortion at any time during gestation need to imagine how they will feel about that stance when they are past their childbearing years and mature enough to have gained a perspective on how they have lived their lives. Are they confident that they will still be proud of their position on abortion? Women need to stop serving as "useful idiots" for progressive politicians who manipulate them for their own purposes. If a person believes that the measure of her freedom as a woman is freedom to abort a fetus, I would argue that something is wrong with her moral compass. To choose to vote for a candidate only because that candidate supports "a woman's right to choose," while ignoring everything else that is wrong in progressive society today, is simplistic and unwise—yet exactly what progressive politicians are relying on women to do for them in future elections.

Is It Good for the Jews?

Progressive anti-Semitism is a specific subset of the general war on religion. Anti-Jewish sentiment has a long history, but the worldwide protests against Israel and Jews following the October 7, 2003, terrorist attacks on Israel merit their own discussion. Progressives are fond of denouncing right-wing anti-Semitism, but for some years now the most ardent and visible anti-Semitism has come from the left of the political spectrum. Jews have been singled out as targets of progressive hatred for two reasons. First, they represent the first monotheistic religion, and their morality set the tone for Western civilization, which makes them a logical target for the anti-religious. Marx was a rabid anti-Semite, and his ideas continue to permeate progressive ideology.

Second, Israel is a Jewish nation, and the idea of nationhood can be traced to the Hebrew Bible. Although rooted in democratic ideas, modern Israel is not a pure democracy, for the simple reason that a majority of Muslims in the state of Israel would again make Jews a vulnerable minority in a hostile Islamic state, defeating the purpose of a modern Jewish state. Progressives choose to view Israel as the "colonizing oppressor" of the Palestinians but ignore the fact that the Palestinians never had a state, while Jews have claimed Israel as their ancestral land for thousands of years and have always maintained a presence there. That Palestinians favor wiping Israel and its Jewish population off the map is considered justified by progressives who are apparently willing to countenance another genocide of Jews, even after the Holocaust. Finally, in the latest iteration of "woke" progressivism, Israelis are seen as having "white privilege"—as we have seen, Sephardic Middle Eastern and African Jews make up the majority of Israel's citizens, and many of them are people of color. There is a growing unholy alliance between white progressives, blacks, and Muslims who espouse anti-Semitic epithets and routinely call for the West to abandon Israel and to boycott and divest from it.

The perverse "morality" of these ideas allows progressive anti-Semites to draw moral equivalencies between Palestinian terrorists who kill and maim civilian men, women, and children and the state of Israel's defense of its people. But what is new, and troubling, is the number of American youth who support Islamic terrorism and anti-Semitism. An October 2023 Harvard/Harris poll conducted online among 2,116 registered voters showed that "26% percent of the youngest age group surveyed (18–24) believes the solution to the Israel-Palestinian conflict is for Israel to be 'ended and given to Hamas and the Palestinians.' Additionally, nearly three in ten of the youngest age group said that the US should back Hamas in the conflict" (Penn, Nesho, and Ansolabehere 2023). A December 2023 Harvard poll suggested that 51 percent of America's youth do not believe that Israel has a right to exist (Harvard Youth Poll 2023). These findings bode poorly for the future of Jews in America, and also suggest that the moral values of young people have been skewed away from traditional Judeo-Christian values to those of progressivism.

Progressives have foisted many lies and distortions on Americans. But they could not have succeeded without a receptive audience, and Americans have been that. Americans have grown decadent, greedy, and self-absorbed—and may no longer have the character required to preserve a once great nation.

CHAPTER 14

Decline and Fall

They want us to be afraid. They want us to be afraid of leaving our homes. They want us to barricade our doors and hide our children. Their aim is to make us fear life itself! They want us to hate. They want us to hate "the other." They want us to practice aggression and perfect antagonism. Their aim is to divide us all! They want us to be inhuman. They want us to throw out our kindness. They want us to bury our love and burn our hope.

—KAMAND KOJOURI (2017)

The result was that the propertied class, the men of real wealth, who had deliberately created the system for their own benefit, drained the life blood from their world and thus destroyed Greco-Roman civilization.

—G. E. M. DE STE. CROIX (1981)

AMERICA IS UNDER SIEGE BY PROGRESSIVE activists and corporate globalists who are determined to transform it from a nation "under God" to one that benefits an atheistic elite. While the religionists' notion of good is the *imitatio Dei,* the progressive definition is the pursuit of power. Instead of Truth, progressives opt for moral relativism and ethical convenience, so that societal agreement concerning what is good becomes impossible.

It's All Relative

Philosopher David Hume (1998) argued that morality cannot be determined rationally and that what is "good" reflects one's emotional preference. Postmodern philosophers have taken it further, by offering a philosophy based on *psychologisms*, that is, mental constructs, and claiming that it is impossible to arrive at objective truth under any circumstance. They have systematically divorced truth from the real world by localizing it in the human mind. As a consequence, progressive reality is contingent, fluid, and based on changing social and cultural trends. All concepts and logic, including mathematics and science, are viewed as culturally conditioned and subject to revision (Feser 2017).

Armed with this flawed ideology, progressives claim that men can become women, that only the "oppressed" deserve a voice in society, and that terrorist atrocities are morally equivalent to a sovereign nation's efforts at defending its citizens. The truth is that the current postmodern progressive perspective is purposefully incoherent so as to make meaningful dialogue impossible. Progressive ideology does not seek a conversation; rather, it uses ideology to cudgel those who disagree. Progressive "inclusiveness" excludes the diversity of ideas and is limited to the diversity of identity. Those who still believe that progressivism represents classical liberal ideas are either ill-informed or purposefully blind, as the current "woke" ideology patently opposes the Enlightenment values of the American experiment.

Chesterton argued, as we have seen, that the assessment of progress should include a decision as to what is "good." Philosopher Alasdair MacIntyre (2016) notes that "moderate realism," a philosophical position expressed by Aristotelian thought, provides a practical definition. "Good," according to Aristotle, is what yields a "flourishing" society. In the animal world, some species flourish by adapting to their environment while others do not. As man has the capacity to modify his environment, those changes will also modify what is judged to be "good." But even in a highly developed and diverse society like America's, it is still possible to identify the conditions under which most citizens will "flourish," while conceding that some will not. This has always been the case. As both Deuteronomy and the Gospel of Mark indicate, the poor will always be among us—as will the sick, the disabled, and other disadvantaged groups. Wishing that it were otherwise will not change reality. History demonstrates that, rather than benefiting the disadvantaged, everyone in society except its ruling elites suffers when notions of equity are artificially imposed by unrealistic ideologues.

Progressives argue that what it means to "flourish" is necessarily subjective. In the *Nichomachean Ethics*, Aristotle defines a "flourishing" society as one that "functions" well. If we apply his notion to American society, most would likely agree that a "good" society is a safe one, one where members are free to engage in commerce that benefits them without harming others, one in which the legal system judges individuals equally and is not corrupt, and one in which honest and open communication is possible. All of that was true of America until recently. If, instead, one defines "good" solely based on the binary choice of supporting the "oppressed" and condemning the "oppressor," neither group can be expected to flourish. If one chooses to define what is "good" as "most free," then freedom itself must be defined. Aristotle and the Judeo-Christian traditions agree that freedom is not solely the unfettered right to do whatever one pleases; it must include concern for the welfare of others in the community. Christianity, by turning inward to emphasize spiritual freedom, inadvertently opened the door to secular notions of freedom, whereas Judaism, because of its focus on Law and the physical world, remained tethered to a notion of freedom with constraints. It is incumbent on both traditions to distinguish their ideas on freedom from those currently being offered by secular progressives.

Up the Revolution!

It has been suggested that people are by nature conservative. Most are largely content with their habits and traditions and generally suspicious of rapid and excessive change. The everyday non-elite citizen is rarely the fomenter of revolution. Instead, ideas for radical change invariably arise in the minds of restless elites who labor under the illusion that their "new" ideas will lead to previously unimagined levels of progress. This is the justification for the Godless Crusade to rid the world of traditional religion and morality. Yet despite what they choose to believe, their ideas are rarely motivated to benefit society. Rather, they are inspired by self-aggrandizement and a lust for power that contradicts the utopian ideas they espouse. This is what is transpiring today, as corporate and political elites push to transform society to consolidate power and riches for themselves. They labor under a flawed ideology that justifies their right to lead society. But their leadership has largely been disastrous. Their goals are corrupt, and they will ultimately fail in their efforts to deceive the public into believing their corruption is imaginary, or that it is being fabricated by enemies of society that must be silenced.

Who supports their misguided project? The answer is those who feel aggrieved and view themselves as victims of society—that is, minorities, unhappy women, the LGBTQ+, the poor, those who are mentally or physically disabled, and so forth. These groups are susceptible to false promises of a better future, free money, and the possibility of at some point being able to exert their own power over others. But they never truly benefit from the transformation of society that the elites promise them. Their primary role is to serve as foot soldiers in the war for deconstructing society, but they lack the vision necessary to create a better society, and they don't realize until it is too late that their true role was to further enrich the elites, as Orwell showed in *Animal Farm*.

Another group of unwitting supporters includes the ill-informed and chronically naïve who support the progressive Democratic Party out of habit or peer pressure. They qualify as Lenin's "useful idiots." Prominent among them are religionists who have abandoned the traditional tenets and demands of their religion for secular ideas to signal their "virtue."

The success of the progressive cultural revolution depends on capturing hearts and minds, and this has been the focus of its propaganda for over a century. Propaganda was used extensively in the Soviet Union to claim success for what was in fact a disastrous centrally planned economy. The Biden administration oversaw a similarly failed economic program characterized by inflation, recession, and energy dependence, yet Biden continued to campaign disingenuously on the lie of "Bidenomics," knowing that that lie would be supported by the progressive press.[1] But the public that must pay more at the gas pump and at the grocery store while increasingly falling into debt knows that something is wrong. Unfortunately, the "disinformation" from the people in power results in confusion and helplessness on the part of a public that no longer knows what to believe and despairs of ever hearing the truth from its government or

---

[1] One example of the big lies the Biden administration was capable of was the claim to have created millions of new jobs over its first two years. The truth is that millions of jobs were lost during the pandemic because mandated lockdowns and government subsidies encouraged people to stay home rather than work. When the pandemic and subsidies ended, people returned to work. Real job creation was essentially zero. To finance extraordinary levels of government spending during the pandemic and subsequently, the government had to borrow and print money, leading to inflation. Supply chain problems related to the pandemic were handled incompetently. In response, the Federal Reserve had to raise interest rates to recent record levels, while the government persisted in increasing spending. The average person must pay more for gasoline, heating his house in winter, and food at the market. The Biden administration's response was to blame the pandemic, Vladimir Putin, and Donald Trump—all of "the usual suspects"—without a hint of truth to its claims.

of having its concerns responded to. When passivity and depression set in, public resistance to the actions of the elites dissipates, which is part of the goal.

Perverting Religion

Amoral progressives encourage the public to embrace the "positive" elements of the Judeo-Christian ethic, such as "love" and "compassion," so as to appear virtuous. By appealing to "the better angels of our nature," they have primed the public over the last sixty years to believe that limit-setting and punishment are harsh and mean-spirited. Psychologists have promoted a progressive ideology focused on self-actualization, which has fed entitled narcissistic notions of individual freedom at the expense of civic-mindedness. Young people have been indoctrinated to believe that America is a racist society and that climate change is an immediate existential threat, the first of which is demonstrably untrue; the second, at best highly questionable. They are taught by progressive activist teachers that it is virtuous to take to the streets and fight for what is "good." Unfortunately, they are also ill-informed and entitled and unaware of the cynical forces that are manipulating their "activism." Their idealism is matched only by their nihilism.

Most parents recognize that young children have difficulty distinguishing fantasy from reality, and that making this distinction is a function of maturity. When young minds are taught to accept fantasy as reality, they will do so. Such fantasies are often seen in totalitarian societies where young people have been fed a diet of lies. One prominent fantasy of childhood is that life is "fair." Young children often complain that a situation is "unfair," as their immature minds cannot distinguish idealized fantasies from harsh realities. In truth, life is not fair, it has never been fair, and it probably never will be.

The notion of equity represents a naïve inability to accept the fact that intelligence, talent, and physical traits are not "normally distributed." Despite this reality, progressive educators insist on training young minds to believe that unequal outcomes are unjust. Similar arguments can be made for the fantasies of diversity and inclusiveness. The progressive claim that these are "religious" values distorts what the Judeo-Christian ethic actually teaches. "Love" without boundaries is not a virtue. Rather, it is often destructive, and unconditional "love" is never the basis for a good society. But it requires a modicum of maturity to recognize that this is true, and it is not surprising that naïve minds of all ages find it unpalatable. Indeed, despite their cynicism and greed, the best progressive minds are immature minds, steeped in childlike fantasies of what might be possible.

In recent years, LGBTQ+ causes have gained acceptance within society. In an effort not to appear bigoted, most Americans have granted these causes legitimacy, but this is ill-advised. The LGBTQ+ community represents a small fraction of society that was tradition-ally marginalized for its "aberrant" behavior. This was in part because of biblical values, but also because its members tended to display behaviors that even secular Americans might find repugnant. While there are members of the LGBTQ+ community who may be ethical and upstanding citizens, a vocal and highly visible faction is intent on corrupting the values of America and especially its youth. To the extent that behaviors exhibited by members of the LGBTQ+ community are disruptive and threaten societal well-being, they deserve to be soundly criticized. Those who behave in this manner often have serious concomitant mental disorders that call for treat-ment, not normalization.

When naked men parade in front of young children at Pride Parades, or transvestites entertain young children at schools or other venues with Drag Queen Story Hour, they should not be applauded, but rather called out for the narcissistic attention-seekers they are. Those who find these antics amusing are wrong to encourage them. Parents should know that transvestites appearing in public schools are not there to provide comic relief; rather, their goal is to groom children into aberrant sex practices and to disrupt the nuclear family.

When nonnormative sexualities were studied in a variety of cultures, they were demonstrated to correlate positively with societal dysfunction (Unwin 1934). Indeed, there are sound sociological reasons the Judeo-Christian ethic frowns on aberrant sexual behaviors. The reason that progressive politicians, big corporations, and the media celebrate the LGBTQ+ community, as well as Black Lives Matter and Antifa, is not to be "tolerant," "diverse," or "inclusive," it is to transform society for their political and globalist benefit. Freud, who focused on the role of sex in human psychology, argued that the sex drive must ultimately be sublimated for the benefit of society (Freud 1930).

Good Judgment

Nonjudgmentalism is a skirting of one's moral responsibilities to one's fellow man. The Hebrew Bible insists that misguided behaviors be judged. As Rusty Reno (2019) notes, it is easy for elites to espouse this notion because their own circles are largely insulated and in practice they continue to insist that standards be met in their families. But imposing this notion on the less privileged has decimated their communities. The book of Psalms repeatedly criticizes elites who take advantage of the weakest members of society. That is what is happening increasingly in America, and it is both unacceptable and certain to lead to national decline.

A society functions well when its citizens make reasoned decisions. But immature minds, in young or old bodies, cannot be expected to do so. MacIntyre (2014) defines reason as "freedom from various traits—ignorance, incapacity to understand a situation, shortsightedness, lack of concern for the common point of view." Progressives fail on all these counts.

Unlike the liberal thinkers of the Enlightenment, progressives are not reliant on either reason or science. These are of secondary importance compared to creating a compliant, amoral society in which they can satisfy their greed and lust for control. This has always been the ultimate goal of totalitarianism, and its promoters can be expected to use all possible tactics to seize and retain power. As Orwell aptly noted, the image of totalitarian society is a "a boot stamping on a human face—forever."

Another progressive strategy has been to encourage the public use of drugs, including marijuana, psychedelics, and opiates. There are few benefits to society in the legalization of mind-altering drugs, except the income that it brings to entrepreneurs and local and state governments. Chronic marijuana use diminishes motivation among adolescents and can promote psychosis and violence in those predisposed—hardly what one would wish for a well-functioning society (Berenson 2019). Claims that marijuana is medicinal, or a panacea for all that ails, are medically questionable and likely placebo in nature (Kradin 2008). While marijuana use may be justified for the relief of pain and anxiety, this constitutes a small fraction of the instances in which it is being used; the vast majority are for recreational and escapist purposes. That marijuana may be no more harmful than alcohol is not an argument for its wholescale legalization, especially as monitoring its use is currently impossible.

Other distractions supported by progressives include the dissemination of pornography and the legalization of prostitution. Sex sells, but when it is used as a commodity, it corrupts society, which is precisely why progressives support it. When you see progressives appear on television protesting, regardless of the cause, one sees heavily tattooed, pierced, purple-haired people prone to emotional outbursts. They are not the best that society has to offer, and they should not be determining America's future.

CHAPTER 15

Can Anything Be Done?

*Never give in, never give in—never, never, never, never—in
nothing great or small, large or petty—never give in except to
convictions of honour and good sense. Never yield to force; never
yield to the apparently overwhelming might of the enemy.*

—WINSTON CHURCHILL (1941)

NOTHING DESCRIBED IN THE PRECEDING CHAPTERS of what is
taking place in America today suggests a flourishing society, to advert
to Aristotle's standard, or a good one, to go by Chesterton's rule.
The fact is, we are losing the war to the Godless crusaders. Traditional religion and morality are being replaced by the malignant and
dysfunctional atheistic religion of "wokeism." Unfortunately, America
will not likely be restored to its former exceptional status, and those
conservatives who yearn nostalgically for the past must come to
grips with reality. Mature Democratic voters continue to support the
progressive agenda, ignoring the fact that it is now far more extreme
than in the past and that, wittingly or not, they are endorsing Marxist
and globalist ideas that will ultimately enslave them (Levin 2023).

In truth, the Enlightenment experiment was never good from a moral perspective. The rejection of God and religion has led the world to its current situation, and while some revel in what they see as their unbounded personal freedoms, most will undoubtedly find the future that progressives have in mind for them hard to tolerate. Too many Americans from both political parties resist acknowledging that America is moving along a path toward totalitarianism. They wish to believe that "it can't happen here." But it can, and it is.

Americans today are more apathetic, self-absorbed, distracted, and politically ignorant and less God-fearing than any generation in the history of the world. Even the ancient pagans, with few exceptions, believed in their gods. Issues of government corruption that would rightfully have inspired the anger and indignation of Americans in the past are currently accepted as "the way things are." Americans have been lulled into ennui by the modern equivalent of "bread and circuses" in much the same way that ancient Romans were as their republic was replaced by tyranny and eventually succumbed altogether to corruption and invading hordes. Despite this looming ominous future, it is an open question whether most Americans will resist it. College-educated urban elites, suburban women, blacks, Hispanics, LGBTQ+ members, and a large percentage of youth are now ardent progressives—and seemingly unconcerned about America's race toward totalitarianism.

If America is to be saved, it will need to renew its commitment to Judeo-Christian values. This will be difficult for many Americans to accept. Few want to hear that they must "repent because the end is near." But America succeeded for more than two centuries because it embraced the Judeo-Christian idea of the good, and if our country is to reverse its current trajectory, Americans will need to make a renewed stand for decency. Suburban women will need to get over their perverse preoccupation with unlimited abortion rights and recognize that a fetus is a living being, and that while ending its life may in rare instances be justified, it is never something to celebrate.

Americans must recognize that progressive calls for diversity, equity, and inclusion in society are not motivated by humanitarian virtue; they are part of a Marxist globalist strategy to eliminate their freedom.

The educational system must be purged of progressive activists, and traditional education must be reinstated, including the Western canon and civic education. The stranglehold of the progressive teachers' unions must be broken, and educational choice be made available through charter schools. Programs granting teaching degrees should be forced to reorient their curricula, and those who refuse should have their government funding rescinded.

Education begins at home, especially moral education. Parents need to make renewed efforts to set examples for their children, if they want them to grow to be responsible adults. Reform synagogues and liberal churches should return to the core traditions of their religions and rethink the Marxist "social justice" that they have committed themselves to.

Sex education has no place in America's grade schools. Children should not be encouraged to read or watch pornography that degrades sexuality, relationships, and the sanctity of marriage. No child should be issued a smartphone until that child is mature enough to use one responsibly, and the many social media platforms that aim at addicting young minds must be recognized for the dangers that they are and appropriately regulated for the good of society. The libertarian argument that these platforms should not be regulated ignores the great harm they are doing to children and society as a whole. A parent who values his or her child's integrity should not bring the child to a Pride Parade or expose the child to drag queens, as these displays are not proper entertainment for anyone, let alone children. Parents who encourage such exhibitions signal their own moral degeneracy and can expect their children to follow suit.

Children must be taught the difference between illusion and reality beginning at an early age. They should learn that when their imagination is totally divorced from reality, it is not necessarily creative; in fact, it may be a path to serious mental disturbance. Men or women who believe that they are not the biological sex they were born into are delusional. For years, psychiatrists agreed on this—as did society—until politics and greed caused them to reconsider. It is an unforgivable moral failure on the part of the mental health and medical professions to have adopted the current misguided and harmful approach to transgenderism without scientific evidence to support it. It is beyond corrupt for medical centers and pharmaceutical companies to profit from gender-affirming care for children. Hopefully, well-aimed lawsuits that rightfully claim malpractice will cure physicians, hospitals, and Big Pharma of this shameful misadventure.

Most states do not sanction smoking or drinking until an individual is twenty-one years of age, as teenagers are judged too immature to make appropriate decisions about their health. On what basis can a five-year-old be allowed to decide about his or her sexual orientation? The answer is that a child that young cannot make that kind of decision, and sane health professionals know this. The psychiatric profession must cease virtue signaling in hope of gaining cultural approval, and medical and psychiatric/psychological professional associations that threaten to delicense health care workers who object should be forced in court to justify their actions based on credible scientific data—which does not exist.

There is much wrong in America today. Adolescence has become interminable. Young men and women who should be marrying, having children, and working to support themselves are living in their parents' basements, with no intention of ever doing the things required of a mature adult. Doting parents afraid of confronting their own children indulge and entitle this immaturity and then bemoan the results.

Authority is viewed as undemocratic and inequitable. Children disrespectfully refer to parents by their first names and know that those parents have failed them. Honoring one's father and mother is one of the Ten Commandments for a good reason, as a child should be grateful for his parents having raised him. The widespread absence of gratitude is poisoning society, and gratitude begins at home. Parents must learn to behave as parents, not as their children's best friend. Disrespect toward parents invariably extends to disrespect toward others in positions of authority. This is the norm in envy-driven revolutionary societies. They lack gratitude, and everyone is referred to as "citizen" or "comrade" to deny the respect due to authority.

Proverbs 9:10 states, "The fear of the Lord is the beginning of wisdom." One can reject God, as atheists do, but one will be forced to live with the consequences of that choice. Nietzsche knew this when he warned that the death of God would have serious negative consequences. Americans are witnessing how abandoning any power greater than ourselves has resulted in increased chaos, greed, hedonism, anxiety, depression, and confusion. For those who can still read the signs, it is evident that the natural order has been disturbed.

Martin Luther King Jr. (1965) famously remarked that "the arc of the moral universe is long, but it bends toward justice." King, a Baptist minister, believed there is an ontological moral order that inheres in the universe. Today man readily accepts the laws of physics but refuses to believe that there may be a metaphysical moral law. We may not see the immediate results of good versus bad behaviors, but in time their fruits always become obvious.

In his explication of what has come to be known as "conservatism," Edmund Burke described the trust required between generations to sustain a flourishing society.

> As the ends of such a partnership cannot be obtained in many generations, it becomes a partnership not only between those who are living, those who are dead, and those who are to be born. Each contract of each particular state is but a clause in the great primaeval contract of eternal society, linking the lower with the higher nature, connecting the visible and invisible world, according to a fixed compact sanctioned by the inviolable

248

oath which hold all physical and moral natures, each in their appointed place (Kirk 1953, 17).

The Talmud (Ta'anis 23b) relates the story of a sage who was journeying on the road when he encountered a man planting a carob tree. He asked him, "How long will it take for this tree to bear fruit?" to which the man replied, "Seventy years." The sage then asked, "Are you certain that you will live another seventy years?" The man answered, "I found grown carob trees when I entered the world. My forefathers planted them for me, so I plant these for my children."

America is that carob tree. It was planted for us by our forebears. They did it out of a sense of moral responsibility extending beyond their own lives. We, in turn, have the same responsibility to see to it that our children and our children's children inherit an America that is upright and flourishing both physically and spiritually, so that they can continue to reap the benefits of the freedom that has been cultivated here for more than two centuries. It should not be sacrificed to the shortsighted greed of corrupt politicians and corporate leaders, or abandoned by a distracted population that has lost sight of what is truly important.

Works Cited

Adler, Alfred. 2024. "A lie would have no sense..." BrainyQuote. Accessed July 21, 2024.

Annenberg Public Policy Center. 2016. "Americans' Knowledge of the Branches of Government Is Declining." September 13, 2016.

Arendt, Hannah. 1976. *The Origins of Totalitarianism.* Orlando, FL: Harvest.

Arnheim, Michael. 2022. *Why Rome Fell: Decline and Fall, or Drift and Change?* New York: Wiley.

Asano, Evan. 2017. "How Much Time Do People Spend on Social Media? [Infographic]." Social Media Today, January 4, 2017.

Assmann, Jan. 2005. *Religion and Cultural Memory: Ten Studies.* Stanford, CA: Stanford University Press.

Atwill, Joseph. 2011. *Caesar's Messiah: The Roman Conspiracy to Invent Jesus.* Charleston, SC: Signature Edition.

Augustine. *Confessions.* 1961. Translated by R. S. Pine-Coffin. New York: Penguin.

Baggini, Julian. 2003. *Atheism: A Very Short Introduction.* Oxford: Oxford University Press.

Bardill, Jonathan. 2012. *Constantine, Divine Emperor of the Christian Golden Age.* Cambridge: Cambridge University Press.

Beck, Judith S., and Aaron T. Beck. 2011. *Cognitive Behavioral Therapy.* New York: Guilford Press.

Berenson, Alex. 2019. *Tell Your Children: The Truth about Marijuana, Mental Illness, and Violence.* New York: Free Press.

Berger, Peter L. 2010. *Between Relativism and Fundamentalism: Religious Resources for a Middle Position.* Grand Rapids, MI: W. B. Eerdmans.

Bohm, David. 1984. *Causality and Chance in Modern Physics.* London: Routledge.

Bork, Robert H. 2003. *Slouching Towards Gomorrah: Modern Liberalism and American Decline.* New York: ReganBooks.

Brown, Anna. 2017. "Republicans, Democrats Have Starkly Different Views on Transgender Issues." Pew Research Center, November 8, 2017.

Bruner, Scott. 2023. *Controligarchs: Exposing the Billionaire Class, Their Secret Deals, and the Globalist Plot to Dominate Your Life.* New York: Sentinel.

Brunton, Paul. 2024. "The divinity is there…" Quotefancy. Accessed July 21, 2024.

Burnham, James. 1966. *The Managerial Revolution.* Bloomington, IN: Indiana University Press.

Burtt, Edwin Arthur. 2016. *The Metaphysical Foundations of Modern Science.* Kettering, OH: Angelico Press.

Camera, Lauren. 2019. "U.S. Students Show No Improvement in Math, Reading, Science on International Exam." *U.S. News and World Report,* December 3, 2019.

Camp, Emma. 2022. "I Came to College Eager to Debate. I Found Self-Censorship Instead." *New York Times,* March 7, 2022.

Carlin, George. 2024. "Forget the politicians…" Goodreads. Accessed July 21, 2024.

Carnegie, Megan. 2023. "Are Gen Z the Most Stressed Generation in the Workplace?" BBC, February 16, 2023.

Chesterton, G. K. 2007. *What's Wrong with the World.* Mineola, NY: Dover Publications.

Chesterton, G. K. 2022. "Heretics." In *Collected Works of G. K. Chesterton.* Orlando, FL: Canva.

Churchill, Winston. 1941. Speech at Harrow School, Harrow, UK, October 29, 1941.

Collins, John J. 1984. *The Apocalyptic Imagination: An Introduction to the Jewish Matrix of Christianity.* Spring Valley, NY: Crossroad.

Corsi, Jerome R. 2023. *The Truth About Neo-Marxism, Cultural Maoism, and Anarchy*. New York: Post Hill Press.

Coughlin, Stephen, and Rich Higgins. 2019. *Re-Membering the Mis-Remembered Left*. Washington, DC: Unconstrained Analytics.

Crawford, Krysta. 2021. "Stanford-led Study Highlights the Importance of Letting Kids Take the Lead." *Stanford News*, March 11, 2021.

Crowell, Rachel. 2021. "Modern Mathematics Confronts Its White, Patriarchal Past." *Scientific American*, August 12, 2021.

Damasio, Antonio. 2000. *The Feeling of What Happens*. New York: Mariner.

Davies, Brian. 2021. *An Introduction to the Philosophy of Religion*. Oxford: Oxford University Press.

Davies, James. 2017. "How Voting and Consensus Created the Diagnostic and Statistical Manual of Mental Disorders (DSM-III)." *Anthropological Medicine* 24: 32–36.

Dawkins, Richard. 2006. *The God Delusion*. Boston: Mariner.

DiAngelo, Robin. 2018. *White Fragility: Why It's So Hard for White People to Talk about Racism*. Boston: Beacon Press.

Dodds, E. R. 1963. *Pagan and Christian in an Age of Anxiety*. Cambridge: Cambridge University Press.

Douglas, Mary. 2001. *In the Wilderness: The Doctrine of Defilement in the Book of Numbers*. Oxford: Oxford University Press.

Douglas, Mary. 2005. *Purity and Danger: An Analysis of Concept of Pollution and Taboo*. London: Routledge.

Dreher, Rod. 2020. *Live Not by Lies: A Manual for Christian Dissidents*. New York: Sentinel.

Dupont, C., D. R. Armant, and C. A. Brenner. 2009. "Epigenetics: Definition, Mechanisms and Clinical Perspective." *Seminars in Reproductive Medicine* 27: 351–55.

Eagleton, Terry. 2014. *Culture and the Death of God*. New Haven, CT: Yale University Press.

Eberstadt, Mary. 2022. *How the West Really Lost God: A New Theory of Secularization*. Philadelphia: Templeton Press.

Economist. 2023. "Legal Action May Change Transgender Care in America." *Economist*, March 7, 2023.

Edelman, Gerald M. 1987. *Neural Darwinism: The Theory of Neuronal Group Selection.* New York: Basic Books.

Eire, Carlos M. N. 2016. *Reformations: The Early Modern World, 1450–1650.* New Haven, CT: Yale University Press.

Eisenhower, Dwight D. 1961. Farewell address, January 17, 1961.

End Wokeness (@EndWokeness). 2023. "Why has everything gone woke these days? ESG scores. Here is BlackRock CEO Larry Fink, along with the CEO of AmEx, explaining his desire to 'force behaviors.'" X, June 4, 2023, 1:46 p.m., https://twitter.com/EndWokeness/status/1665414711188287489.

Erikson, Erik H. 1995. *Young Man Luther: A Study in Psychoanalysis and History.* New York: W. W. Norton.

Rita Felski. 2012. "Critique and the Hermeneutics of Suspicion," *M/C Journal* 15, no. 1.

Fernandez, Ephrem, and Sheri L. Johnson. 2016. "Anger in Psychological Disorders: Prevalence, Presentation, Etiology and Prognostic Implications." *Clinical Psychology Review* 46: 124–35.

Feser, Edward. 2008. *The Last Superstition: A Refutation of the New Atheism.* South Bend, IN: St. Augustine's Press.

Feser, Edward. 2017. *Five Proofs of the Existence of God: Aristotle, Plotinus, Augustine, Aquina, Leibniz.* San Francisco: Ignatius Press.

Feser, Edward. 2019. *Aristotle's Revenge: The Metaphysical Foundations of Physical and Biological Science.* Neunkirchen, Austria: Editiones Scholasticae.

Feynman, Richard P. 1998. *The Meaning of It All: Thoughts of a Citizen-Scientist.* New York: Basic Books.

Feynman, Richard P. 2011. *Six Easy Pieces: Essentials of Physics Explained by Its Most Brilliant Teacher.* New York: Basic Books.

Filoramo, Giovanni. 2024. "Rather than a cognitive procedure..." Quotefancy. Accessed July 21, 2024.

Fondas, Nanette. 2013. "The Many Myths about Mothers Who 'Opt Out.'" *The Atlantic*, May 25, 2013.

Fox, Robin Lane. 2006. *The Classical World: An Epic History from Homer to Hadrian.* New York: Basic Books.

Frank, Erica, Zhuo Zhao, and Yifeng Fang. 2021. "Experiences of Work-Family Conflict and Mental Health Symptoms by Gender Among Physician Parents During the COVID-19 Pandemic." *JAMA Network Open* 4: e2134515.

Frankfurt, Harry G. 2006a. *On Truth*. New York: Knopf.

Frankfurt, Harry G. 2006b. *Taking Ourselves Seriously & Getting It Right*. Stanford, CA: Stanford University Press.

Frankl, Viktor E. 1992. *Man's Search for Meaning: An Introduction to Logotherapy*. Boston: Beacon Press.

Frazer, James George. 2019. *The Golden Bough: A Study in Religion and Magic*. Mineola, NY: Dover Publications.

Fredriksen, Paula. 2017. *Paul: The Pagans' Apostle*. New Haven, CT: Yale University Press.

Freud, Sigmund. 1914. *On Narcissism*. London, Hogarth Press.

Freud, Sigmund. 1922. *Beyond the Pleasure Principle*. London: Hogarth Press.

Freud, Sigmund. 1924. "The Passing of the Oedipus Complex." *International Journal of Psycho-Analysis* 5, no. 4: 419–24.

Freud, Sigmund. 1930. *Civilization and Its Discontents*. London: Hogarth Press.

Freud, Sigmund. 1953–1974a. "Notes on a Case of Obsessional Neurosis." In *The Standard Edition of the Complete Psychological Works of Sigmund Freud*. Edited by James Strachey. London: Hogarth Press.

Freud, Sigmund. 1953–1974b. "Obsessive Actions and Religious Practices." In *The Standard Edition of the Complete Psychological Works of Sigmund Freud*. Edited by James Strachey. London: Hogarth Press.

Freud, Sigmund. 1953–1974c. "On Narcissism: An Introduction." In *The Standard Edition of the Complete Psychological Works of Sigmund Freud*. Edited by James Strachey. London: Hogarth Press.

Freud, Sigmund. 1975. *The Future of an Illusion*. New York: W. W. Norton.

Freud, Sigmund. 1989. *Totem and Taboo*. Translated by James Strachey. New York: W. W. Norton.

Freud, Sigmund. 2010. *Moses and Monotheism*. Eastford, CT: Martino Fine Books.

Fromm, Erich. 1960. *Escape from Freedom*. New York: Vintage.

Gay, Peter. 1987. *A Godless Jew: Freud, Atheism, and the Making of Psychoanalysis*. New Haven, CT: Yale University Press.

Gibbon, Edward. 1993–1994. *The Decline and Fall of the Roman Empire*. 6 vols. Everyman's Library.

Gleick, James. 1987. *Chaos: Making a New Science*. New York: Viking.

Goldberg, Jonah. 2018. *Suicide of the West: How the Rebirth of Tribalism, Populism, Nationalism, and Identity Politics Is Destroying American Democracy*. New York: Simon & Schuster.

Goldfarb, Stanley. 2022. *Take Two Aspirin and Call Me by My Pronouns*. New York: Bombardier Books.

Gottfried, Jeffrey, et al. 2022. "Journalists Sense Turmoil in Their Industry amid Continued Passion for Their Work." Pew Research Center, June 14, 2022.

Gould, Stephen Jay. 1999. *Rocks of Ages: Science and Religion in the Fullness of Life*. New York: Ballantine.

Gray, John. 2003. *Straw Dogs: Thoughts on Humans and Other Animals*. New York: Farrar, Straus and Giroux.

Gray, John. 2018. *Seven Types of Atheism*. New York: Farrar, Straus and Giroux.

Greenblatt, Stephen. 2011. *The Swerve: How the World Became Modern*. New York: W. W. Norton.

Griffiths, Paul J. 2000. "The Very Idea of Religion." *First Things*, May 1, 2000.

Gross, Neil. 2008. "The Religious Convictions of College and University Professors." In *The American University in a Postsecular Age*. Edited by Douglas Jacobsen and Rhonda Jacobsen. Oxford: Oxford University Press.

Gutwinski, Stefan, et al. 2021. "The Prevalence of Mental Disorders among Homeless People in High-Income Countries: An Updated Systematic Review and Meta-Regression Analysis." *PLoS Medicine* 18.

Haidt, Jonathan. 2012. *The Righteous Mind: Why Good People Are Divided by Politics and Religion*. New York: Pantheon Books.

Hancock, Graham, and Glenn Kreisberg, eds. 2010. *Lost Knowledge of the Ancients: A Graham Hancock Reader*. Rochester, VT: Bear & Co.

Harari, Yuval Noah. 2015. *Sapiens*. New York: Harper Perennial.

Harvard Youth Poll. 2024. "The Spring 2024 Harvard Youth Poll."

Hayek, Friedrich A. 1988. *The Fatal Conceit: The Errors of Socialism.* Edited by W. W. Bartley III. Chicago: University of Chicago Press.

Hayes, Nicky, and Stephen Joseph. 2003. "Big 5 Correlates of Three Measures of Subjective Well-Being." *Personality and Individual Differences* 34: 723–27.

Heather, Peter, and John Rapley. 2023. *Why Empires Fail: Rome, America, and the Future of the West.* New Haven, CT: Yale University Press.

Hecht, Jennifer Michael. 2003. *Doubt: A History: The Great Doubters and Their Legacy of Innovation from Socrates and Jesus from Thomas Jefferson and Emily Dickinson.* New York: HarperOne.

Higgins, Sean. 2011. "Pelosi, the Bishops, and Immigration." *Catholic World Report*, May 4, 2011.

Hobbes, Thomas. 2021. *Leviathan.* Edited by David Johnston. New York: W. W. Norton.

Holmes, Kim R. 2016. *The Closing of the Liberal Mind: How Groupthink and Intolerance Define the Left.* New York: Encounter Books.

Horowitz, Juliana Menasce, Anna Brown, and Kiana Cox. 2019. "Race in America 2019." Pew Research Center, April 9, 2019.

McLean Hospital. 2024. "The Social Dilemma: Social Media and Your Mental Health."

Hume, David. 1998. *An Enquiry Concerning the Principles of Morals.* Oxford World's Classics. Edited by Peter Millican. Oxford: Oxford University Press.

Huntington, Samuel P. 1998. *The Clash of Civilizations and the Remaking of World Order.* New York: Basic Books.

Jackson, Michael, et al. 2021. "National Household Education Surveys Program of 2019." Institute of Education Sciences, US Department of Education. January 2021.

James, William. 1963. *The Varieties of Religious Experience: A Study in Human Nature.* New Hyde Park, NY: University Books.

James, William. 2017. *The Will to Believe.* CreateSpace.

Jaschik, Scott. 2017. "Professors and Politics: What the Research Says." *Inside Higher Ed*, February 26, 2017.

Jefferson, Thomas. 1800. Letter to William Hamilton, April 22, 1800.

Jefferson, Thomas. 2004. *The Jefferson Bible*. New York: Akashic Books.

Jerusalem Post Staff. 2024. "Nearly Half of Young Jewish Voters Feel Biden Overly Supports Israel—Poll." *Jerusalem Post*, January 9, 2024.

John Paul II. 1988. Letter of His Holiness to Reverend George V. Coyne, S. J., Director of the Vatican Observatory, June 1, 1988.

Johnson, Paul. 1988. *Intellectuals: From Marx and Tolstoy to Sartre and Chomsky*. New York: Harper Perennial.

Jonas, Hans. 1958. *The Gnostic Religion*. Boston: Beacon Press.

Jonas, Hans. 1984. *The Imperative of Responsibility*. Chicago: University of Chicago Press.

Jonas, Hans. 2010. "Seventeenth Century and After: The Meaning of Scientific and Technological Revolution." In *Philosophical Essays: From Ancient Creed to Technological Man*. Edited by Carl Mitcham. New York: Atropos Press.

Jones, Jeffrey M. 2022. "Belief in God in U.S. Dips to 81%, a New Low." Gallup.

Joseph, Rhawn. 1992. *The Right Brain and the Unconscious: Discovering the Stranger Within*. New York: Plenum Press.

Josephus, Flavius. 1981. *The Jewish War*. Translated by G. A. Williamson. Harmondsworth, UK: Penguin.

Jung, Carl Gustav. 1912. "Psychology of Religion." In *The Collected Works of C. G. Jung*. Edited by Herbert Read, Michael Fordham, and Gerhard Adler, vol. 7. Princeton, NJ: Princeton University Press.

Jung, Carl Gustav. 1950. *Modern Man in Search of a Soul*. New York: Harcourt, Brace & World.

Jung, Carl Gustav. 1972. *Psychological Types*. Princeton, NJ: Princeton University Press.

Jung, Carl Gustav. 1973. *Letters*. Translated by R. F. C. Hull. Edited by Gerhard Adler and Aniela Jaffé. Vol. 1: 1906–1950. Milton Park, Oxfordshire, UK: Routledge.

Jung, Carl Gustav. 1976. "Two Essays on Analytical Psychology." In *The Collected Works of C. G. Jung*. Edited by Gerhard Adler and R. F. C. Hull, vol. 7. Princeton, NJ: Princeton University Press.

Jung, Carl Gustav. 1989. *Memories, Dreams, Reflections*. Recorded and edited by Aniela Jaffé. New York: Vintage.

Kahane, Meir. 1972. *Never Again! A Program for Survival*. Hameir L'David.

Kaku, Michio. 2005. *Parallel Worlds: A Journey through Creation, Higher Dimensions, and the Future of the Cosmos*. New York: Anchor Books.

Kellner, Menachem. 2006. *Maimonides' Confrontation with Mysticism*. Liverpool: Littman Library of Jewish Civilization.

Kendi, Ibram X. 2023. *How to Be an Antiracist*. New York: One World.

Keyes, Ralph. 2004. *The Post-Truth Era: Dishonesty and Deception in Contemporary Life*. New York: St. Martin's Press.

King, Martin Luther. 1965. "Keep Moving from This Mountain." Sermon at Temple Israel, Hollywood, CA, February 25, 1965.

King, Stephen. 1999. *Storm of the Century*. Greengrass Productions.

Kirk, Russell. 1953. *The Conservative Mind: From Burke to Eliot*. Chicago: Regnery Publishing.

Koenig, Harold G. 2012. "Religion, Spirituality, and Health: The Research and Clinical Implications." *ISRN Psychiatry*, December 16, 2012.

Kojouri, Kamand. 2017. "They Want Us to Be Afraid." KamandKojouri. net. June 11, 2017.

Kradin, Richard. 2007. "Minding the Gaps: The Role of Informational Encapsulation and Mindful Attention in the Analysis of Transference." *Journal of Jungian Theory and Practice* 1: 1–13.

Kradin, Richard. 2008. *The Placebo Response: The Power of Unconscious Healing*. New York: Routledge.

Kradin, Richard. 2016. *Parting of the Ways: How Esoteric Judaism and Christianity Influenced the Psychoanalytic Theories of Sigmund Freud and Carl Jung*. New York: Academic Studies.

Kradin, Richard. 2018. *Out of Control: Apocalyptic Psychology in the Age of Trump*. Boston: Richard Kradin.

Kradin, Richard. 2020. *Breakdown: How Progressive Ideology Is Eroding Morality and Redefining Mental Health in America*. Conroe, TX: Defiance Press & Publishing.

Kradin, Richard. 2021. *Judaism: Moral Psychology for a Secular World*. New York: JEP.

Kradin, Richard. 2022. *Unhealthy: Corruption and Malpractice in the American Health System*. Conroe, TX: Defiance Press & Publishing.

Krugman, Paul. 2008. "Clinging to a Stereotype" (opinion). *New York Times*, April 18, 2008.

Kurlansky, Mark. 2016. *Paper: Paging through History*. New York: W. W. Norton.

Lagatta, Eric. 2024. "Disease X: What to Know about the Hypothetical Pandemic World Leaders Hope to Prevent." *USA Today*, January 17, 2024.

Lasch, Christopher. 1979. *The Culture of Narcissism: American Life in an Age of Diminishing Expectations*. New York: W. W. Norton.

Le Bon, Gustave. 1899. *The Psychology of Socialism*. New York: Macmillan.

Lefroy, Emily. 2023. "Millennials Are 'The Biggest Liars' of All Generations, Survey Reveals." *New York Post*, updated July 6, 2023.

Levin, Mark R. 2023. *The Democratic Party Hates America*. New York: Threshold Editions.

Levine, Amy-Jill, and Marc Zvi Brettler. 2020. *The Bible with and without Jesus*. New York: HarperOne.

Lifton, Robert Jay. 2000. *The Nazi Doctors: Medical Killing and the Psychology of Genocide*. New York: Basic Books.

Lifton, Robert Jay. 2014. *Thought Reform and the Psychology of Totalism*. Mansfield Center, CT: Martino Publishing.

Locke, John, George Berkeley, and David Hume. 1990. *The Empiricists*. New York: Anchor Books/Doubleday.

Longfellow, Henry Wadsworth. 2002. *Kavanaugh: A Tale*. Boston: Ticknor and Fields, 1856.

Lukianoff, Greg, and Jonathan Haidt. 2018. *The Coddling of the American Mind: How Good Intentions and Bad Ideas Are Setting Up a Generation for Failure*. New York City: Penguin Press.

Luneau, Delphine. 2023. "Human Rights Campaign: Extremists at CPAC Laid Bare Hatred at Root of Vile Legislation Targeting Trans People." Human Rights Campaign, March 6, 2023.

Mac Donald, Heather. 2023. *When Race Trumps Merit*. Nashville: DW Books.

Mac Donald, Heather. 2018. *The Diversity Delusion*. New York: St. Martin's Press.

Mac Donald, Heather. 2016. *The War on Cops: How the New Attack on Law and Order Makes Everyone Less Safe*. New York: Perseus.

Machiavelli, Niccolò. 1847. *The History of Florence, The Prince, and Various Historical Tracts*. London: H. G. Bohn.

MacIntyre, Alasdair. 2014. *Whose Justice? Which Rationality?* South Bend, IN: University of Notre Dame Press.

MacIntyre, Alasdair. 2016. *Ethics in the Conflicts of Modernity*. Cambridge: Cambridge University Press.

Mandel, Bethany, and Karol Markowicz. 2023. *Stolen Youth*. Nashville: DW Books.

Manent, Pierre. 2022. *The Illusion of Our Times*. South Bend, IN: Saint Augustine's Press.

Martin, Mike W. 2006. *From Morality to Mental Health*. Oxford: Oxford University Press.

Marx, Karl. 1998. *The Communist Manifesto*. New York: New York University Press.

Marx, Karl. 2023. *Critique of the Gotha Program*. Translated by Kevin B. Anderson and Karel Ludenhoff. Oakland, CA: PM Press/Spectre.

Marx, Karl. 1843. Letter to Arnold Ruge.

Masterton, Matt. 2022. "Chicago Tops 630 Homicides, 2,600 Shootings in 2022: Police." WTTW, December 1, 2022.

McGilchrist, Iain. 2018. *The Master and His Emissary: The Divided Brain and the Making of the Western World*. New Haven, CT: Yale University Press.

McGilchrist, Iain. 2021. *The Matter with Things: Our Brains, Our Delusions, and the Unmaking of the World*. London: Perspective Press.

McMahon, Darrin M. 2023. *Equality: The History of an Elusive Idea*. New York: Basic Books.

McNally, Richard J. 2011. *What Is Mental Illness?* Cambridge, MA: Belknap Press.

McWhorter, John. 2021. *Woke Racism: How a New Religion Has Betrayed Black America*. New York: Penguin.

Meacham, Jon. 2012. *Thomas Jefferson: The Art of Power*. New York: Random House.

Meissner, W. W. 2013. "Winnicott's Legacy: On Psychoanalyzing Religious Patients." *Psychoanalytic Inquiry* 33.

Miles, Lynn. 2021. *The Christian Left: How Liberal Thought Has Hijacked the Church*. Savage, MN: BroadStreet.

Mill, John Stuart. 1946. *On Liberty, and Considerations on Representative Government*. Edited by R. B. McCallum. Oxford: B. Blackwell.

Mitchell, Alex. 2023. "Left-Wing Extremism Linked to Psychopathy and Narcissism: A Study." *New York Post*, May 25, 2023.

Monroe-Hamilton, Terresa. 2023. "Shocking 40 Percent of Students at Elite Ivy League School Say They're LGBTQ+." BizPac Review: Business & Politics, July 10, 2023.

Murray, Charles. 2012. *Coming Apart: The State of White America, 1960–2010*. New York: Crown Forum.

Murray, Charles. 2021. *Facing Reality: Two Truths about Race in America*. New York: Encounter Books.

Nagel, Thomas. 1997. *The Last Word*. Oxford: Oxford University Press.

Narayan, Jyoti, et al. 2023. "Elon Musk and Others Urge AI Pause, Citing 'Risks to Society.'" Reuters, April 5, 2023.

NBC News. 2023. "Poll: Nearly 3 in 4 Americans Say Country Is on 'Wrong Track.'" NBC News, June 25, 2023.

Neusner, Jacob, and Bruce Chilton, eds. 2009. *The Golden Rule: The Ethics of Reciprocity in World Religions*. Lanham, MD: University Press of America.

Nietzsche, Friedrich. 2003. *Beyond Good and Evil*. Translated by R. J. Hollingdale. London: Penguin Classics.

Nietzsche, Friedrich. 2012. *The Gay Science*. Translated by Thomas Common. Mineola, NY: Dover Publications.

Nirenberg, David. 2013. *Anti-Judaism: The Western Tradition*. New York: W. W. Norton.

Nixey, Catherine. 2017. *The Darkening Age: The Christian Destruction of the Classical World*. New York: Mariner.

Obama, Barack. 2011. "Remarks by the President in State of the Union Address," The White House, January 25, 2011.

Orwell, George. 1968. *An Age like This, 1920–1940. The Collected Essays, Journalism and Letters of George Orwell.* Edited by Sonia Orwell and Ian Angus, vol. 1. New York: Harcourt, Brace & World.

Orwell, George. 1983. *1984: A Novel.* New York: New American Library.

Otto, Rudolf. 1936. *The Idea of the Holy.* New York: Oxford University Press.

Pagels, Elaine H. 1981. *The Gnostic Gospels.* New York: Vintage Books.

Päs, Heinrich. 2023. *The One: How an Ancient Idea Holds the Future of Physics.* New York: Basic Books.

Patterson, Orlando. 1991. *Freedom: Volume I: Freedom in the Making of Western Culture.* New York: Basic Books.

Penn, Mark, Dritan Nesho, and Stephen Ansolabehere. 2023. "Approval and Mood of Country." Harvard CAPS/Harris Poll. October 19, 2023.

Pew Research Center. 2009. "A Religious Portrait of African-Americans." January 30, 2009.

Pew Research Center. 2015. "America's Changing Religious Landscape." May 12, 2015.

Pew Research Center. 2017. "The Partisan Divide on Political Values Grows Even Wider." October 5, 2017.

Pew Research Center. 2021. "Jewish Americans in 2020." May 11, 2021.

Phillips, Alek. 2023. "How Many Mass Shootings Have Been Carried Out by Transgender People?" *Newsweek*, March 28, 2023.

Piereson, James. 2013. *Camelot and the Cultural Revolution: How the Assassination of John F. Kennedy Shattered American Liberalism.* New York: Encounter Books.

Pinker, Steven. 2018. *Enlightenment Now: The Case for Reason, Science, Humanism, and Progress.* New York: Penguin.

Plato. 1925. *Statesman. Philebus. Ion.* Translated by Harold North Fowler and W. R. M. Lamb. Loeb Classical Library No. 164. Cambridge, MA: Harvard University Press.

Plato. 1998. *Plato's Republic for Readers: A Constitution.* Translated by George A. Blair. Lanham, MD: University Press of America.

Plato. 2001. *Dialogues of Plato: The Complete Texts of the Apology, Crito, Phaedo and Symposium, and Extensive Selections from the Republic.* Edited by Justin B. Kaplan. Translated by Benjamin Jowett. New York: Washington Square Press.

Plato. 2003. *Gorgias and Timaeus.* Mineola, NY: Dover Publications.

Pluckrose, Helen, and James Lindsay. 2020. *Cynical Theories: How Activist Scholarship Made Everything about Race, Gender, and Identity—and Why This Harms Everybody.* Durham, NC: Pitchstone Publishing.

Podhoretz, Norman. 2009. *Why Are Jews Liberals?* New York: Doubleday.

Popper, Karl. 1994. *The Open Society and Its Enemies.* Princeton, NJ: Princeton University Press.

Prager, Dennis. 2023. "2 Education Down." Pragertopia, October 24, 2023.

Ramaswamy, Vivek. 2021. *Woke, Inc.: Inside Corporate America's Social Justice Scam.* New York: Hachette Books.

Ramaswamy, Vivek. 2022. *Nation of Victims: Identity Politics, the Death of Merit, and the Path Back to Excellence.* New York: Hachette Books.

Rawls, John. 1971. *A Theory of Justice.* Cambridge: Harvard University Press.

Reilly, Katie. 2016. "Read Hillary Clinton's 'Basket of Deplorables' Remarks about Donald Trump Supporters." *Time*, September 10, 2016.

Reis, Shulamith, et al. 2021. "Pathological Narcissism and Emotional Responses to Rejection: The Impact of Adult Attachment." *Frontiers in Psychology* 12.

Reno, R. R. 2016. *Resurrecting the Idea of a Christian Society.* Washington, DC: Salem Books.

Reno, R. R. 2019. *Return of the Strong Gods: Nationalism, Populism, and the Future of the West.* Washington, DC: Regnery Gateway.

Rieff, Philip. 1966. *Triumph of the Therapeutic: Uses of Faith after Freud.* Chicago: University of Chicago Press.

Rieff, Philip. 1979. *Freud: The Mind of the Moralist.* Third Edition. Chicago: University of Chicago Press.

Rindsberg, Ashley. 2021. *The Gray Lady Winked: How the New York Times's Misreporting, Distortions & Fabrications Radically Alter History.* Midnight Oil Publishers.

Rizzuto, Ana-Maria. 1998. *Why Did Freud Reject God?: A Psychodynamic Interpretation.* New Haven, CT: Yale University Press.

Rogers, Guy MacLean. 2021. *For the Freedom of Zion: The Great Revolt of Jews Against Romans, 66–74 CE.* New Haven, CT: Yale University Press.

Rommen, Heinrich. 1998. *The Natural Law: A Study in Legal and Social History and Philosophy.* Indianapolis: Liberty Fund Inc.

Rose, Matthew. 2024. "A Rabbi for Christians." *First Things* 340: 41–48.

Rosin, Hanna. 2013. "The Dirty Little Secret: Most Gay Couples Aren't Monogamous." *Slate*, June 26, 2013.

Ross, George. 2018. "The Absent Father: One Explanation of Behavioral Problems among African American Males." PhD dissertation, University of Missouri, St. Louis.

Rossi, Neto R., et al. 2012. "Gender Reassignment Surgery—a 13 Year Review of Surgical Outcomes." *International Brazilian Journal of Urology* 38, no. 1: 97–107.

Rothman, Noah. 2022. *The Rise of the New Puritans: Fighting against Progressives' War against Fun.* New York: Broadside Books.

Royal College of Psychiatrists. 2014. "Royal College of Psychiatrists' Statement on Sexual Orientation." March 2014.

Rubin, Dave (@RubinReport). 2020. "Progressivism is a mental disorder…" X, July 22, 2020, 11:06.

Rubinstein, Gidi. 2010. "Narcissism and Self-Esteem Among Homosexual and Heterosexual Male Students." *Journal of Sex & Marital Therapy* 36: 24–34.

Rufo, Christopher F. 2023. *America's Cultural Revolution: How the Radical Left Conquered Everything.* New York: Broadside Books.

Saad, Lydia. 2019. "Socialism as Popular as Capitalism among Young Adults in U.S. Gallup Poll." Gallup, November 2019.

Saad, Lydia. 2024. "U.S. Women Have Become More Liberal; Men Mostly Stable." Gallup, February 7, 2024.

Sacks, Jonathan. 2003. *The Dignity of Difference: How to Avoid the Clash of Civilizations.* 2nd edition. London: Bloomsbury Continuum.

Sacks, Jonathan. 2020. *Morality: Restoring the Common Good in Divided Times*. New York: Basic Books.

Salzman, Leon. 1977. *Treatment of the Obsessional Personality*. Northvale, NJ: Jason Aronson.

Samuels, David. 2016. "The Aspiring Novelist Who Became Obama's Foreign-Policy Guru." *New York Times Magazine*, May 5, 2016.

Sanders, E. P. 1985. *Jesus and Judaism*. Philadelphia: Fortress Press.

Sapolsky, Robert M. 2017. *Behave: The Biology of Humans at Our Best and Worst*. New York: Penguin.

Schenker, Joseph G. 2008. "The Beginning of Human Life." *Journal of Assisted Reproduction and Genetics* 25: 271–76.

Scholem, Gershom. 1995. *The Messianic Idea in Judaism: And Other Essays on Jewish Spirituality*. New York: Schocken.

Schweitzer, Peter. 2021. *Profiles in Corruption: Abuse of Power by America's Progressive Elite*. New York: Harper.

Scully, Emer. 2019. "Hundreds of Transgender Youth Who Had Transgender Reassignment Surgery Wish They Hadn't and Want to Transition Back, Says Trans Rights Champion." *Daily Mail*, updated October 7, 2019.

Shapiro, David. 1981. *Autonomy and Rigid Character*. New York: Basic Books.

Sheldon, J. P., et al. 2007. "Beliefs about the Etiology of Homosexuality and about the Ramifications of Discovering Its Possible Genetic Origin." *Journal of Homosexuality* 52, no. 3–4: 111–150.

Shirer, William L. 1960. *The Rise and Fall of the Third Reich: A History of Nazi Germany*. New York: Simon & Schuster.

Shoemaker, Karl. 2011. *Sanctuary and Crime in the Middle Ages, 400–1500*. New York: Fordham University Press.

Shpancer, Noam. 2020. "The Deal with Daycare: What Do the Data Denote?" *Psychology Today*, February 1, 2020.

Simpson, James. 2021. *Who Was Karl Marx? The Men, the Motives and the Menace behind Today's Rampaging American Left*. Baltimore: Simpson Publishing.

Smith, Adam. 2015. *The Wealth of Nations*. New York: Fall River Press.

Smith, Nicholas D., Fritz Allhoff, and Anand Vaidya. 2008. *Ancient Philosophy: Essential Readings with Commentary*. Malden, MA: Blackwell.

Snow, C. P. 1959. *The Two Cultures and the Scientific Revolution*. Oxford: Oxford University Press.

Soloveitchik, Joseph B. 1992. *The Lonely Man of Faith*. New York: Doubleday.

Soloveitchik, Joseph B. 2006. *Kol Dodi Dofek: Listen—My Beloved Knocks*. Brooklyn, New York: KTAV Publishing House.

Sowell, Thomas. 1975. *Affirmative Action Reconsidered: Was It Necessary in Academia?* Washington, DC: American Enterprise Institute for Public Policy Research.

Stanley, Jason. 2015. *How Propaganda Works*. Princeton, NJ: Princeton University Press.

Stark, Rodney. 1996. *The Rise of Christianity: A Sociologist Reconsiders History*. Princeton, NJ: Princeton University Press.

Ste. Croix, G. E. M. de. 1981. *Class Struggle in the Ancient Greek World*. London: Duckworth.

Steele, Shelby. 2007. *White Guilt: How Blacks and Whites Together Destroyed the Promise of the Civil Rights Era*. New York: Harper Perennial.

Storm, Ingrid. 2015. "Morality in Context: A Multilevel Analysis of the Relationship between Religion and Values in European Politics and Religion." *Politics and Religion* 1: 28.

Sulloway, Frank J. 1979. *Freud: Biologist of the Mind*. New York: Basic Books.

Talmud Bavli. 2012. Vol. 1: Berachhot. Edited by Adin Steinsalz. 2012. Jerusalem: Koren.

Thomas, Helen. 1984. "Reagan: Politics and Religion Inseparable." UPI, August 23, 1984.

Thomas, Val, ed. 2022. "'Woke' Therapy Weakens the Client," *Critical Therapy Antidote*, February 5, 2022, https://criticaltherapyantidote.org/2022/02/05/woke-therapy-weakens-the-client/.

Thomas, Val, ed. 2023. *Cynical Therapies: Perspectives on the Antitherapeutic Nature of Critical Social Justice*. Jacobs Well, Australia: Ocean Reeve.

Tigue, Kristopher. 2022. "Experts Debunk Viral Post Claiming 1,100 Scientists Say 'There's No Climate Emergency.'" Inside Climate News, August 23, 2022.

Tocqueville, Alexis de. 2000. *Democracy in America*. Translated, and with an introduction by Harvey C. Mansfield and Debra Winthrop. Chicago: University of Chicago Press.

Turco, Arielle Del. 2023. "Hostility against Churches: Supplemental Report—First Quarter 2023." Family Research Council.

Twenge, Jean M. 2014. *Generation Me: Why Today's Young Americans Are More Confident, Assertive, Entitled—and More Miserable than Ever Before*. New York: Atria Books.

Twenge, Jean M. 2023. *Generations: The Real Differences between Gen Z, Millennials, Gen X, Boomers, and Silents*. New York: Atria Books.

Tyson, Alec, Cary Funk, and Brian Kennedy. 2023. "What the Data Says about Americans' Views of Climate Change," Pew Research Center, August 9, 2023.

University of Michigan. 2024. "Monitoring the Future" study, Institute for Social Research.

Unwin, J. D. 1934. *Sex and Culture*. Oxford: Oxford University Press.

Vaillant, George E. 1977. *Adaptation to Life*. Boston: Little, Brown.

Venker, Suzanne, and Phyllis Schlafly. 2011. *The Flipside of Feminism: What Conservative Women Know—and Men Can't Say*. Washington, DC: WND Books.

von Franz, Marie-Louise. 1985. *Projection and Re-collection in Jungian Psychology*. London: Open Court Publishing.

Wallis, R. T. 1972. *Neoplatonism*. Indianapolis: Hackett.

Ward, Michael. 2013. "Science and Religion in the Writings of C.S. Lewis." *Science and Christian Belief* 25: 3–16.

Waterfield, Robin. 2023. *Plato of Athens: A Life in Philosophy*. Oxford: Oxford University Press.

Weber, Max. 2002. *The Protestant Ethic and the Spirit of Capitalism: And Other Writings*. New York: Penguin Classics.

Wells, H. G. 2023. *The Time Machine*. Fingerprint! Publishing.

Wilson, James Matthew. 2017. *The Vision of the Soul: Truth, Goodness, and Beauty in the Western Tradition*. Washington, DC: The Catholic University of America Press.

Wilson, Russell. 2024. "God is good…" A-Z Quotes. Accessed June 20, 2024.

Wilson, Sheryl C., and Theodore X. Barber. 1983. "The Fantasy-Prone Personality: Implications for Understanding Imagery, Hypnosis, and Parapsychological Phenomena." In *Imagery: Current Theory, Research, and Application*. Edited by Anees A. Sheikh. New York: Wiley.

Wilson, William Griffith ("Bill W."). 1957. *A. A. Comes of Age*. Chicago: A. A. Publishing.

Wolin, Sheldon S. 2017. *Democracy, Incorporated: Managed Democracy and the Specter of Inverted Totalitarianism*. Princeton, NJ: Princeton University Press.

Wood, Gordon S. 1990. *The Rising Glory of America, 1760–1820*. Boston: Northeastern University Press.

Wright, Alyssa. 2020. "Trans-Tech Is a Budding Industry: So Why Is No One Investing in It?" *Forbes*, December 8, 2020.

Zhao, Mike. 2022. *Critical Race Theory and Woke Culture: America's Dangerous Repeat of China's Cultural Revolution*. Maitland, FL: Liberty Hill Publishing.

Zitner, Aaron. "America Pulls Back from Values That Once Defined It." *Wall Street Journal*, March 27, 2023.

Zorzi, Graedon. 2022. "The Pagan Roots of Democrats' Abortion Extremism." *The Hill*, October 1, 2022.

Acknowledgments

THIS TEXT HAS BEEN SEVERAL YEARS in the making, as it required reviewing a wealth of information from a variety of fields. While I hold advanced degrees in medicine, psychology, physics, and comparative religion, I am not a philosopher or a political scientist, and as the text addresses these areas, I hope and trust that I have done justice to them.

I have made a conscious effort to avoid authoring a compendium of the ideas of others, as much ink has been spilled in recent years concerning what is transpiring in the culture today. I have also adopted a psychological perspective to explain many of the differences in how conservatives and Progressives view the world, especially God and religion—an angle that has largely been ignored, yet one that arguably is necessary for understanding what is presently taking place.

While it was not my intention to author a polemic, I have not avoided expressing my reasons for believing that progressivism has been a consistent source of bad ideas that disrupt society. My positions on God and religion are also unapologetically conservative. In addition, while I argue that by adopting an overly spiritualized approach to religion, Christianity inadvertently fostered secularism and misguided progressive ideas of "freedom," I recognize that most Christian orthodoxies continue to share the belief that man is not "the measure of all things" and that a divinely inspired morality is essential to maintaining the well-being of society.

I am grateful to Alfred Regnery of Republic Books for recognizing the value of the ideas in this text and choosing to take it to publication.

I cannot sufficiently thank Elizabeth Kantor for her expert editorial efforts in helping to make the text more accessible to the reading public.

I thank Siobhan Cashman for having read the text and making insightful suggestions for how to improve it.

Lucas Klein has been a great help in publicizing my ideas about the current misdirection of the mental health field in his popular online podcasts.

Finally, although Rafi my *very* cute Havanese did not read the text, as he was too busy burying bones and begging for food, he did object to the amount of time that my writing took away from our time playing together. Thankfully, he does not write book reviews.

About the Author

DR. RICHARD KRADIN is a physician at Massachusetts General Hospital, a psychoanalyst, and professor emeritus at Harvard Medical School. He holds a post-graduate degree in comparative religion from Harvard University, and lectures nationally and internationally. Dr. Kradin is the recipient of the Gradiva Award for best paper in psychoanalysis, the Upjohn award for excellence in cancer research, and the Small Prize (summa cum laude, Harvard).

He has authored multiple texts in the areas of medicine, psychotherapy, and religion including *The Herald Dream* (2006, Karnac), *The Placebo Response and the Power of Unconscious Healing* (2008, Routledge), *Pathologies of the Mind/Body Interface* (2012, Routledge), *The Parting of the Ways: How Esoteric Judaism and Christianity Influenced the Psychoanalytic Theories of Sigmund Freud and Carl Jung* (2015, Academic Studies Press), *Out of Control: Apocalyptic*

Psychology in the Age of Trump (2018), *Breakdown: How Progressive Ideology is Eroding Morality and Redefining Mental Health in America* (2020, Defiance Press), *Never Trump: Why Obsessional Elites are Undermining the Future of America* (2021, Defiance Press), *Judaism: Moral Psychology for a Secular World* (2021, JEP), and *Unhealthy: Corruption and Malpractice in the American Health System* (2022, Defiance Press).

www.ingramcontent.com/pod-product-compliance
Lightning Source LLC
Chambersburg PA
CBHW012043230825
31500CB00005B/145